THE
PHILOSOPHER'S
DICTIONARY

———

Robert M. Martin

rd
dition

The Philosopher's Dictionary

"Martin's *Dictionary* is one that professionals can rely on and recommend to students with confidence. But Martin also presents philosophy in a witty, lively, and engaged manner; the reader gets the rewarding sensation of a discipline in motion, an ongoing conversation between past, present and future."
Edric Sobstyl, University of Texas at Dallas

"... clearly [the dictionary] best-suited for introductory philosophy students."
Dialogue

"As interesting to the general reader as it is useful to the student."
David Copp, Bowling Green University

"Very valuable ... an excellent first place to look for explanations of philosophical concepts."
Thomas Hurka, University of Toronto

The central aim of *The Philosopher's Dictionary* is to provide a comprehensive and up-to-date guide to philosophical terms. Definitions are brief, clear, and user-friendly. Notes on usage, spelling and pronunciation are included, and there are brief entries on hundreds of the best-known philosophers. Throughout, Martin writes in a style at once informal and authoritative, making difficult concepts intelligible without distorting them.

The third edition has been revised throughout, and includes many new entries on philosophical concepts, from *Berry's paradox* and the *Chinese room example* to *perfectionism* and *satisfice*. The number of entries on active philosophers has also been considerably increased.

the author: Educated at Columbia University and the University of Michigan, Robert M. Martin is a Professor in the Philosophy Department at Dalhousie University. His other works include *The Meaning of Language* (MIT Press, 1987), *There Are Two Errors in the the the Title of this Book* (Broadview, 2/e 2002), and *Scientific Thinking* (Broadview, 1997).

The Philosopher's Dictionary

Third Edition

Robert M. Martin

broadview press

©2002 Robert Martin

All rights reserved. The use of any part of this publication reproduced, transmitted in any form or by any means, electronic, mechanical, photocopying, recording, or otherwise, or stored in a retrieval system, without prior written consent of the publisher — or in the case of photocopying, a licence from CANCOPY (Canadian Copyright Licensing Agency), One Yonge Street, Suite 1900, Toronto, Ontario M5E 1E5 — is an infringement of the copyright law.

National Library of Canada Cataloguing in Publication Data

Martin, Robert M.
   The philosopher's dictionary

3rd ed.
ISBN 1-55111-494-1

   1. Philosophy—Dictionaries.   I. Title

B41.M37 2002   103   C2002-901005-5

Broadview Press Ltd. is an independent, international publishing house, incorporated in 1985

North America
Post Office Box 1243, Peterborough, Ontario, Canada K9J 7H5
3576 California Road, Orchard Park, NY 14127
Tel: (705) 743-8990; Fax: (705) 743-8353;
e-mail: customerservice@broadviewpress.com

United Kingdom and Europe
Plymbridge North (Thomas Lyster, Ltd.)
Units 3 & 4a, Ormskirk Industrial Park, Burscough Rd, Ormskirk,
Lancashire L39 2YW Tel: (1695) 575112; Fax: (1695) 570120;
E-Mail: books@tlyster.co.uk

Australia
St. Clair Press, P.O. Box 287, Rozelle, NSW 2039
Tel: (02) 818-1942; Fax: (02) 418-1923

www.broadviewpress.com

Broadview Press gratefully acknowledges the financial support of the Book Publishing Industry Development Program, Ministry of Canadian Heritage, Government of Canada.

Typesetting and assembly: True to Type Inc., Mississauga, Canada.
PRINTED IN CANADA

To Fran, who loves five-dollar words.

I love words but I don't like strange ones. You don't understand them and they don't understand you.

Will Rogers

feather: 1a: one of the light horny epidermal outgrowths that form the external covering of the body of birds and that consist of a shaft bearing on each side a series of barbs which bear barbules which in turn bear barbicels commonly ending in hooked hamuli and interlocking with the barbules of an adjacent barb to link the barbs into a continuous vane.

Webster's Seventh New Collegiate Dictionary

About This Dictionary

PHILOSOPHERS HAVE THEIR OWN technical vocabulary—perhaps more of it than in any other academic field—and often use ordinary words in special ways. Thus this dictionary.

I have tried to locate terms in here where you'd likely look for them first, but there is a great deal of cross-reference, in case you look somewhere else. Alphabetization ignores spaces and punctuation. Phrases are almost always defined in entries alphabetized according to the real order of the words: for example, there is an entry defining 'general will' among the G's, cross-referenced under 'will, general' among the W's. Contrasting or very closely related terms are often defined together: thus 'analytic' and 'synthetic' are both defined in the entry for 'analytic / synthetic', to which the entry for 'synthetic' will refer you. Slashes are used to separate such related terms.

Some definitions use words I define elsewhere; where it might be helpful for you to look up these words, they are in SMALL CAPITALS. For brevity I ignore obvious variations (for example, 'CONSISTENT' in one definition refers the reader to the entry titled '**consistency**'). When there are several numbered senses in the entry referred to, I indicate the relevant sense by a superscript number following the word in small capitals; thus '*See* DIALECTIC[5].' refers you to the fifth numbered entry under '**dialectic**'. Often the word in small capitals is just the first word of the title of the cross-referenced entry; for example, 'ANALOGY' in one entry refers you to another titled '**analogy / disanalogy**'. When a term inside a definition is defined elsewhere, but not under its own heading, the entry in which it is defined is noted in a '*See* ...' comment. So when the word 'synthetic' occurs in a definition, you'll find '*See* ANALYTIC / SYNTHETIC'. I note related terms which it might be helpful for you to consult in a '*See also* ...' comment.

Before modern times, people were formally referred to often by their first names. So, for example, the entry for 'Thomas Aquinas' is alphabetized under the T's (though cross-referenced under the A's). I have often given philosophers' full names when they are commonly referred to only by a shorter name. Parentheses tell you what to leave out when mentioning them. For example, J(ohn) L(angshaw) Austin is almost always called J. L. Austin, and we talk of Auguste Comte, not (Isidore) Auguste (Marie François) Comte.

I have given spelling variations, warnings about common misspellings, usage directions, and pronunciations, where useful, in square brackets. When it would be uncommon, or pretentious, or very difficult for English speakers to use the original pronunciation of words or names that come from other languages, I have given the best acceptable English (mis)pronunciation. In pronunciations, I have indicated the German 'ch', a throaty hiss, by CH (in small capitals); and the French nasalized vowel followed by m or n by putting these letters in small capitals. Pronounce them if you can.

There is a Greek or Latin name associated with almost every philosophical concept talked about before 1600, and there is a non-English word for many concepts associated with non-English-speaking philosophers. I have included non-English words when they are likely to be found untranslated in English philosophical writing. The non-English terms are in *italics*, though most of them have been naturalized into working philosophical English and need not be underlined or italicized in your writing.

To keep this book short enough to be handy and inexpensive, I have kept definitions brief and basic. There is much more to be said! Longer works have much more detailed discussions, include very uncommon terms, and make a more substantial effort than I have to include philosophical ideas and authors outside the Western tradition. See:

- *The Cambridge Dictionary of Philosophy* ed. by Robert Audi (Cambridge, 1999)
- *The Concise Routledge Encyclopedia of Philosophy* (Routledge, 1999)
- *The Encyclopedia of Philosophy* (New York: Macmillan, 1967)
- *The Oxford Companion to Philosophy* ed. by Ted Honderich (Oxford, 1995)

- *The Oxford Dictionary of Philosophy by* Simon Blackburn (Oxford, 1996)

On-line resources include

- The Internet Encyclopedia of Philosophy: http://www.utm.edu/research/iep/
- The Stanford Encyclopedia of Philosophy: http://plato.stanford.edu/contents.html

And, of course, there's no substitute for reading philosophical works themselves.

I hope that you'll find this book friendly, informal, and helpful. My aim has been to give definitions that can be understood by people who don't already know what the defined term means. (Dictionaries do not always manage this!) I have tried to include all the basic philosophical words, and to be even-handed; but this book must reflect my own philosophical biases and training. If you find unhelpful definitions, or important words left out, or implicit philosophical bias, please write me at the Philosophy Department, Dalhousie University, Halifax, Nova Scotia, Canada B3H 4P9. Your suggestions will be gratefully acknowledged, and will be considered for future revised editions.

I have several people to thank for their help: the editors and anonymous readers for Broadview Press, and (in alphabetical order) Charles Anderson, David Braybrooke, Keith Burgess-Jackson, Steven Burns, Doug Butler, Rich Campbell, George Fogarasi, Michael Hymers, Gérald Lafleur, Roderick T. Long, Jack MacIntosh, Mary MacLeod, Robert Nadeau, Josefine Papst, Jeff Pelletier, Roland Puccetti, Shelagh Ross, Robin Smith, Aga Skotowski, Paul C. L. Tang, Terry Tomkow, Tom Vinci, Sheldon Wein, and Anna Zaniewska.

A

---

abduction   The process involved in finding plausible explanatory HYPOTHESES, as distinguished from the VERIFICATION of one of them. There has been a good deal of progress in the search for the LOGIC of the latter process, but not of the former.

Abélard,   (or Abailard), Peter (or Pierre) (1079-1142) French philosopher with works mainly on THEOLOGY, LOGIC, METAPHYSICS, and ETHICS. Noted for his position on UNIVERSALS: he argued that only INDIVIDUALS exist, and that general terms stand for ABSTRACTIONS of the mind.

absent qualia   *See* ZOMBIES.

absolute   'Absolute' as used in philosophy often means 'complete, perfect, independent, unchanging, not RELATIVE'. Some IDEALIST philosophers think that something exists called 'the Absolute', the basis of all being. HEGEL identified the "absolute spirit" with God, and thought that it manifests itself in developments in the world (*see* HISTORICAL MATERIALISM / IDEALISM). Other philosophers with similar views are FICHTE, SCHELLING, ROYCE, and BRADLEY. Sometimes capitalized: 'the Absolute'; 'Absolute Spirit'.

absolute idealism   *See* ABSOLUTE.

absolute space and time   The view that space and time exist independently of the objects and events in them. This was Newton's view, rejected by (among others) Einstein (*see* SCIENTISTS).

absolute spirit   *See* ABSOLUTE.

absolutism, ethical / cultural   *See* RELATIVISM / ABSOLUTISM.

absorption   A rule of INFERENCE: 'If P then Q' implies 'If P, then P and Q'. In symbols: P ⊃ Q therefore P ⊃ (P & Q).

abstract / concrete entities / ideas   Abstract entities (sometimes called "abstracta") are supposed not to be locatable in space or time, not perceptible, without causes or effects, necessarily existing. Putative examples are properties, UNIVERSALS, SETS, geometrical figures, and numbers. Something is, by contrast, concrete when it is particular and spatially and temporally locatable—perhaps material (*see* MATERIALISM). There's a long history of philosophical argument about the reality of certain abstracta. Clearly some of them aren't real, for example, the average American family, with its 2.6 children. The FALLACY of misplaced concreteness mistakenly argues that something abstract is real (*see* REIFICATION). There's also debate about whether we can even have ideas of them. We experience only particulars, so abstract ideas were a problem for the classical EMPIRICISTS, who thought that every IDEA was a copy of an experience. LOCKE thought that we 'abstract' the general idea of dogs from particular ideas of Fido, Spot, etc. BERKELEY insisted that all ideas were particular, but argued that we could use the particular Fido-idea to stand also for Spot, etc. But perhaps (as PLATO and others have argued) we must have innate abstract ideas, not originating with sensation, in order to be able to classify the particulars (*See* FORM[1].)

absurdity   **1.** Something clearly false or SELF-CONTRADICTORY. Deriving an absurdity in this sense from the denial of what is to be proved is what happens in a *reductio ad absurdum*—an INDIRECT PROOF. **2.** Something unreasonable, meaningless, inappropriate, without structure, incoherent, failing to make sense. EXISTENTIALISTS hold that reality, and our place in it, are absurd in this sense; CAMUS made much of the confrontation of our ideas of justice and rationality with a senseless and indifferent universe.

Abunaser   *See* AL-FĀRĀBĪ

abusive *ad hominem* argument   *See* AD HOMINEM

Academy   The *Akademia* (Academy) was the place in Athens where PLATO taught, and thus was used for the school of PLA-TONISTS which survived for almost 900 years. The word came to refer more generally (with a lower-case 'a'), to any association of scholars (whence the term 'academic'). Don't be too hasty to dismiss some point as "purely academic" if you are in an academy.

access, privileged   *See* PRIVILEGED ACCESS.

accident   **1.** *See* ESSENCE / ACCIDENT. **2.** A FALLACY in which one reasons from a GENERALIZATION that is by-and-large true to a specific case in which it does not apply; for example: "It's a free country; therefore I have the right to drive while I'm drunk." Converse accident, also known as hasty generalization, argues fallaciously from an insufficient number of cases to a generalization: "Uncle Fred smoked two packs a day and lived till 95; so smoking must not be all that harmful."

accidental quality / characteristic   *See* ESSENCE / ACCIDENT.

Achilles and the tortoise   *See* ZENO OF ELEA.

acquaintance, knowledge by   *See* KNOWLEDGE BY ACQUAIN-TANCE / BY DESCRIPTION.

acrasia   *See* WEAKNESS OF THE WILL.

act / agent moralities   Some moral philosophers think that the basic sort of thing ethics evaluates is the worth of ACTIONS people do (act morality); others think that what's basic to moral theory is the worth of the person who acts (AGENT morality). KANT argued that good actions were those done by people with the right sort of motives, so his ethical theory is one species of agent morality; another is VIRTUE ethics. The UTILITARIANS thought that the basic kind of ethical thought evaluates actions (via their consequences), whatever the motives or moral worth of the people who do them, so their ethics is a variety of act morality.

action A human action is distinguished from just any bodily movement, usually on the basis that an action must be intended. Thus your accidentally spilling your coffee is not an action; neither is the motion of your tongue while you drink your coffee, because you do not think about that motion, or intend that it be the way it is. ('Act' is used in the same way.)

action at a distance The effect that one thing can have on another that it is not touching and to which it is not connected by something in-between. Gravitation is an example. Some philosophers and scientists—e.g., LEIBNIZ—thought that this was impossible. One way they tried to explain gravitation is to suppose that bodies that gravitationally attract each other are connected by some intervening invisible thing that fills the space between them and transfers the gravitational force.

action theory The branch of philosophy that considers questions about ACTION. Examples of these are: What differentiates an action from other movements? Can there be actions that are refrainings from acting? Where does an action end and its consequences begin? What sort of EXPLANATION is suitable for actions? Moral questions (about, for example, ACTS / OMISSIONS) and the questions of FREE WILL and responsibility are sometimes included in action theory.

active euthanasia *See* EUTHANASIA.

acts / omissions An act is doing something, by contrast with an omission (or refraining), which is merely failing to do something. Some philosophers think that there can be a moral difference between these even when they have the same motives and outcome. For example, it has been argued that an act of killing someone is worse than merely refraining from saving someone's life, even when they have exactly the same motive and results.

acts, speech   *See* SPEECH ACTS.

actual world   *See* POSSIBLE WORLDS.

act utilitarianism   *See* UTILITARIANISM.

Adams,   Marilyn McCord (b. 1943) American philosopher, primarily working on MEDIEVAL philosophy and philosophy of religion.

Adams,   Robert Merrihew (b. 1937) American philosopher, with work in philosophy of religion, ethics, and other fields.

ad baculum   (Latin: "to the stick"—that is, "to force") A logically mistaken (but sometimes persuasive) form of ARGUMENT in which someone supports a position by threatening or predicting dire consequences for non-belief. Example: "Druid non-Euclidianism has the only correct philosophical view on this matter. If you don't think so, wait to see what mark I give you on the next exam." Sometimes called 'appeal to force'. One of the informal FALLACIES. ['ad BAK-you-lum']

addition   A rule of INFERENCE: P therefore P or Q.

addition theorem / rule   The principle that the PROBABILITY that at least one of two independent events **x** and **y** will happen is the probability of **x** + the probability of **y** – the probability that both will happen. If the two events are MUTUALLY EXCLUSIVE, the probability of at least one happening is merely the probability of **x** + the probability of **y**. (*See also*: MULTIPLICATION THEOREM / RULE.)

ad hoc (Latin: "to this"—that is, "specially for this purpose")
An *ad hoc* ASSUMPTION is one that is introduced illicitly in an attempt to save some position from a contrary ARGUMENT or COUNTEREXAMPLE intended to show that the position is false. It is illicit because it is designed especially to accommodate the argument or counter example, and has no independent support. An example of *ad hoc* reasoning (adapted from AUGUSTINE):

"Suicide is always wrong."

"Well, how about all those women who in early Christian times killed themselves rather than being raped by pagan soldiers, and whom you count as saints?"

"That doesn't show that suicide is permissible. In those cases, they must have been acting under direct secret orders from God, so what they did was OK."

ad hominem (Latin: "at the person") A logically mistaken (but sometimes persuasive) form of ARGUMENT which comes in several kinds: (1) the "abusive ad hominem" in which, instead of giving good reasons against some position, one irrelevantly attacks or abuses the person who held that position. An example: "Plato's theory of forms can't be correct because Plato was a known, practising homosexual." (2) the "circumstantial ad hominem" which makes appeal to the special position of some person: "His argument against putting the dump there is no good—obviously he only thinks that because he lives nearby." (3) The "*tu quoque*" (Latin: "you also"): "You tell me not to drink so much, but you put away a good deal of booze yourself." One of the informal FALLACIES. Also refers to the non-fallacious practice of arguing for a conclusion on the basis of assumptions you do not accept, but your audience does.['ad' + 'HAH-ma-nem']

ad ignorantiam (Latin: "to ignorance") A logically mistaken (but sometimes persuasive) form of ARGUMENT in which one supports a position by claiming that nobody can show that it's false (or that a position is false because no one can prove that it is true). Example: "God must exist, because it's impossible to give any definite disproof of His existence." One of the informal FALLACIES. ['ad' + 'ig-na-RANT-ee-am' or 'ig-na-RANCE-ee-am']

ad misericordiam   (Latin: "to pity") A logically mistaken (but sometimes persuasive) form of ARGUMENT in which one supports a position by making a (strictly speaking, irrelevant) appeal to the audience's sympathies or mercy—for example, the sort of argument frequently made to a jury by defense lawyers. One of the informal fallacies. ['ad' + 'miz-uh-ri-CORD-ee-am']

Adorno,   Theodor [Wiesengrund] (1903-1969) German philosopher, member of the FRANKFURT SCHOOL; known also for his work in sociology and musicology.

ad populum   (Latin: "to the people") A logically mistaken (but sometimes persuasive) form of ARGUMENT in which someone supports a position by making an inappropriate appeal to the prejudices or emotions of the audience. Also called 'appeal to emotion'. One of the informal FALLACIES. ['ad POP-you-lum']

ad verecundiam   (Latin: "to modesty") A logically mistaken (but sometimes persuasive) form of ARGUMENT in which someone supports a position by appeal to a supposed authority who in fact has no special expertise in the matter. Advertising using celebrity endorsement encourages this fallacy. Also known as the argument from (or appeal to) authority. One of the informal FALLACIES. ['ad' + 'ver-uh-KUN-di-am']

adverbial theory of perception   When you hallucinate something blue, it is tempting to say that you are seeing an internal blue SENSE-DATUM. But those who object to this sort of peculiar object prefer to say that there's no blue thing which is the object of your perception at all. All that is happening is that you are perceiving in a certain way—as it were, "blue-ly".

17

A / E / I / O propositions   This distinction among kinds of statements, used in TRADITIONAL LOGIC, is best explained by
examples:

    A: All pigs are mammals.
    E: No pigs are mammals.
    I: Some pigs are mammals.
    O: Some pigs are not mammals.

See also QUALITY / QUANTITY (OF A PROPOSITION).

aesthetics   The philosophical study of art, of our reactions to
it, and of similar reactions to things that are not works of art.
Typical questions here are: What is the definition of 'art'?
How can we judge aesthetic worth? Is this an objective matter (*see* SUBJECTIVE / OBJECTIVE)? Are the artist's intentions
relevant to artistic interpretation? Is there a special frame of
mind (an "aesthetic attitude") appropriate for appreciating
art? ['es-THET-iks'; sometimes (especially in the US) spelled
'esthetics', though this is more often the name of the science
of hair dying, nail polishing, etc.]

aether   *See* ETHER.

aetiology   The causes of something or the study of these causes. ['ee-tee-AH-lo-jee'; sometimes (especially in the US)
spelled 'etiology']

affirming the antecedent   A correct form of reasoning involving the CONDITIONAL, in which one derives the consequent
from a conditional plus its antecedent. Example:

    If it rained this morning, the pavement would be wet now.
    It rained this morning.
    Therefore the pavement must be wet now.

DENYING THE CONSEQUENT is a similar form of correct reasoning. And compare the incorrect forms: AFFIRMING THE
CONSEQUENT, DENYING THE ANTECEDENT.

affirming the consequent   An incorrect form of reasoning
involving the CONDITIONAL, in which one derives the
antecedent from a conditional plus its consequent. Example:

If it rained this morning, the pavement would be wet now.
The pavement is wet.
Therefore it must have rained this morning.

DENYING THE ANTECEDENT is a similar form of incorrect reasoning. And compare the correct forms: AFFIRMING THE ANTECEDENT, DENYING THE CONSEQUENT.

a fortiori   (Latin: "from what is stronger") Means 'with even stronger reason', 'even more so'. "You owe thanks to someone who lets you use his car for a day. So *a fortiori*, you should really be grateful to Fred, who let you have his car for a whole month." [usually 'ay FOR-she-OR-eye', sometimes 'ah FOR-tee-OR-ee']

after-image   The image remaining in your visual field after some comparatively intense stimulus has ceased, for example, after you see a camera's flash. This sort of thing—an image without a present object—motivates the SENSE-DATA theory.

agape / philia / eros   (All Greek words for "love" of various sorts.) *Agape* is unselfish love for all persons; Christians often use this word for what they take to be ideal love. Sometimes contrasted with *philia* (brotherly love, fondness, or friendship) and with *eros* (passionate or erotic love; by extension, the unifying force in the universe; some philosophers have extended this to represent the love of perfect beauty, the mystical union with Being, etc.). ['AH-ga-pay', 'FILL-ee-ah', 'EE-ros' or 'EH-ros']

agathon   (Greek: "a good" or "the good") The object of all human activity; PLATO identified it with the source of all being. ['AH-ga-thon']

agent   An agent is one who can perform a genuine INTENTIONAL[1] ACTION, and who is thus morally responsible for what he/she does. This excludes people, for example, who are unable to perceive relevant facts, or who can't reason about consequences. In law the term is used to refer to a person who, by mutual consent, acts for another person who is known as the principal.

agent / event causation   Often it is thought that causes and effects must be events—for example, human actions and decisions. This leads to problems (*see* FREE WILL and DETERMINISM). In response, some philosophers have argued that the cause of our actions is not a (determined) event (such as a decision), but rather an AGENT (the person who acts). In a more general way, 'agent causation' is the idea that things, not events, are causes: that rock caused the dent in my car.

agent moralities   *See* ACT / AGENT MORALITIES.

Age of Reason   *See* ENLIGHTENMENT.

agnosticism   *See* ATHEISM / THEISM / AGNOSTICISM.

agreement, method of   *See* MILL'S METHODS.

AI   *See* ARTIFICIAL INTELLIGENCE.

akrasia   *See* WEAKNESS OF THE WILL.

Albertus Magnus,   Saint (or Albert the Great; original name Albert, Count von Bellstädt) (c. 1206-1280) German SCHOLASTIC philosopher and theologian, known for his efforts to combine Greek, Arabic, and Christian thought; teacher of THOMAS AQUINAS.

alchemy   The MEDIEVAL (pseudo-)science which attempted to find the philosopher's stone which would turn base metals into gold, the panacea which would cure all disease, and the elixir of longevity.

alethic   Means 'having to do with necessity and possibility'. Alethic logic is that branch of MODAL LOGIC concerned with the connections between sentences involving the alethic modalities: 'necessary', 'possible', 'impossible', etc. 'It's necessary that P' is often symbolized '□P'; and 'it's possible that P' as '◇P'. ['ah-LEE-thick']

al-Fārābī   Abu Nasr, also called Abunaser, and, in Latin, Alpharabius (870-950) Persian philosopher of Turkish origin, considered one of the greatest Muslim philosophers. His views were based on PLATO and ARISTOTLE, modified by the doctrines of Islam.

al-Ghazālī   Abu Hamìd Muhammad (1058-1111) Persian Islamic theologian who argued that real knowledge arose from divine REVELATION rather than from rational thought.

algorithm   A mechanical method (i.e., one determined by strict rules, needing no creativity or ingenuity to apply) for carrying out a given calculation in a finite number of steps. Also called 'decision procedure' or 'effective procedure'.

alienation   Estrangement, separation. HEGEL discussed the possibility of human estrangement from the natural world. The EXISTENTIALISTS thought that our alienation from nature and from each other was an important and inevitable part of the human condition. In MARX, 'alienation' means the separation from the products of our labour (as employees, we don't own what we produce) as well as from society and from ourselves.

allegory of the cave   *See* CAVE.

Alpharabius   *See* AL-FĀRĀBĪ.

Alston,   William P[ayne] (b. 1921) American philosopher, best known for his contributions to EPISTEMOLOGY and philosophy of religion.

Althusser,   Louis (1918-1990) French philosopher associated with the STRUCTURALISTS, known for his application of that theory to MARXIST thought. ['al-too-sair']

altruism **1.** Generosity. **2.** The philosophical position that one ought to act for the benefit of others. Contrast with EGOISM.

ambiguity Susceptibility of multiple interpretation regarding meaning (contrast with VAGUENESS). A sentence may show lexical ambiguity when it is not clear which of the meanings of a word is appropriate: for example, "I ran into a bank" might describe a hurried financial transaction or a boating accident. ("Lexical" here means having to do with a lexicon—i.e., a dictionary.) Or structural ambiguity (also known as 'amphiboly' ['am-FIB-uh-lee']) in which grammatical matters are unclear: "Fred had lunch with Tom and his sister." Whose sister? Fred's or Tom's? The FALLACY of amphiboly is mistaken reasoning arising from structural ambiguity. This fallacy, together with the fallacies of EQUIVOCATION, ACCENT, and COMPOSITION / DIVISION, are all classified as fallacies of ambiguity, sometimes called 'sophisms'.

ambiguous middle, fallacy of the A form of FALLACIOUS SYLLOGISM in which the MIDDLE TERM (see MAJOR / MIDDLE / MINOR TERM / PREMISE) shifts meaning from one premise to the other. A silly example:

Some triangles are obtuse.
Everything that is obtuse is stupid.
Therefore some triangles are stupid.

amorality *See* IMMORALITY / AMORALITY.

ampersand The symbol '&', meaning 'and'. *See* SYMBOLS OF SENTENTIAL LOGIC.

amphiboly *See* AMBIGUITY.

analogy / disanalogy An analogy is a similarity of two things. Reasoning from (or by) analogy—the 'analogical argument'—concludes that because two things share one or more characteristics, they share another. For example, some philosophers think they can solve the PROBLEM OF OTHER

MINDS by analogy: other people share my general outward appearance and behaviour, so that's evidence that they also have minds. (This argument is associated with MILL.) A disanalogy is a difference between compared things; disanalogies between things reduce the strength of an argument from analogy.

analysis   Some things are capable of being understood in terms of their component parts; analysis takes them apart into their simpler elements. RUSSELL, MOORE, and (at times) WITTGENSTEIN thought that the job of philosophy was the analysis of CONCEPTS. (*See* ANALYTIC PHILOSOPHY.) REDUCTIVE analysis aims to show that what is analyzed does not constitute a basic existent—or need not be thought of as existing at all. The 'paradox of analysis' points out that for a statement giving the analysis of some term to be meaningful to you, you must already understand that term; but this implies that no analysis can possibly be informative. What is to be analyzed is called the 'analysandum', and what provides the analysis is called the 'analysans'.

analysis, linguistic   *See* ANALYTIC PHILOSOPHY.

analytical behaviourism   *See* BEHAVOURISM.

analytical definition   *See* GENUS / SPECIES.

analyticity   *See* ANALYTIC / SYNTHETIC.

analytic philosophy   'Analytic' philosophy was so-called because of its emphasis on ANALYSIS of CONCEPTS; but this name has spread to cover a much wider variety of philosophy, associated with the English-speaking philosophers following the revolt against IDEALISM[2] begun by RUSSELL and MOORE at the beginning of the twentieth century. Because of its emphasis on language, it is sometimes called 'linguistic philosophy' or 'linguistic analysis'; and sometimes 'Oxford philosophy', after the university association of some of its most influential practitioners. Analytic philosophers often tended to be EMPIRICISTS and UTILITARIANS, in the British tradition of HUME and MILL, rather than in the CONTINENTAL tradition of SPECULATIVE philosophy, coming from HEGEL and HUSSERL. Nowadays both the analytic and the continental traditions include such a broad variety of approaches that these distinctions aren't very precise; the names 'analytic', 'speculative' and so on tend mostly to be used as derogatory epithets for the competition.

analytic / synthetic These words were introduced by KANT, referring to the difference between two kinds of JUDGMENT. Kant called a judgment analytic when the "PREDICATE was contained in the subject"; thus, for example, the judgment that all bachelors are unmarried is analytic because the subject ('bachelors') "contains" the predicate ('unmarried'). This possibly makes the notion the same as that of CONCEPTUAL TRUTH. Later philosophers prefer to make this distinction in terms of sentences and meanings: a sentence is analytic when the meaning of the subject of that sentence contains the meaning of the predicate: 'unmarried' is part of the definition of 'bachelor'. In other words, an analytic sentence is one that is true merely because of the meanings of the words. 'It's snowing or it's not snowing' is true merely because of the meaning of the words 'or' and 'not', so perhaps we should count this as analytic too. But since the relevant words in this case are "*logical*" words, this sentence is more particularly known as a LOGICAL TRUTH. A synthetic truth is a sentence that is true, but not merely because of the meaning of the words. 'Pigs don't fly' is true *partially* because of the meaning of the words, of course: if 'pigs' meant 'woodpeckers', then that sentence would be false. But since the definition of 'pig' tells us nothing about flying, this sentence is not true merely because of the meaning of the words. One can speak also about analytically false sentences, for example, 'There exists a married bachelor'. Be careful to distinguish among the analytic / synthetic, LOGICAL TRUTH / FALSITY, NECESSARY / CONTINGENT, and *A PRIORI / A POSTERI-*

ORI. For example, analytic sentences are necessarily true, and may (sometimes) be known *a priori*; but there may also be synthetic a priori statements (Kant thought there were). QUINE argued that the analytic / synthetic distinction is not a good one, because one cannot distinguish between matters of meaning of the words of a sentence and matters of fact.

analytic, transcendental   *See* TRANSCENDENTAL ANALYTIC.

anamnesis   *See* RECOLLECTION.

anaphora   Linguistic situation in which one term (the 'anaphore') gets its reference through an earlier term (the 'antecedent'). In 'Arnold scratched himself', 'himself' is the anaphore, 'Arnold' is the antecedent.

anarchism   The view that government has no right to coerce citizens, and that the best society is one with the least government, or with no government at all. A well-known advocate of philosophical anarchism is PROUDHON.

Anaxagoras   (c. 500-428 B.C.) PRE-SOCRATIC Greek META-PHYSICIAN and COSMOLOGIST. His writings contain speculations on the origins of the universe and the constituents of matter. ['an-ak-SAG-uh-rus']

Anaximander   (c. 610-546 B.C.) PRE-SOCRATIC Greek scientist and METAPHYSICIAN. Believed in a single SUBSTANCE (called "the indefinite") out of which everything was formed, by distillation of hot, cold, dry, and wet elements. ['uh-NAX-uh-man-der']

Anaximenes   (d. c. 528 B.C.) PRE-SOCRATIC Greek METAPHYSICIAN and COSMOLOGIST. His candidate for the single SUBSTANCE that composed all existence was air (or mist), condensed or evaporated. ['an-ax-IH-muh-neez']

ancient philosophy   Ancient philosophy began in primitive form, we suppose, in prehistory; the earliest Western philosopher of whose work we have a historical account is THALES (c. 580 B.C.). The end of this period is often marked by the beginning of MEDIEVAL PHILOSOPHY, with the work of AUGUSTINE (about 400 A.D.).

angoisse *See* EXISTENTIAL ANGUISH.

angst *See* EXISTENTIAL ANGUISH.

anguish *See* EXISTENTIAL ANGUISH.

animism The view that things not normally thought to be so are alive, or at least are understandable in terms of features normally associated only with living things. This is usually associated with primitive religion, but a recent animistic view in science is the Gaia hypothesis—that the earth is (or is in some ways like) a living organism. *See also* ANTHROPO-MORPHIC.

anomalous monism This view, associated with Donald DAVIDSON, grants to physical MONISM that each "mental" state is really some physical—physiological—state; but it denies the possibility of REDUCTION of such states, arguing that laws identifying or otherwise relating TYPES of mental states to types of physical states are impossible.

Anscombe, G[ertrude] E[lisabeth] M[argaret]. (1919-2001) English philosopher; pupil, editor, and translator of WITTGEN-STEIN; influential anti-EMPIRICIST writer on ACTION and CAUSATION; conservative Catholic ethicist.

Anselm, Saint (1033-1109) Italian-born, English SCHOLASTIC theologian / philosopher, Archbishop of Canterbury. An important philosopher of the early middle ages; known for his defense of rational THEOLOGY and the ONTOLOGICAL ARGUMENT FOR GOD'S EXISTENCE.

antecedent conditions The events or states of affairs that come

before a given event and that cause it, or are necessary or sufficient (*See* NECESSARY / SUFFICIENT CONDITIONS) for it to
happen.

antecedent, affirming /denying   *See* AFFIRMING THE ANTE-
CEDENT *and* DENYING THE ANTECEDENT.

antecedent / consequent   *See* CONDITIONAL.

anthropic principle   Sometimes stated as: the laws and conditions of the universe are not completely arbitrary, but are
constrained to be consistent with our existence. For some
philosophers, this is an argument that the universe was
designed with us in mind (compare the TELEOLOGICAL
ARGUMENT); but for others, it merely states the obvious: that
what we observe is restricted by the conditions necessary for
our presence as observers, and that scientists can expect to
find that the characteristics of the current universe are not
fatal to humans.

anthropocentrism   *See* SPECISM.

anthropomorphic   Having human form, human-like. PRIMITIVE
thought, for example, anthropomorphized nature, seeing it as
characterized by aims, emotions and desires (for instance,
seeing a thunderstorm as a manifestation of anger). Some
religious thought conceives of God anthropomorphically, in
that God is thought of as having human desires and aims.
['AN-throw-po-MOR-fick']

antilogism   An inconsistent (*see* CONSISTENT) set of three sentences: two of them premises of a valid SYLLOGISM, and the
third the negation of its conclusion. (*See* ARGUMENT) ['an-
TIL-uh-jizm']

antinomy   In general, a PARADOX. In KANT, the "antinomies of
pure reason" derive contradictions from the improper use of
principles of space and time, human freedom, and GOD. ['an-
TIN-uh-mee']

antirealism   *See* REALISM / ANTIREALISM.

antithesis   *See* DIALECTIC[5].

anxiety   *See* EXISTENTIAL ANGUISH.

apodictic / assertoric / problematic   Apodictic (sometimes spelled 'apodeictic') statements assert that something is (**a**) necessary (or impossible); or (**b**) CERTAINLY, INDUBITABLY true (or false); or (**c**) demonstrably, provably true (or false). (Philosophers sometimes have not disentangled these notions, which are (**a**) METAPHYSICAL; (**b**) EPISTEMOLOGICAL; and (**c**) LOGICAL.) An assertoric statement says merely what actually is (or isn't); and a problematic statement what might be (or might not be). *See also* NECESSARY / CONTINGENT TRUTH.

apodosis / protasis   Old-fashioned names for (respectively) the consequent and the antecedent of a CONDITIONAL.

Apollonian / Dionysian   NIETZSCHE distinguished these two sorts of approaches to art and, more generally, to life. The former tends toward order, rationality, harmony, clarity, and intellect; the latter toward disorder, spontaneity, imagination, energy, and creativity. Nietzsche associated Dionysian attitudes with the WILL TO POWER.

apologist   One who defends a doctrine. The term is used historically especially for the early Christian teachers who wrote apologies for (defenses of) their religion. In this technical use, the term does not carry the implication that the apologist expresses regret and begs pardon for what he did.

aporia   (Greek: literally "with no pathway", figuratively "puzzle", "difficulty".) An inconsistent but individually plausible group of statements; the presence of evidence both for and against something. Discussions in PLATO sometimes pose these puzzles without solving them. ARISTOTLE thought that philosophy aimed at finding their solutions. ['uh-POR-ee-uh']

a posteriori   *See* A PRIORI / A POSTERIORI.

appearance / reality   The difference between the way things seem to us and the way they really are. Philosophers have often been concerned with this difference, wondering what reasoning could establish that things ever are as they seem.

apperception   LEIBNIZ'S term for the mind's apprehension of its own states. KANT distinguished between EMPIRICAL apperception, present in our own ordinary mental states, for example, when we become aware we believe something, and TRANSCENDENTAL apperception, implicit in the unity of one's experiences in one subject, making experience possible.

a priori / a posteriori   (Latin, "from before / from after") Two different ways in which something might be known to be true (or false). It can be known *a priori* if it can be known before, or independently of, sense-experience of the fact in question. It can be known *a posteriori* if it can be known on the basis of, after, sense-experience of the fact. One can know that all bachelors are unmarried a priori; one doesn't need to observe even one bachelor to know this is true. In this case (but perhaps not in all cases) a priori knowledge is possible because what's known is a CONCEPTUAL TRUTH or because the sentence that expresses this truth is analytic (*see* ANALYTIC / SYNTHETIC) or LOGICALLY TRUE. The terms are associated with KANT, who argued that certain a priori truths (for example, that every event has a cause) were not conceptual or analytic. A priori truths are sometimes called 'TRUTHS OF REASON'. A priori reasoning is sometimes called PURE REASON[2]. ['ay' or 'ah' + 'pre-OR-ee' / 'pos-tee-ree-OR-ee' The Latin phrase has been accepted into philosophical English so thoroughly that it need not be italicised]

a priori **probability**   *See* PROBABILITY.

A proposition   *See* A / E / I / O PROPOSITIONS.

Aquinas,   Saint Thomas *See* THOMAS AQUINAS.

arche   (Greek: "beginning" or "origin") The word was extended to mean 'principle' or 'FOUNDATION', and thus to refer to
the basis of political authority, existence, or knowledge.
['AR-kay']

archetypes   *See* FORM[1] *and* Jung in entry for SCIENTISTS.

Arendt,   Hanna (1906-75). Influential German-born American
political theorist; critic of contemporary mass society.

arete   Greek: "excellence", "virtue", with the association of
fulfilment of function and potential. ['AH-reh-tay']

argument   An argument in ordinary talk is a debate, especially
a heated one. But in philosophical usage, an argument is one
or more statements (called 'premises'; singular 'premise' or
'premiss') advanced in order to support another statement
(the conclusion). Thus philosophers need not get angry when
they argue. Premises actually support a conclusion only
when there is the appropriate sort of logical connection
between the premises and the conclusion. In DEDUCTIVE
arguments, the conclusion must be true given the truth of the
premises; in an INDUCTIVE argument, the truth of the premises makes the conclusion more probable. Any deductive argument in which the premises really do have the appropriate
logical connection with the conclusion is called a 'valid'
argument; in invalid arguments, this connection is lacking. A
valid argument may, however, fail to support its conclusion
because one or more of its premises is false—for example:
   All pigs fly.
   All flying things are lighter than air.
   Therefore all pigs are lighter than air.
This argument is valid, but it fails to convince because both
of its premises are false. An argument with at least one false

premise is called 'unsound'; a sound argument is a valid argument all of whose premises are true. A sound argument provides a proof of its conclusion (though in logic it's often said that a proof is provided merely when the argument is valid). [Note to students: please don't spell this word 'arguement']

argument from analogy　*See* ANALOGY.

argument from authority　*See* AD VERECUNDIAM.

argument from design　*See* TELEOLOGICAL ARGUMENT.

argument from evil　*See* PROBLEM OF EVIL.

argument from illusion / hallucination　The argument (against NAÏVE REALISMS) that the existence of perceptual ILLUSIONS and hallucinations shows that we really directly perceive only SENSE-DATA and not an independent world.

argument of a function　*See* FUNCTION.

argument, open question　*See* OPEN QUESTION ARGUMENT.

arguments for God's existence　*See* the following well-known ones:
> COMMON CONSENT ARGUMENT
> DEGREES OF PERFECTION ARGUMENT
> FIRST CAUSE ARGUMENT
> MORAL ARGUMENT
> MYSTICAL EXPERIENCE ARGUMENT
> ONTOLOGICAL ARGUMENT
> PASCAL's Wager
> TELEOLOGICAL ARGUMENT.

***argumentum ad ...**　See* particular forms of FALLACIOUS ARGUMENT known under traditional Latin names:
> *AD BACULUM*—"to the stick"—i.e., from force

AD HOMINEM—at the man / person
AD IGNORANTIAM—to ignorance
AD MISERICORDIAM—to pity
AD POPULUM—to the [prejudices of] the people
AD VERECUNDIAM—"to modesty"—false authority.

Aristippus   (c. 435-356 B.C.) Greek SOPHIST, founder of the CYRENAIC school; follower of SOCRATES, known for his HEDONISTIC ethics. ['ar-is-TIP-us']

Aristotle   (384-322 B.C.) Hugely influential Greek philosopher and scientist; some think the greatest philosopher. He was PLATO'S student; like his teacher, he was centrally concerned with knowledge of reality and of the right way to live. Unlike Plato, however, he accepted the reality of the EMPIRICAL, changing world, and attempted to discover what sort of understanding we must have in order to have knowledge of it. He argued that INDIVIDUAL things must be seen as belonging to kinds of things, each of which has ESSENTIAL properties that give it potential for change and development. (For Aristotle's distinction of kinds of properties, *see* FOUR CAUSES.) Investigation into the essential properties of humans can tell us what human good is: he conceived it as a life lived in accord with the moral and intellectual VIRTUES. Aristotle's writings cover all sorts of areas in natural science and philosophy. He began the systematic study of LOGIC. For 'Aristotelian definition' *see* GENUS / SPECIES. For 'Aristotelian logic' *see* TRADITIONAL LOGIC.

Armstrong,   David M[alet] (b. 1926) Australian METAPHYSICIAN, best known for his influential hard-nosed MATERIALISM.

Arrow's theorem / paradox   *See* VOTER'S PARADOX[2].

art   **1.** The process and the product involved in painting, sculpture, etc. (*See also* AESTHETICS.) **2.** Also, in a wider sense, in any intentional creation (ARTIFACT). **3.** A 'term of art' (also called 'technical term') is thus a term used in a special, tech-

nical way. Looking at this dictionary will show you that philosophy is full of terms of art.

artifact   A product of human work, as distinguished from a naturally occurring object. In science, a piece of data or experimental result which has been produced or significantly
altered by the process of observation. (Also spelled 'arte-
fact')

artificial intelligence   An area of study in computer science
and psychology that involves building (or imagining)
machines, or programming computers, to mimic certain
complex intelligent human activities. The creation of a program that can play chess at a high level is one of its successes. Artificial intelligence is of philosophical interest insofar
as it might shed light on what human mentality is like, and
insofar as its successes and failures enter into arguments
about MATERIALISM. [sometimes abbreviated 'AI']

artificial / natural language   A natural language is one used by
some actual group of people, that has developed on its own,
culturally and historically. An artificial language is one
developed for some purpose. Philosophers use the term to
refer especially to IDEAL LANGUAGES. Computer languages
are artificial language; SYMBOLIC LOGIC provides other
examples.

asceticism   The practice of living under extremely simple conditions, with minimal enjoyment, pleasure, and comfort.
Sometimes ascetics even intentionally produce pain or dis-
comfort. Certain religious enthusiasts thought this was a
good idea. AUGUSTINE and SCHOPENHAUER gave philosophical arguments in favour of certain forms of asceticism. ['ah-
SET-a-sizm']

assertability, warranted   *See* WARRANTED ASSERTABILITY.

assertion   A statement or sentence used to state a fact, to make a claim, true or false, about the way things are; or the act of saying or writing such a sentence. Distinguished from sentences or acts that express feelings, ask questions, etc. and so are neither true nor false. An indicative sentence that does not state anything that is true or false ('Tuesdays more than twelve pounds long juggle deeply') may be poetic, but isn't an assertion.

assertion sign   *See* SYMBOLS OF SENTENTIAL LOGIC.

assertoric   *See* APODEICTIC / ASSERTORIC / PROBLEMATIC.

association   A rule of INFERENCE allowing mutual replacement of these equivalents:
(P v (Q v R)) is equivalent to ((P v Q) v R);
(P & (Q & R)) is equivalent to ((P & Q) & R)

association of ideas   One thought produces another: when you think about shoes, maybe this drags along the thought of socks. Associationism is the view that this sort of thing was at the core of our mental life, and that its laws constitute a scientific cognitive psychology.

assumption   **1.** Something taken to be true, without argument or justification. *See also* AXIOM / POSTULATE / POSIT. **2.** = premise (*see* ARGUMENT).

A statement   *See* A / E / I / O PROPOSITIONS.

asymmetric   *See* SYMMETRIC / ASYMMETRIC / NONSYMMETRIC.

ataraxia   Greek: peace of mind, tranquility. The STOICS and EPICUREANS took this to be the aim of life. ['at-a-RAX-ee-ah']

atheism / theism / agnosticism   Atheists believe that God doesn't exist. They sometimes (but not always) think, in addition, that religious practice is foolish, or that the morality fostered by religion is wrong. Because atheism has been so unpopular, atheistic philosophers have sometimes disguised their views. LUCRETIUS and HUME were probably atheists. RUSSELL was open about his atheism, and got into trouble for it. Not every religion includes the belief in God—Buddhism, for example, is sometimes said to be an atheistic religion. Atheism is contrasted with its opposite, theism, the view that God does exist, and also with agnosticism, the view that there isn't any good reason to believe either that God exists or that He doesn't. [Note the way 'atheist', 'atheism', 'theist', and 'theism' are spelled: 'e' before 'i']

atomic facts / propositions   *See* LOGICAL ATOMISM.

atomism   The view that things are composed of elementary basic parts. From ancient times till the present, physics was often atomistic (though what's now called an 'atom' is no longer regarded as a basic component—contemporary physicists think that much smaller parts might be basic). Philosophical atomism is associated with DEMOCRITUS, EPICURUS, LUCRETIUS, and many more recent philosophers of nature. (*See also* CORPUSCULARIANISM, LOGICAL ATOMISM.)

attitude, propositional   *See* PROPOSITIONAL ATTITUDE.

attribute   *See* QUALITY / ATTRIBUTE / PROPERTY.

attributes, divine   *See* DIVINE ATTRIBUTES.

Augustine,   Saint (354-430) Philosopher and theologian, born in N. Africa; converted to Christianity in 386. An important figure in the establishment of Christianity as an intellectual and political force, and in the transition from ancient to MEDIEVAL thought; the first important Christian philosopher. He is often called Augustine of Hippo, to distinguish him from the other Saint Augustine (of Canterbury), who is important for establishing Christianity in England, but not as a philosopher. ['aw-GUS-tin', or sometimes 'AW-gus-teen']

Aureol [Auriol; Aureoli; Aureolus],   Peter [Petrus] *See* PETER AUREOL.

Austin,   John (1790-1859) English legal philosopher known for his position that LAW[1] is the command of the sovereign.

Austin,   J(ohn) L(angshaw) (1911-1960) English philosopher; a leading figure in ORDINARY LANGUAGE PHILOSOPHY. He drew philosophical conclusions from ANALYSES of our uses of language in general, and of particular philosophically relevant words, for example, about the nature of knowledge from subtle facts about the way we use the word 'know'.

authenticity   *See* BAD FAITH / GOOD FAITH / AUTHENTICITY / INAUTHENTICITY.

authoritarian   A government, church, etc., that demands strict and unquestioning obedience, and thus denies freedom of thought or action, is authoritarian.

authority, appeal to   *See AD VERECUNDIAM.*

autological   *See* SELF-REFERENCE.

automata   These are (arguably) mindless devices that imitate the intelligent and goal-directed actions of people—robots, for example. DESCARTES thought that animals were automata—merely physical "mechanisms", without mind. ['automata' is plural; singular 'automaton'; 'aw-TOM-a-ta', 'aw-TOM-a-ton'] *See also* ARTIFICIAL INTELLIGENCE, CYBERNETICS.

autonomy / heteronomy   Autonomy is self-governance—the ability or right to determine one's own actions and beliefs. Some ethical theories—for example, KANT'S—see the respect for autonomy as a central ethical principle. Heteronomy is its opposite: dependence on others. *See also* PATERNALISM.

average / total utilitarianism   UTILITARIANISM needs to specify how to understand the greatest good for the greatest number of people. Is a society better when it produces the greatest average UTILITY, or when it produces the greatest total? Make sure you understand why these are not the same thing.

Averroës   *See* IBN RUSHD.

Avicenna   *See* IBN SĪNĀ.

axiology   *See* VALUE THEORY.

axiomatic theory   *See* AXIOM / POSTULATE / POSIT.

axiom / postulate / posit   An axiom is a statement regarded as obviously true, used as a starting point for deriving other statements. An axiomatic THEORY is one that is based on axioms. Not every theory is axiomatic: some don't have such basic statements. 'Postulate' (as a noun) is often used to mean the same thing, though sometimes it refers only to such statements within a particular theory, while axioms are basic and obvious statements common to many theories (for example, the basic laws of LOGIC). The verb 'to postulate' means the act of postulation—ASSUMPTION, often of the existence of something, for theoretical purposes. A posit is an assumption, especially some thing assumed to exist; to posit something is to assume it (*see* THEORETICAL ENTITIES / CONSTRUCTS).

Ayer,   (Sir) A(lfred) J(ules) (1910-1989) English philosopher; his book *Language, Truth and Logic* presented LOGICAL POSITIVISM in a vigorous and influential way. ['AY-er']

B

Bachelard, Gaston (1884-1962) French anti-POSITIVIST subjectivist theorist of science. ['bash-eh-lar']

Bacon, Francis (Baron Verulam and Viscount St. Albans) (1561-1626) English philosopher and scientist. An early advocate of EMPIRICISM and enemy of appeal to authority in science; often considered the father of modern science.

Bacon, Roger (c. 1214-1292) English philosopher and scientist, known as 'Doctor Mirabilis'. An influential commentator on ARISTOTLE, early EPISTEMOLOGIST, theorist of scientific method.

bad faith / good faith / authenticity / inauthenticity Bad faith is, in general, self-deception. In SARTRE'S EXISTENTIALISM, bad faith (in French, '*mauvaise foi*' ['mo-vase fwa']) is the attempt to deny one's own FREEDOM, thus to escape EXISTENTIAL ANGUISH, the anxiety recognition of one's freedom brings). Bad faith is the pretence that one's actions, values, or preferences are determined by something in one's past—heredity, environment, social expectations, objective values, personality, etc. Good faith, its opposite, is the accepting that one is the author of, and responsible for, actions, values, and preferences. Authenticity in HEIDEGGER is an intentional awareness and taking-charge of the self by the self. It is, for the existentialists, a praiseworthy state of good faith, in which one actively creates one's long- and short-term ideals, projects, and plans, and owns up to having them and to having created them.

Baier, Annette (b. 1929) American philosopher with important work on HUME and ethics. ['BUY-er']

Baier, Kurt [Erich Maria] (b. 1917) Austrian/Australian/American philosopher influential in his thinking about the connections between moral, practical, and theoretical reasoning. ['BUY-er']

bald man paradox *See* SORITES.

"ball of wax" example DESCARTES used this THOUGHT EXPERIMENT to show the necessity of believing in physical SUBSTANCE. Imagine you see a ball of wax, at room temperature. Put it next to the fire, and in a while, all its characteristics have changed: its shape, colour, odour, hardness, etc. Yet it is the same object we saw earlier (not something else). This sameness cannot be explained in terms of having the same characteristics; so there must be something other than characteristics—an unchanging and invisible substance—which accounts for it. *See also* IDENTITY[4], PROBLEM OF IDENTITY, QUALITY / ATTRIBUTE / PROPERTY.

barber paradox Imagine a barber who shaves all and only those men in the town who don't shave themselves. Does this barber shave himself? If he does, he doesn't. If he doesn't, he does. This is something like a SELF-REFERENCE paradox, similar in form to RUSSELL'S PARADOX, but there is a simple solution here: we have simply proven that there is no such barber.

Barth, Karl (1886-1968) Influential Swiss theologian, known for his opposition to the modern humanistic religious emphasis on feelings and individual spirituality, and advocacy of the Reformation's emphasis on sinfulness and the message of the Bible. ['bart']

Barthes, Roland (1915-1980) French philosopher associated with the STRUCTURALISTS, known for his application of that theory to literary criticism. ['bar-t']

base, epistemological *See* BASING RELATION.

base, supervenience   *See* SUPERVENIENCE.

basic action   If someone did **x** by doing **y**, then **x** is not a basic ACTION (it's a non-basic action). Sally murdered Sam by shooting him, so Sally's murdering Sam is not a basic action. Sally shot Sam by discharging her revolver, so Sally's shooting Sam isn't a basic action either. What action of Sally's was basic? Perhaps her moving her finger (when she shot the revolver)—she didn't do this by doing something else. This distinction has relevance in ACTION THEORY.

basic statement   The truth or falsity of some statements is determined by appeal to some others (by means of LOGIC or scientific method), but some philosophers think that there must be a starting point: basic statements. Whether there are basic statements, what they are, and why they are acceptable, are all controversial questions. *See also* BASING RELATION / AXIOM / POSTULATE, LOGICAL ATOMISM, PROTOCOL SEN-TENCES.

basing relation   In EPISTEMOLOGY, the relation between one belief and a second, where the first is the "basis" or "base" of the second—the evidence for it, or the reason for believing it.

Bayesian   An adjective referring to a variety of related aspects of PROBABILITY theory, associated with the work of Thomas Bayes (1702-1761), English mathematician. **1.** Bayes' theorem is a mathematical formula relating conditional and prior probability. **2.** 'Bayesianism' sometimes refers to the view that probability should be understood as subjective; or **3.** to the view that rational choice is choice that maximizes EXPECTED UTILITY. [Pronounced 'bayz', 'BAYZ-ian']

Bayle,   Pierre (1647-1706) French ENLIGHTENMENT philoso-pher. His destructive SCEPTICAL attacks on accepted views (including religion) were an influence on HUME and VOLTAIRE.

Beauvoir,   Simone de (1908-1986) French writer and philosopher, known for her combination of EXISTENTIALISM and FEMINISM. ['bow-vwar']

becoming / being   Being is whatever exists. Some philosophers thought that in the real realm of being, nothing changes; thus the realm of becoming, the visible world where things change, was thought to be unreal or "less real". Philosophers who hold this view face the necessity of explaining how we know about the real world, and what the visible world has to do with it. These worries were a central feature of ancient Greek philosophy, and often also concerns of MODERN PHILOSOPHY and science.

Bedeutung   *See* DENOTATION / CONNOTATION.

beetle in the box   WITTGENSTEIN tells the following philosophical fable:

> Suppose each person had something he/she calls a 'beetle' in a box, but could see only what's in his/her box. It's possible that each person has something different, or even nothing at all, in his/her box, or that the contents of some person's box are constantly changing. The word 'beetle' would then have no use in our language.

This fable can be taken to be an attack on the idea that there are PRIVATE[2] objects—for example, mental events that only the person having them can know about; or at least on the idea that we can talk about such private things in public language (*see* PRIVATE LANGUAGE ARGUMENT).

begging the question   *See* CIRCULAR REASONING / DEFINITION.

behaviourism   Early in the twentieth century, many psychologists decided that INTROSPECTION was not a good basis for the science of the mind; instead they advocated reliance on external, observable behaviour (*see* PRIVACY[2]). Methodological (psychological) behaviourism is the view that only external behaviour should be investigated by science. METAPHYS-

ICAL or ANALYTICAL behaviourism is the philosophical view that public behaviour is all there is—that this is what we're talking about when we refer to mental events or characteristics in others, and even in ourselves. It's a form of MATERIALISM. J. B. Watson and B. F. Skinner (*See* SCIENTISTS) were foremost behaviourist psychologists. [The American spelling of these words omits the 'u']

being   *See* BECOMING / BEING.

being for itself / in itself   *See* IN ITSELF / FOR ITSELF.

belief   *See* KNOWLEDGE / BELIEF.

benevolence   *See* SYMPATHY / EMPATHY / BENEVOLENCE.

Bennett,   Jonathan F[rancis] (b. 1930) New Zealand-born philosopher known for his revisionist work on historical philosophers, and his writings on rationality.

Bentham,   Jeremy (1748-1832) English founder of UTILITARIANISM, influential in moral, political, and legal theory.

Bergson,   Henri (Louis) (1859-1941) French philosopher in whose work EVOLUTION plays a central role. Among his central notions is the "ÉLAN VITAL" ['ay-LAN vee-tal'] the non-MATERIALISTIC vital force supposed to cause change and development. He was a champion of INTUITION against rationalistic "conceptual" thought. ['bairg-SON']

Berkeley,   George (1685-1753) Irish philosopher, Bishop of Cloyne; known for his EMPIRICIST EPISTEMOLOGY and IDEALIST METAPHYSICS. Berkeley rejected the idea that a world independent of PERCEPTIONS can be inferred from them; perceptions are all there is. (But they can exist externally and independently of us—in the mind of God.) Since only individual particular perceptions are possible, he argued against the possibility of ABSTRACT IDEAS. His views may be construed as a form of PHE-

NOMENALISM. ['BARK-lee': 'BERK-lee' is the pronunciation of the name of the California city named after the philosopher]

Berlin, Isaiah (1909-1997) Born in Latvia, but worked in England; known primarily for his work in the history of ideas and his liberal political theory.

Berry's paradox There are various ways of referring to numbers: 'thirty-seven', 'the sum of 8 and 5', 'the number of bears Goldilocks met'. Consider this: 'the smallest integer not nameable in less than nineteen syllables'. What integer is that? If that eighteen-syllable phrase names some integer, that integer is nameable in less than nineteen syllables, so the phrase doesn't name it.

best of all possible worlds A phrase associated with LEIBNIZ, who believed that God, being perfectly good, knowing, and powerful, could not have created anything less than perfect; thus this world (despite how it sometimes appears, especially on Monday morning) is the best of all possible worlds (*see* PROBLEM OF EVIL).

biconditional A material biconditional (sometimes called a material equivalence or simply a biconditional) is a TRUTH-FUNCTIONAL connective. It is true when both sentences it connects are true, or when both are false; it is false when the sentences have different TRUTH VALUES. It is symbolized by the triple-bar ($\equiv$) or the double-arrow ($\leftrightarrow$), and may be interpreted as "if and only if" (sometimes abbreviated 'iff'). It is called the biconditional because it means the same as a CONJUNCTION[1] of two CONDITIONALS: $P \equiv Q$ is equivalent to $(P \supset Q) \& (Q \supset P)$. A logical biconditional is a biconditional that is LOGICALLY TRUE.

bioethics The ethics involved in various sorts of biology-related activities, mostly centring on medical matters. Examples of issues considered in bioethics are abortion, genetic control, EUTHANASIA, and *in vitro* fertilization.

binary predicate   *See* PREDICATE.

binary relation   *See* RELATIONS.

biting the bullet   What philosophers are said to do when they choose to accept the unlikely counterintuitive (*see* INTUITION) consequences of their position, rather than taking them as COUNTEREXAMPLES. The phrase comes from old movies, in which wounded cowboys bit down on a bullet to help them stand the pain of surgery without anaesthetic.

bivalence   *See* law of the excluded middle, in LAWS OF THOUGHT.

Black,   Max (1909-88) Born in Russia, educated in England, worked in the US; important work in logic and philosophy of language.

black box   When a mechanism is identified merely by its functional properties, without reference to, or even knowledge of, the internal structure responsible for those properties, it is said to be thought of as a black box. FUNCTIONALISM and BEHAVIOURISM both think of the modules responsible for human behaviour as black boxes.

Blanshard,   Brand (1892-1987) American philosopher, known for his attacks on ANALYTIC PHILOSOPHY and ethical noncognitivism (*see* COGNITIVISM / NONCOGNITIVISM), and his defenses of RATIONALISM and IDEALISM.

bleen   *See* GRUE.

blindsight   People with certain brain injuries report blindness in regions of the visual field, but are nevertheless able to "guess" at what's represented in that field with great accuracy. An interesting result for EPISTEMOLOGY.

Block,   Ned (b. 1942) American philosopher important in contemporary philosophy of mind.

bodily interchange   This is what would happen if the same person existed at one time in one body and at another time in another body, for example, through REINCARNATION, or through a variety of science-fiction techniques such as brain or memory transplant. The topic is important not only in religious contexts or as entertainment, but as a THOUGHT EXPERIMENT about PERSONAL IDENTITY.

Boethius,   Anicius Manlius Severinus (c. 480-524) Roman philosopher and statesman, translator of Aristotle. Best known for his influential work in LOGIC, and for his book *The Consolation of Philosophy*. ['bo-EE-thee-us']

Bolzano,   Bernard (1781-1848) Czech philosopher, theologian, logician, and mathematician. His work in EPISTEMOLOGY and LOGIC, relatively unrecognized in his time, has received recent attention.

Bonaventure   (in Italian, Bonaventura), Saint (Original name, Giovanni di [John of] Fidanza) (1221-1274) Italian SCHOLASTIC philosopher / theologian. His work was strongly influenced by AUGUSTINE.

Bonhoeffer,   Dietrich (1906-1945) German theologian. Active in the resistance to Hitler, he died in a Nazi concentration camp. His radically secularized and ecumenical religious views have been of great interest in contemporary THEOLOGY.

Boole,   George (1815-1864) English mathematician responsible for the development of the idea of treating variables in logic (*see* SYMBOLS OF QUANTIFIER LOGIC) in ways analogous to those in algebra; this was the first real step in the development of modern logic. One obvious difference between the "Boolean interpretation" of CATEGORIAL statements and the ARISTOTELIAN (TRADITIONAL) interpretation is that in the latter, but not the former, UNIVERSAL statements have EXISTENTIAL IMPORT.

book of life   In the Bible, a record of those destined for heaven. For MEDIEVAL and contemporary philosophers, a book that recorded your destiny or the details of your life in advance was a thought experiment about DETERMINISM, FOREKNOWLEDGE, and FREE WILL.

borderline case   *See* VAGUENESS.

Bosanquet,   Bernard (1848-1923) He and BRADLEY were the leading British ABSOLUTE IDEALISTS of the beginning of the twentieth century. ['boz-an-KET']

bound variable   *See* SYMBOLS OF QUANTIFIER LOGIC.

bourgeoisie / proletariat   Names of the two social/economic classes important in MARX'S analysis. The former is the capitalist CLASS[2]—employers, financiers, landlords, etc., though more generally now the bourgeoisie is taken to include middle class wage-earners as well. The latter is the working class. ['boor-zhwa-zee']

Boyle,   Robert *See* SCIENTISTS.

Bowsma,   O[ets] K[olk] (1898-1978) American ORDINARY-LANGUAGE PHILOSOPHER; his specialty was exposing, in a WITTGENSTEINIAN fashion, the nonsense of certain philosophical pronouncements.

bracketing   HUSSERL'S term, referring to the process of suspending normal ASSUMPTIONS[1] and PRESUPPOSITIONS. He thought that by "bracketing off" the assumptions of science we could see things as they fundamentally appear to CONSCIOUSNESS. *See also* PHENOMENOLOGY.

Bradley,   F(rancis) H(erbert) (1846-1924) English IDEALIST philosopher, known for his works on LOGIC, METAPHYSICS, and ethics. His work was largely outside the British EMPIRICIST tradition, more in the CONTINENTAL HEGELIAN spirit.

His central metaphysical notion is "the ABSOLUTE"—a coherent and comprehensive whole that harmonizes the diversity and SELF-CONTRADICTIONS of appearances.

brain in a vat Imagine that you are, and always have been, merely a brain suspended in a vat of nutritive liquid, connected to a computer that feeds you electronic signals, thereby simulating sense experience. All your experiences are thus hallucinations (*see* ILLUSION / HALLUCINATION / DELUSION). Have you any good reason to think this story is false? This THOUGHT EXPERIMENT, suggested by Hilary PUTNAM, is used by philosophers to consider SCEPTICISM about the external world.

brain transplants THOUGHT-EXPERIMENTS involving moving one brain, complete with memories and personalities, into another body. Where is the original person, post-transplant? A way of considering questions of PERSONAL IDENTITY.

Braithwaite, Richard Bevan (1900-90) English EMPIRICIST philosopher of science.

Brandt, Richard B[ooker] (1910-1997) American ethicist, with important work on rule-UTILITARIAN and naturalistic ethics. (*See* ETHICAL NATURALISM.)

Brentano, Franz (1838-1917) German philosopher and psychologist, an important influence on later CONTINENTAL philosophers; known for his theory of INTENTIONALITY[2] – the reference of mental states to (sometimes "inexistent") things beyond themselves, the "aboutness" of mental states. "Brentano's thesis" is the view that this intentionality is what distinguishes the mental from everything else.

Broad, C(harlie) D(unbar) (1887-1971) English philosopher who contributed to a wide variety of topics; a collector and systematizer of traditional philosophical ideas who nevertheless took account of contemporary philosophy and science.

Brouwer, Luitzen Egbertus Jan (1881-1966) Dutch mathematician, a founder of mathematical INTUITIONISM, with important work in the philosophy of mathematics.

Bruno, Giordano (1548-1600) Italian Renaissance philosopher. He worked in various European countries after religious persecution forced him to flee Italy; burned as a heretic. His work is now seen as an important step toward the scientific views of nature that followed.

Buber, Martin (1878-1965) Austrian Jewish philosopher and theologian, worked in Germany and Palestine. Best known for his thought on the special "I-thou" relationship we can have with other people.

bundle theory In general, the view of classical EMPIRICISTS who argued that things are nothing more than bundles of properties, and that there is no need to think of SUBSTRATA. The phrase most often refers to a special case of this general theory: HUME'S theory of PERSONAL IDENTITY. He argued that since we can't perceive any continuing self in us, our idea of a person, which has to come from PERCEPTION to be valid, can't be of a continuing mental SUBSTANCE. All we can perceive in ourselves is a continuously changing "bundle" of mental events, so this is what our CONCEPT of the self must consist of.

burden of proof When there is a disagreement, it's sometimes the case that one side is expected to prove its case, and if it can't, the other wins by default. The side that must provide proof is said to have the burden of proof. It may be the side with the position that is surprising, or unorthodox, or that runs counter to other well-accepted beliefs. Thus, for example, people who claim that we have been regularly visited by aliens from outer space have the burden of proof. Because they can't prove their case, they lose the argument, despite the fact that nobody can prove we haven't been visited.

Burge, Tyler (b. 1946) American philosopher of mind, logic, and language.

Buridan, Jean (c. 1300-1358) French philosopher and scientist; work on physics, LOGIC, and METAPHYSICS. He argued that one must do what and only what seems to one to be the greatest good, but that the will can put off choosing when there's no clearly best option. One problem raised by this position is illustrated by the story known as Buridan's ass (though Buridan himself is not responsible for this story): imagine a hungry ass standing between two equal and equidistant piles of hay. Neither would seem more desirable to it than the other, so if Buridan's principle were right, the animal would starve to death.

Burke, Edmund (1729-1797) British statesman and political thinker, associated with conservative political views.

Butler, Judith (b. 1956) American FEMINIST with influential writings in many fields including legal and social theory.

Butler, Bishop Joseph (1692-1752) English theologian and moralist, known for his work on moral psychology and THEOLOGY.

C

calculus An abstract system of symbols, aimed at calculating something. Some philosophers think of the various sciences as interpreted calculi. One can call each symbol-system of SYMBOLIC LOGIC a 'calculus': for example, the SENTENTIAL and QUANTIFIER calculi. The system for calculating PROBABILITIES is called the 'probability calculus'. A calculus is interpreted (given a "valuation") when its symbols are given meaning by relating them to things in the real world; uninterpreted, it is just a bunch of symbols with syntax but no semantics (*See* SEMANTICS / SYNTAX / PRAGMATICS.) 'The calculus' names a branch of mathematics independently and somewhat differently developed by LEIBNIZ and Newton (see SCIENTISTS) during the late seventeenth century. ('Calculus' is singular; plural: 'calculi'.)

calculus, felicity / felicific / pleasure-pain / hedonic / happiness. *See* FELICIFIC CALCULUS.

Calvin, John (original name Jean Chauvin or Caulvin) (1509-1564) French (lived in Switzerland) theologian and religious reformer. His moral, theological, and social views ("Calvinism") have been influential, and he was a key figure in the Protestant Reformation.

Cambridge change / property An example of a Cambridge change is when Fred becomes the smartest kid in the class because Sally, formerly the smartest, moves away. This is not a real change in Fred; it's a change only in a RELATIONAL, 'Cambridge' property. But it's hard to draw a very good distinction here: would becoming a parent be a real or a Cambridge change?

Cambridge Platonists A school of seventeenth-century English clergy, moralists, and philosophers; you won't be surprised to hear that they were centered around Cambridge University and shared an enthusiasm for PLATO. None of the members of this school had substantial later influence, and you probably won't recognize any of their names: Benjamin Whichcote, Ralph Cudworth, Henry More, John Smith, Gilbert Burnet... Their interest nowadays is largely the result of their being a definite exception to the general rule that English philosophy is utilitarian and empiricist.

Camus, Albert (1913-1960) Algerian-born French novelist and philosopher, associated with the EXISTENTIALISTS.

canon A basic and important rule.

Cantor, Georg (1845-1918) Russian-born German mathematician and logician, best known for his creation of SET theory.

capitalism An economic system characterized by private property and a free market, contrasted with SOCIALISM / COMMUNISM.

cardinal / ordinal scale / ranking A cardinal scale assigns some number to each item on a list; the number reflects the "size" of each item. Thus, for example, a cardinal ranking of the UTILITY of actions would assign a utility to each item reflecting its degree of value. We would expect that an item with a utility of 1000 is ten times as good as an item with a utility of 100. An ordinal scale arranges items on a list merely in order of their size, without giving absolute values. Thus, if one action is higher on an ordinal list of utilities, that means that it has more utility; but we aren't told how much more.

Carnap, Rudolf (1891-1970) German-born philosopher who spent his later life in the U.S., to which he transplanted LOGICAL POSITIVISM when the VIENNA CIRCLE disbanded in pre-World War II Austria. He is important also for his work on philosophy of science and LOGIC.

Cartesian This means 'pertaining to DESCARTES'. Cartesian-
ism is a school of thought derived from Descartes' philosophy. "Cartesian doubt" names Descartes' philosophical
method in which he begins by doubting all his beliefs, even
the ordinary common-sense ones, because of the possibility
that he is dreaming or is being fooled by a "Cartesian
demon" (an EVIL GENIUS). He then searches for a starting
point that is INDUBITABLE. "Cartesian DUALISM" strongly
separates mind and body into wholly different metaphysical
categories; the "Cartesian ego" is a purely thinking thing (a
"*RES COGITANS*") with no physical characteristics. The "Cartesian circle" is this bit of apparently CIRCULAR REASONING
Descartes gives in the *Meditations*: God's existence guarantees the reliability of my CLEAR AND DISTINCT ideas; but the
proof of God's existence depends on the reliability of the
clear and distinct premises of that proof.

Cartwright, Nancy (b. 1943) American-born philosopher of
science, with important works in the history and philosophy
of physics and economics.

Cassirer, Ernst (1874-1945) German neo-Kantian philosopher
with wide-ranging work on language, science, mythology,
and history of culture.

Castañeda, Héctor-Neri. (b. 1924) American ANALYTIC philosopher, known for his work in METAPHYSICS, logic, and
philosophy of language.

casuistry The determination of right and wrong by reasoning
involving general principles applied to particular cases, taking into account their particular characteristics. Because religious casuists sometimes reasoned in overly complex ways
to silly conclusions, this word has come to have disparaging
overtones. ['KAZH-you-is-tree']

categorial logic The theory of the logical relations between
sentences with the following forms:

All A's are B's
No A's are B's
Some A's are B's
Some A's are non-B's

These are the standard forms of the categorial propositions—
the A / E / I / O PROPOSITIONS.

categorical / hypothetical imperative KANT's distinction. An
imperative is a command. 'Categorical' means absolute—not
dependent on particular aims or circumstances; 'hypothetical' means relative to, depending on, particular aims or circumstances. Thus, 'Tell the truth' is a categorical imperative,
but 'If it is to everyone's benefit, tell the truth' and 'If you
want others to trust you, tell the truth' are hypothetical imperatives. Kant argued that hypothetical imperatives, while
sometimes giving useful practical advice, do not express the
standards of morality, which are expressed only by categorical imperatives. He argued further that there is one command
central to all morality—*the* categorical imperative: Act in a
way such that the general rule behind your action could consistently be willed to be a universal law. He argued that this
was equivalent to saying that others should be treated as
ends, never as means only.

categorical / hypothetical proposition A hypothetical PROPO-
SITION is one of the form 'if P then Q'—nowadays more
often called "CONDITIONAL". A categorical proposition is one
not hypothetical. This distinction may not be a very useful
one: "if P then Q" is logically equivalent (see BICONDITION-
AL) to "not-P or Q"; so in some sense they mean the same
thing. The first clearly has hypothetical form; but should we
call the second categorical?

categories **1.** A synonym for 'classes' (*See* SET[2].) The logic of
categories is CATEGORIAL LOGIC. **2.** ARISTOTLE and KANT
called our most basic concepts the 'categories'. Kant thought
these were *A PRIORI*, and they included CAUSATION and SUB-
STANCE.

categorematic   *See* SYNCATEGOREMATIC / CATEGOREMATIC.

category mistake   Gilbert RYLE gave this example of a category mistake: someone is shown a number of classroom and
administrative buildings, libraries, student residences, etc.,
but says, "I have seen all those, but where is the university?"
His mistake was to think that the university is just another
building, whereas the university is in a different category.
Ryle argued that some philosophical mistakes—for instance,
the separation of mind from body and its behaviour—are
thus made by people who don't understand what categories
their concepts belong in.

catharsis   ARISTOTLE's term for the purging or cleansing of the
emotions that he thought happened to the audience at the end
of a dramatic tragedy, when pity and terror produced in the
audience are calmed. [Also spelled '*katharsis*']

causal chain   A series of events in which each event causes the
next.

causal explanation   *See* EXPLANATION.

causal theories   A variety of theories that make the notion of
cause basic in some way. The causal theory of knowledge
proposes, as a condition of 'P knows that **x**', that P's belief
be causally connected in some appropriate way to the fact
that **x**. The causal theory of perception points out that a
"blue sensation" is one normally caused by a blue thing,
and tries to avoid SENSE-DATA by explaining that what is
happening when there is no blue thing there is that the sensation is one that would have been caused by a blue thing,
were the situation normal. For the causal theory of mind,
see FUNCTIONALISM. The causal theory of meaning / reference makes the meaning /reference of terms a matter of the
causal connections their uses have with the external world;
an important example of this is the causal theory of PROPER
NAMES.

causa sui   *See* CAUSE-OF-ITSELF.

causation   The relation that holds between a cause and its effect. Also called 'causality'. Long-standing philosophical problems are concerned with the nature of cause, and how we find out about it. HUME argued that a supposed "power" in **x** to bring about **y** "NECESSARILY" would not be EMPIRICAL, so that idea is illegitimate; all we can observe is that **x**s have regularly been followed by **y**s in the past (i.e., have been "constantly conjoined" with **y**s). Critics object that this fails to distinguish between causal connections and mere accidental but universal regularities. For other controversies about cause, *see* DETERMINISM *and* AGENT / EVENT CAUSATION *and* REASONS / CAUSES. [The adjectival form of 'cause' is 'causal'—please don't spell this 'casual']

cause, false   *See* FALSE CAUSE.

cause-of-itself   (Latin; *causa sui* ['COWS-ah SOO-ee']) Narrowly, a thing that causes itself to exist (or to be the way it is). God is commonly thought to be the only thing that is capable of this. This notion is difficult to understand, given that, in the common notion of cause, for **x** to cause **y**, **x** must exist before **y** does, and it's nonsense to think of something existing before it itself does. A broader (and more old-fashioned) notion thinks of cause as EXPLANATION. This does not lead to the same absurdity, but has its own problems: how can something provide the explanation for its own existence?

cause, proximate / remote   *See* PROXIMATE / REMOTE CAUSE.

causes, efficient / formal / material / final   *See* FOUR CAUSES.

causes / reasons   *See* REASONS / CAUSES.

causes, the four   *See* FOUR CAUSES.

cave   In *The Republic*, PLATO imagines a group of prisoners chained inside a cave, who never see anything in the outside world; all they see are shadows cast on the wall of the cave by objects inside the cave that are copies of real things outside. This "allegory of the cave" is presented as an analogy to the way Plato sees our status: what we experience is not reality, but merely a shadowy representation of it. The philosopher's job is to figure out what reality might be like. (*See also* FORM[1].)

central-state materialism   *See* MATERIALISM.

certainty   A belief is called 'certain' in ordinary talk when it is believed very strongly, or when one is unable to think, or even imagine, that it might be false. Philosophers often don't want to rely on a subjective and psychological test for certainty, and demand proof that some belief really is beyond rational doubt. Some philosophers think that all our knowledge must have a certain FOUNDATION. 'Moral certainty' means sufficiently warranted to justified action; 'metaphysical certainty' means warranted not merely by fallible perception of particulars, but rather by some presumably more reliable reasoning about all being; 'logical certainty' is the extremely strong warrant we get for a proposition which is in some sense a truth of logic. None of these three terms is very precise in sense or application; all are best avoided.

ceteris paribus   (Latin: "other things being equal") This is used in comparing two things while assuming they differ only in the one characteristic under consideration. For example, it could be said that, *ceteris paribus*, a simple theory is better than a complicated one; though if everything else is not equal—if, for example, the simpler theory has fewer true predictions—then it might not be better. ['KEH' or 'SEH' + '-ter-iss PAR-uh-bus']

chain, causal   *See* CAUSAL CHAIN.

Chain of Being   *See* GREAT CHAIN OF BEING.

chance   1. Something happens by chance when it is not fully DETERMINED by previous events—when previous events do not necessarily bring it about, or make it the way it is; in other words, when it's a random event. We can sometimes know the PROBABILITY of chance events in advance. **2.** Sometimes, however, we speak of chance events as those we're unable to predict with CERTAINTY, though they might be determined in unknown ways; for example, how a flipped coin turns up may be fully determined by how it's flipped, but in practice, we don't and can't do the measurements and calculations, so we say it's a matter of chance. **3.** A third way of using this term refers to an event as merely coincidental with another; thus we might say that it was mere chance that it rained on Fred's birthday. We don't mean here that either event was uncaused or unpredictable.

change, Cambridge   *See* CAMBRIDGE CHANGE.

chaos   1. Early philosophers used this term to refer to the unformed and disorderly state of things which, they supposed, preceded the imposition of order that produced the universe (the COSMOS). **2.** The term has been used recently (in 'chaos theory') to refer to a branch of mathematical study concerned with complex phenomena which show some unpredictable features.

charity, principle of   *See* PRINCIPLE OF CHARITY.

chimera   In Greek mythology, this is a monster with a lion's head, goat's body and snake's tail. By extension, in philosophy this means a non-existent object which we imagine by combining features of real things. ['ky-MEER-a' or 'kuh-MEER-a']

Chinese room example   SEARLE asks us to imagine a huge room containing a worker and an enormous library. Somebody writes a question in Chinese on a slip of paper and feeds it into the room. The worker who understands no

Chinese finds the Chinese characters, just by their look, in books, and follows complicated instructions which eventuate in his writing other characters on the paper, which in fact answer that question, and feeds it back out. This room (so to speak) behaves outwardly like a person who understands Chinese, but Searle argues that once we know what's going on inside, it's clear that there's no comprehension of Chinese involved. Searle concludes that external behaviour is not sufficient for attribution of some mental characteristics. (This example is also known as the "Chinese Box".)

Chisholm,   Roderick M[ilton] (1916-1999) American ANALYTIC philosopher, surprisingly influenced by the PHENOMENOLOGICAL methods of BRENTANO and MEINONG.

Chomsky,   (Avram) Noam (b. 1928) American linguist (known for ground-breaking work in semantic theory—*See* SEMANTICS / SYNTAX / PRAGMATICS) and philosopher (associated with the INNATENESS hypothesis). Recently in the public eye for his strong left-wing political views.

Chrysippus   (280-207 B.C.) Prolific Greek philosopher—widely quoted by the ancients, though none of his works survive. Central figure in STOICISM.

Church,   Alonzo (1903-1995) American logician and mathematician; responsible for some of the basic results of contemporary mathematical logic.

Churchland,   Paul M[ontgomery) (b. 1942) Canadian philosopher known for his advocacy of eliminativist MATERIALISM.

Cicero,   (Marcus Tullius) (106-43 B.C.) Roman orator and statesman, writer of works on politics and oratory.

circle, vicious   *See* CIRCULAR REASONING / DEFINITION.

Circle, Vienna   *See* VIENNA CIRCLE.

circle, virtuous   *See* CIRCULAR REASONING / DEFINITION.

circular reasoning / definition   A DEFINITION is (viciously) circular (and thus useless) when the term to be defined, or a version of it, occurs in the definition; for example, the definition of 'free action' as 'action that is freely done'. (*See* list of other sorts of DEFINITION.) (Viciously) circular reasoning defends some statement by assuming the truth of that statement; e.g.:

>"Why do you think what the Bible says is true?"
>"Because the Bible is the Word of God."
>"How do you know that it is the Word of God?"
>"Because it says so in the Bible, and everything there is true."

Some philosophers argue that not all circles are vicious, and that some sorts of circular reasoning are acceptable—"virtuously circular"—for example, when the circle is wide enough. A dictionary, for example, must be circular, defining words in terms of other words; but this is okay.

Circular reasoning is also known as 'begging the question'. Careless speakers sometimes think that this means 'raising the question'; it doesn't. Begging the question is sometimes called by its Latin name, '*petitio principii*' ['peh-TIT-ee-oh prin-KIP-ee-ee' or 'pi-TISH-ee-oh prin-SIP-ee-ee'] "postulation of the beginning".

circumstantial *ad hominem* argument   *See* AD HOMINEM.

civil disobedience   A deliberate, conscientious, public, often non-violent law violation, with the aim of protesting what is thought to be the injustice of the law or of some other state policy.

civil rights   *See* RIGHTS.

clairvoyance   EXTRA-SENSORY PERCEPTION or PRECOGNITION by means of "visions". A PARANORMAL PHENOMENON about whose existence mainstream science is sceptical.

class   **1**. *See* SET. **2**. An economic and/or social division of
society, important in MARX and other more recent political
theory. Marx thought that the BOURGEOISIE and proletariat
were doomed to warfare, and that this "class struggle" would
propel society toward socialist society.

clear and distinct ideas   DESCARTES (and others) have used this
to refer to the kind of ideas they thought philosophers should
seek as the FOUNDATION for any other beliefs, and which are
completely reliable or CERTAIN. An idea is clear according to
Descartes, when it is "present and apparent to an attentive
mind"; and distinct when it is "so precise and different from
other objects that it contains within itself nothing but what is
clear." There is some problem in interpreting just what
Descartes meant here, and in showing why this sort of idea
might be especially or completely reliable.

clear / hard case   A clear case in law is one in which, if all the
facts (including the facts of legal history) were known, all
reasonable people would agree on what legal outcome was
proper. Reasonable people could disagree on the proper outcome of a hard case despite this full knowledge.

closure / closed under ...   Closure under some relation **R**
means that if **P** is in some set, and if **P** is related to **Q** by **R**,
then **Q** is in that set too. For example, if belief is closed under
implication (*see* INFERENCE / IMPLICATION / ENTAILMENT[1]),
then if **A** believes **P**, and **P** implies **Q**, then **A** believes **Q**. (It
seems that belief is not closed under implication.)

coercion   *See* COMPULSION.

coextensive   Two TERMS or PREDICATES are coextensive when
they in fact apply to exactly the same objects (*see* EXTENSION
/ INTENSION).

cogito ergo sum   (Latin: "I think, therefore I exist") DESCARTES'
famous argument (sometimes called 'the cogito' for short),

which he took to be the starting point in his search for CER-
TAINTY. Whatever else he might be mistaken about, he reasoned, he could not be mistaken that he was thinking,
because even mistaken thinking is thinking. It followed that
he must exist—at least as a thinking thing. In French: "Je
pense donc je suis." ['KO-' or 'KAH-' + 'gee-toe air-go soom';
'zhuh PANZ donk zhuh swee']

cognitive / emotive meaning   The former is what a sentence
states—what makes it true or false. The latter is its "expressive" content—the speaker's feelings that it communicates,
rather than any beliefs. *See* COGNITIVISM / NONCOGNITIVISM.

cognition   The operations of the mind; sometimes particularly
believing and awareness; sometimes, more particularly, the
mental process by which we get KNOWLEDGE.

cognitive science   A recently-developed discipline combining
philosophers, psychologists, and computer scientists, devoted to providing theories of COGNITION.

cognitivism / noncognitivism   Cognitivism is the position that
something can be known. Ethical cognitivism is the view that
ethical statements are statements about (supposed) facts and
thus are true or false, and might be known to be true or false.
This is opposed to the noncognitivist position that ethical
statements are not knowable. A species of ethical noncognitivism is EMOTIVISM, which argues that ethical statements are
not fact-stating, but are expressions of approval or disapproval (like 'Hooray for that!'), or invitations to action (like
'Please do that!') and are thus neither true nor false, and not
knowable. Cognitivists thus think that ethical statements
have COGNITIVE MEANING; and non-cognitivists that they do
not—that they have perhaps emotive meaning only.

coherence / incoherence   A SET of beliefs or sentences is
coherent when it fits together in a logical way—that is, when
everything in the set is consistent, or when the items in it

CONFIRM others in it. A set in which one item would be false, or probably false, given the truth of others is not coherent (is incoherent). *See* COHERENCE THEORY OF TRUTH.

coherence theory of truth   The idea that the truth of something is constituted by the fact that it fits into a COHERENT set: the SET of true sentences is the one that fits together best. For a list of competing theories, *see* TRUTH.

collectively / distributively   What applies to a group collectively applies to it as a whole only, i.e., not to its individual members (not distributively). The atoms that constitute a pig collectively, but not distributively, outweigh a fly. (*See also* COMPOSITION / DIVISION.)

collective responsibility   The controversial idea that a group or nation or culture can bear RESPONSIBILITY as a whole for bad acts: for example, the whole German nation for Nazi atrocities.

Collingwood,   R[obert] G[eorge] (1889-1943) English historian and IDEALIST philosopher.

commensurability / incommensurability   Different things are commensurable when they can be measured on the same scale. UTILITARIANISM, at least in some versions, assumes that different people's different pleasures are commensurable on a common scale of utilites; but it has been argued that there's no way to make sensible quantity comparisons. Another example of supposed incommensurability is in the comparison of science and religion: some philosophers think that it's foolish to criticize religious statements using the criteria of scientific adequacy. WITTGENSTEIN is strongly associated with the view that various human activities should be seen as incommensurable, assessable only by their own internal standards.

commitment   **1.** A binding OBLIGATION voluntarily undertaken by the person thus obligated. EXISTENTIALISTS hold that one freely and arbitrarily makes up one's commitments, and that this is the only source of one's moral obligation. 2. *See* ONTOLOGICAL commitment.

common consent argument for God's existence   The supposed fact that so many cultures in all historical periods have believed in God is given as evidence of His existence. Objections: not all cultures share belief in God, and it wouldn't prove anything even if they did. Here's a particularly bad version of this argument:

> "The Bible has been translated into hundreds of different languages, but in every single translation, it says that God exists! So He must exist."

common sense   1. Until the eighteenth century or so, this term named the supposed mental faculty which combined input from different senses to give us a unified idea of an external object, combining, for example, the smell, taste, look and feel of a peach. **2.** More recently, it has come to mean the mental faculty which all people are supposed to possess "in common", for knowledge of basic everyday truths. Some philosophers have counted this as an answer to SCEPTICAL doubts about the obvious truths that there exists an external world, other minds, etc. The eighteenth-century Scottish "common sense philosophers" (most notably Thomas REID), and, later, PEIRCE and MOORE relied heavily on this notion, attempting to vindicate the views of ordinary people attacked by HUMEAN scepticism.

common-sense realism   *See* NAÏVE REALISM.

commons, tragedy of the   *See* TRAGEDY OF THE COMMONS.

communism   *See* SOCIALISM / COMMUNISM.

communitarianism   Advocates the position in social philosophy that the RIGHTS of individuals are not basic—that groups, or society as a whole, can have rights that are not constituted by the individual rights of the members of those groups, and that these group rights may override claims to individual rights. FASCISM is a rather extreme example of communitarianism. A form of HOLISM in social theory; the contrast is with individualism.

commutation   A rule of INFERENCE which allows the replacement or mutual inference of the equivalent expressions (P & Q) and (Q & P), and also of (P v Q) and (Q v P).

commutativity   *See* SYMMETRIC / ASYMMETRIC / NONSYMMETRIC.

compatibilism   Any philosophical position that claims that two things are compatible (they can both exist at once). In particular, this word is often used to refer to the view that FREE WILL and DETERMINISM are compatible—that is, that people's ACTIONS are (sometimes) free even though they are fully causally determined. They argue that we're not free when we're acting under COMPULSION (that is, *forced* to act), but that this is a different thing from the action's being determined or caused.

complement   The complement of one SET is another set containing everything not in the first. The complement of the set of pigs includes all non-pigs (cows, planets, toes, days of the week, etc.). If 'P' stands for the set of pigs, then '-P' or 'p̄' stands for its complement. The complement of the term 'pigs' is the term 'non-pigs'.

completeness / incompleteness   These terms have a variety of technical senses, but in a common use, a LOGICAL system is complete when every LOGICALLY TRUE sentence is DERIVABLE; otherwise incomplete.

complex ideas   *See* SIMPLE / COMPLEX IDEAS.

complex question   An informal fallacy: a question is asked so as to presuppose the truth of some assumption. The classic (sexist) example of this is the question, "When did you stop beating your wife?"

composition / division (fallacies of)   The fallacy of composition is the incorrect reasoning from properties of parts of a whole to properties of the whole itself. For instance, it's true that each atom of a pig weighs less than one gram, but it's a mistake to conclude that since the pig is composed of nothing but these atoms, the pig weighs less than one gram. The fallacy of division runs in the other direction: illicitly reasoning that since a collection has a property, then so must a part of that collection: Elephants are becoming rare; Jumbo is an elephant; therefore Jumbo is becoming rare.

compulsion   An ACTION is said to be done under compulsion (also known as 'constraint' or 'coercion') when it is "forced" by internal or external circumstances, and thus the doer of that action can't be held morally RESPONSIBLE for doing it. If you steal something, for example, because someone is forcing you to do it at gunpoint, or because you are a kleptomaniac (i.e., you have the psychological disorder that is supposed to create an irresistible tendency to steal), that doesn't make your action any better, but it does mean that you're not to blame. COMPATIBLISTS about FREE WILL argue that compulsion is the sort of cause that makes one unfree and not responsible, but when one's action is caused (DETERMINED) but not due to compulsion, one is free and responsible.

Comte,   (Isidore) Auguste (Marie-François) (1798-1857) French POSITIVIST philosopher. He emphasized the evolution of thought toward scientific, EMPIRICAL explanation. He is credited with founding the science of sociology. ['кOMT']

conatus   A mental tendency, process or event of the sort that initiates action. "Conation" names the general aspect of mentality that initiates action.

concept **1.** In ordinary talk, this word often has little meaning, and is best omitted when it's just a pretentious synonym for 'idea'. **2.** Philosophers may use this word to refer to the ability to categorize things; thus to say that someone has the concept of *duck* is to say that that person can sort things correctly into ducks and non-ducks. A concept is sometimes distinguished from a percept, which is a particular mental item had while sensing a particular thing. A concept, then, may be thought to be a generalization or abstraction from one or many percepts (*see* ABSTRACT / CONCRETE ENTITIES / IDEAS). Thus a percept is sometimes called a particular idea, and a concept a general or abstract idea.

conceptual analysis   *See* ANALYTIC PHILOSOPHY.

conceptualism   *See* UNIVERSALS.

conceptual scheme   The most general framework of someone's view of the world—a structured system of CONCEPTS that divide that person's world into kinds of things. It has sometimes been supposed that two people's conceptual schemes might differ so much that one would never be able to understand or translate what the other said.

conceptual truth   A statement that is true merely because of the nature of the CONCEPTS that make it up. The fact that all bachelors are unmarried is a conceptual truth, because the concept of being a bachelor involves being unmarried. Compare the fact that snow is white: this is not a conceptual truth, because being white, despite being true of snow, is not part of the concept of snow. We can imagine, consistent with our concept of snow, that snow is always green. (Substitute 'word' for 'concept' in this definition, and it turns into the definition of 'ANALYTIC TRUTH'.)

conclusion   *See* ARGUMENT.

conclusion markers   Terms which indicate what the conclusion of an argument is, for example, 'therefore', 'hence', 'accordingly', 'thus'.

concomitant variation (method of)   *See* MILL'S METHODS.

concrete   *See* ABSTRACT / CONCRETE ENTITIES / IDEAS.

Condillac,   Étienne Bonnot de (1715-1780) French philosopher, one of the ENCYCLOPEDISTS, with influential works on theory of knowledge. ['kon-dee-yak']

conditional   A statement of the form 'if P then Q', for example, 'If it's raining, then you'll get wet'. What this sort of statement means (and what would make it true) is a surprisingly complicated matter, but a core of that meaning is MODELLED by the (much simpler) material conditional in SENTENTIAL LOGIC. A material conditional of the form 'if P then Q' is defined as a statement that is true when P is false or Q is true (or both); so it is false only when P is true and Q is false. The first clause in this material conditional is called the 'antecedent', the second the 'consequent'. (Or sometimes by the old-fashioned terms 'protasis' and 'apodosis'; or 'implicans' and 'implicate'.) To symbolize this sentence we connect letters representing the antecedent and consequent by the horseshoe (⊃) or the arrow (→) (*see* SYMBOLS OF SENTENTIAL LOGIC). To see why the material conditional is only a rough match for the English conditional, consider the English sentence 'If Bolivia is in Asia, then pigs fly.' Is this true or false or neither? It's hard to say. But suppose we translate this into symbolic logic as 'B ⊃ P'. Now the antecedent of this material conditional 'B' ('Bolivia is in Asia') is false, so 'B ⊃ P' is true. This and other strange results of modeling the English conditional by the material conditional are known as the PARADOXES of material IMPLICATION. It's clear also that the material conditional does not model the COUNTERFACTUAL. A material conditional is also known as a material implication, though 'implication' can also refer to a relation between whole statements. Material conditionals should be distinguished from strict implications: these are conditionals that are LOGICALLY TRUE, for example, 'If some pigs are sloppy eaters, then some sloppy eaters are pigs'.

conditional, contrary-to-fact   *See* COUNTERFACTUAL.

conditional probability   *See* PROBABILITY.

conditional proof   The rule of INFERENCE that permits one to infer a CONDITIONAL once one has derived the consequent from the antecedent.

condition, necessary / sufficient   *See* NECESSARY / SUFFICIENT CONDITION.

Condorcet,   Antoine Caritat, Marquis de (1743-1794) French mathematician, philosopher, and social theorist, one of the ENCYCLOPEDISTS. For 'Condorcet paradox' *see* VOTER'S PARADOX^2. ['kon-dor-say']

confirmation / disconfirmation / verification / falsification   Confirmation is the collection of evidence for a statement. Because there might be some evidence even for a false statement, a statement might be confirmed though false. Collecting evidence that a statement is false is called 'disconfirmation'. 'Verification' means 'confirmation' and 'falsification' means 'disconfirmation', though one tends to speak of a statement as having been verified (or falsified) only if the statement is really true (or false), and has been shown to be so by the evidence. Confirmation theory is the attempt to give a general account of what counts as confirmation. This is a surprisingly difficult job; the paradoxes of confirmation appear to show what is wrong with some attempts. (*See* GRUE, RAVEN PARADOX.)

conjunction   **1.** The logical relation expressed in English by connecting two sentences by 'and'; also the sentence thus formed. The sentences connected in a conjunction are called 'conjuncts'. A conjunction is true when both conjuncts are true, and false otherwise. Thus the sentence 'It's raining and it's Tuesday' is true when both 'It's raining' and 'It's Tuesday' are true. If one or both conjuncts are false, the conjunction is false. A conjunction is symbolized in logic by connecting letters standing for the conjuncts with an ampersand (&) or a dot (·) or a carat (^). **2.** The rule of INFERENCE: P, Q; therefore P and Q.

connectionism   The position that the best MODEL for COGNITIVE systems is a "neural net"—a network of interconnected transmitting units that can excite or inhibit others. After several processing cycles, these networks can learn.

connotation   *See* DENOTATION / CONNOTATION.

connotative definition   *See* DENOTATION / CONNOTATION.

conscience   This is the sense of right and wrong. It is sometimes supposed that this is a way we have of knowing moral truths, perhaps by some sort of reliable internal "voice" or sense-perception (*see* MORAL SENSE THEORY), perhaps provided by God, which tells us moral facts. [Students sometimes confuse this word with 'CONSCIOUS']

consciousness   **1.** The state that we are in when awake: mental events are going on. **2.** Awareness of something. (You aren't usually conscious of the position of your tongue). **3.** = mind (though it might be that the mind exists even while we are asleep or not aware of anything). The fact that we are conscious is supposed by some to distinguish people from machines and other non-living things, and perhaps from (at least the lower) animals. *See also* SELF-CONSCIOUSNESS.

consequent   *See* CONDITIONAL.

consequentialism   The position that people's actions are right or wrong because of their consequences (their results). This sort of ethical theory is also called 'TELEOLOGICAL', and is contrasted with deontological theories (associated with KANT and others)—those that hold that results of actions are morally irrelevant. Thus, for example, a Kantian might think that lying is always wrong just in itself, whereas a consequentialist might think that lying is morally permissible in those circumstances in which the lie results in good consequences overall.

consistency   A SET of statements is consistent if it is logically possible that all the statements in that set are true. It is inconsistent if one statement CONTRADICTS another, or if a contradiction results from reasoning from the set. For example, these three statements form an inconsistent set:

Fred is good at logic.

Nobody who failed this test is good at logic.

Fred failed this test.

Note that there can be a consistent set in which some, or all, the statements are false. The two false statements, 'Pigs fly' and 'Grass is always purple' make a consistent set: they don't contradict each other, and no contradiction arises from assuming both of them. Each is false, but each might have been true, and both could have been true together. The set consisting of this one statement 'It's raining and it's not raining' is inconsistent, because this statement is SELF-CONTRADICTORY.

constant   *See* SYMBOLS OF QUANTIFIER LOGIC.

constant conjunction   *See* CAUSATION.

constative   *See* PERFORMATIVE / CONSTATIVE.

constitutive / regulative rule   A regulative rule merely tells people what to do or not to do (e.g., 'Keep off the grass'). Constitutive rules (according to SEARLE) may "create or define new forms of behaviour" and "often have the form: **x** counts as **y**". Thus, the rule 'Moving the ball across the goal line while in play counts as a touchdown' creates a new form of behaviour (a touchdown, non-existent without this rule). ['con-STIT-you-tiv']

constraint   *See* COMPULSION.

constructive dilemma   *See* DILEMMA.

constructive existence proof   In mathematics, one gives a constructive existence proof of some mathematical entity when one produces an example of it, or at least gives a method for producing an example. INTUITIONISTS in mathematics may, for example, reject the existence of infinity because no constructive existence proof of it can be given.

construct, theoretical   *See*   THEORETICAL ENTITIES / CONSTRUCTS.

contemplation   Meditation, thoughtfulness. Some philosophers think that the contemplative life—one filled with thought (especially philosophical thought!)—is the best or happiest. It's not obvious that this is true.

content, wide / narrow   *See* WIDE / NARROW CONTENT.

context   The relevant surroundings of something. In LOGIC, the context of a group of words is the rest of the words in its sentence. One logically interesting distinction between contexts is their OPAQUE / TRANSPARENT character; and *see also* INTENTIONAL. In ethics, context is relevant to those who think that the surroundings of some act are relevant to its rightness or wrongness. In epistemology, contextualism stresses that justification of one hypothesis does not rule out every logically possible alternative; it only needs to rule out those alternatives which are relevant given the context of accepted belief.

contiguity   Proximity (touching) in space or time ('spatial' or

'TEMPORAL contiguity'). Two events are spatially and temporally contiguous when there is neither space nor time between them.

Continental philosophy   This expression is used by philosophers in English-speaking countries to refer to what they take to be the "SPECULATIVE" style of philosophy done on the European Continent during the 19th and 20th centuries. The contrast implied is with ANALYTIC philosophy. Continental philosophers include HEGEL, HUSSERL, HEIDEGGER, SARTRE, FOUCAULT, HABERMAS, and DERRIDA; but none of them calls himself "Continental" and it's a misleading term insofar as it implies that their work is alike in method or content. It's more informative to refer to more particular continental schools, including ABSOLUTE IDEALISM, PHENOMENOLOGY, EXISTENTIALISM, STRUCTURALISM, DECONSTRUCTIONISM.

contingency   To say that a statement is contingent is to say that it is neither NECESSARY nor impossible. METAPHYSICAL contingency is contrasted with what must be true or false; logical contingency is contrasted with what is a LOGICAL TRUTH / FALSITY. Both sorts are sometimes simply called 'contingency'. This makes things confusing.

contingency argument for God's existence   *See* FIVE WAYS.

contingents, problem of future   *See* FUTURE CONTINGENTS.

continuum   **1.** A process of gradual development with no sudden changes. **2.** A series with no gaps in it, i.e., continuous, not composed of discrete elements. Time is a continuum if between any two times, no matter how close, there is a third. ['con-TIN-you-um']

contra-causal freedom   LIBERTARIANS sometimes believe that a free ACTION—one we're RESPONSIBLE for—could only be one that is not caused by previous events. Thus, the sort of freedom they attribute to some of our actions is contra-causal (*see* FREE WILL).

contract / contractarianism   *See* SOCIAL CONTRACT.

contradiction / contrary   Two statements are contradictories
when the truth of one logically requires the falsity of the
other, and the falsity of one requires the truth of the other—
in other words, when it is impossible that both are true, and
it is impossible that both are false. 'It's raining' and 'It's not
raining' are contradictory: exactly one of them must be true.
Two statements are contraries when it is impossible that they
are both true, though they might both be false. 'No pigs fly'
and 'All pigs fly' are contraries, not contradictories. It is logically impossible that both of them are true, though they both
might be false (were it the case that some, but not all, pigs
fly). One can also call a SELF-CONTRADICTION a 'contradiction'. *See also* SUBCONTRARIES.

contradiction, law / principle of   *See* LAWS OF THOUGHT.

contraposition   1. A rule of SENTENTIAL LOGIC that says that
from any sentence of the form 'If P then Q' one may reason
correctly to the corresponding sentence of the form 'If not Q
then not P'. **2.** A rule of CATEGORIAL LOGIC that says that one
may create a logically equivalent sentence from any categorial sentence by replacing its subject terms with the COMPLE-
MENT of its PREDICATE term, and by replacing its predicate
term with the complement of its subject term. For example,
the contrapositive of 'All bats are mammals' is 'All non-
mammals are non-bats'.

contrary   *See* CONTRADICTION / CONTRARY.

contrary-to-fact conditional   *See* COUNTERFACTUAL.

convention   A convention is a general (perhaps TACIT) agreement for coordinated behaviour. David LEWIS has written
about conventions that arise when people have a coordination problem—when it would be to everyone's advantage
that actions be coordinated in any one of a variety of arbitrary ways—and the convention picks one of these ways.

Thus, it is a (North American) convention that one drives to the right.

conventionalism   *See*   REALISM / ANTIREALISM; *see also* RIGHTS.

conventional rights   *See* RIGHTS.

conversational / conventional implicature   *See* INFERENCE / IMPLICATION / ENTAILMENT[2].

converse accident   *See* ACCIDENT[2].

converse / obverse   Terms of TRADITIONAL LOGIC. The converse of a statement is obtained by interchanging the subject and PREDICATE[2] (the process called 'conversion'); thus, the converse of 'All pigs are sloppy eaters' is 'All sloppy eaters are pigs'. The process is called 'conversion', and the statement to be converted is called the 'convertend'. (You can see that conversion is not always a correct way to reason.) The obverse of a statement is obtained by changing 'No' to 'All' (or vice versa), or by changing 'Some...are' to 'Some...are not' (or vice versa); and by changing the predicate term to its COMPLEMENT. Thus, the obverse of 'No pigs are non-mammals' is 'All pigs are mammals', and the obverse of 'Some pigs are non-flying things' is 'Some pigs are not flying things'. The process is called 'obversion' and the statement to be obverted is called the 'obvertend'. All obversions are valid (*see* ARGUMENT).

Conway,   Anne (full name: Ann Finch, Viscountess Conway of Newcastle) (c. 1631-c. 1679) English philosopher; writer on DESCARTES, HOBBES, and SPINOZA; correspondent with LEIBNIZ.

coordination problem   *See* CONVENTION.

Copernicus,   Nicolaus *See* SCIENTISTS.

copula   In TRADITIONAL LOGIC, the words that connect subject and PREDICATE[2], such as 'is', 'are', 'are not', etc. ['COP-you-luh']

co-referential   Two TERMS[2]—nouns or noun phrases—are co-referential when they REFER to exactly the same thing, or the same group of things. Co-referential terms do not always have the same meaning. In QUINE'S example, 'animals with hearts' and 'animals with kidneys' are co-referential (because all and only animals with hearts are animals with kidneys), but these two terms have different meanings. The terms 'Mount Everest' and 'the tallest mountain on earth' are co-referential.

corner quotes   Also known as corners or quasi-quotes. A logical notation invented by QUINE to provide a brief way of referring to any expression of such-and-such a kind. Suppose you want to say that any two WELL-FORMED sentences connected by '⊃' is itself a well-formed sentence. Let ϕ and ψ be VARIABLES in the META-language ranging over well-formed sentences. But you can't say

'$\phi \supset \psi$' is well-formed

because it isn't: those two Greek letters aren't sentence letters. What you want to say is that any statement of this form (where those two places are filled by well-formed sentences) is well formed. For this you use corner quotes:

$\ulcorner \phi \supset \psi \urcorner$ is well-formed.

corporeal substance   *See* SUBSTANCE.

corpuscularianism   Seventeenth-century version of ATOMISM; held that all material objects were composed of tiny particles—"corpuscles". Corpuscularians included GASSENDI, Boyle (*see* SCIENTISTS) and LOCKE.

correspondence theory of truth   Something is true when it corresponds with the facts. This is a commonsense view, but some philosophers have rejected it because they find that the notion of "correspondence" is completely unclear, or that we never have any grounds for thinking that a sentence or belief "corresponds" with external facts—all we have direct contact with is other beliefs. (For a list of competing theories, *see* TRUTH.)

corrigibility   *See* INCORRIGIBILITY.

cosmogony   Theory about the origins of the universe. ['koz-MOG-uh-nee']

cosmological argument for God's existence   *See* FIRST CAUSE ARGUMENT.

cosmology   Philosophical or scientific theorizing about the COSMOS. Early philosophers often had ideas about where the cosmos came from, how it developed into the current form, and what its basic structure and laws were.

cosmos   The universe as a whole, especially as the Greeks saw it. [sometimes spelled the way it's transliterated from Greek: '*kosmos*'] *See also* CHAOS.

counterexample   An example intended to show that some general claim is false. Reasoning by counterexample is frequently a useful philosophical tactic for arguing against some position. (Also called 'counterinstance'.)

counterfactual   A counterfactual (also called a 'counterfactual conditional' or a 'contrary-to-fact conditional') is a CONDITIONAL statement whose antecedent is false. The subjunctive is used in English counterfactuals: 'If Fred were here, you wouldn't be doing that'. (This is properly said only when Fred isn't here.) One important and controversial area in modern LOGIC is concerned with the TRUTH-CONDITIONS for counterfactuals. A powerful and widely accepted way of understanding counterfactuals (associated with KRIPKE, David LEWIS and others) uses the notion of POSSIBLE

WORLDS: a counterfactual is true when the consequent is true in the nearest possible world (i.e., a world as much as possible like ours) in which the antecedent is true.

counterinstance   *See* COUNTEREXAMPLE.

counterintuitive   *See* INTUITION.

counterpart theory   Nixon might have lost the election in 1968, and many philosophers like to explain possibilities like this by saying that what's possible happened in a POSSIBLE WORLD; so in this case, it seems, there is a possible world in which Nixon lost that election. In the view of David LEWIS and others, however, we should not think of the same thing (person in this case) existing in various worlds. Instead it is proposed that in a nearby possible world there is a different but extremely similar person who lost that election—this is Nixon's "counterpart".

count / mass noun / sortal   A mass noun names a type of stuff, 'water', for instance. A count noun names an individual thing, 'book', for example. It makes sense to count things named by count nouns: how many books? But stuff named by a mass noun isn't counted: asking how many waters doesn't make sense. Instead one measures quantity: how much water? A similar (perhaps identical) distinction is between a 'sortal' and a 'non-sortal' term. It has been said (and denied) that the count / mass distinction is a syntactic distinction, having to do with what's allowed in the language ('some air' but not 'two airs'), but the sortal / non-sortal distinction is SEMANTIC, having to do with truth conditions: a sortal term is one with clear single principles for correct individuation and counting. Thus 'thing' is a count noun—'three things' makes sense—but not a sortal, because it's not clear, in some contexts, where the boundaries of one thing are, and how to count things.

covering law   A general LAW[3] applying to a particular instance. The covering law theory (or "MODEL") of EXPLANATION (also called the 'Deductive-Nomological' or 'D-N' theory) says that a particular event is explained by providing one or more covering laws that, together with particular facts, IMPLY the event. For example, we can explain why a piece of metal rusted by appealing to the covering law that iron rusts when exposed to air and moisture, and the facts that this metal is iron, and was exposed to air and moisture. This theory of explanation is associated with MILL and HEMPEL.

creationism   The religious doctrine that the world was created by a divine being, or that it owes its present form to divine agency. This term is frequently used to refer to the fundamentalist idea that the world was created in exactly the way the Bible says it was, that living things did not develop by the natural process of EVOLUTION, but were created in their present form by God. Creationists sometimes claim that their theory is an alternative scientific hypothesis to Darwinism; for most philosophers, the only question here is whether creationism is a false scientific theory with abundant disconfirmation, or not an attempt at science at all.

criterion   A test or standard for the presence of a property, or for the applicability of a word, or for the truth or falsity of a PROPOSITION. This word is singular; its plural is 'criteria'.

critical idealism / realism   "Critical idealism" sometimes refers to KANT'S theory, sometimes to HEGEL'S. "Critical realism" is supposed to be a view between the extremes of IDEALISM[2] and REALISM, holding in common with the latter that objects are real, external, and objective, and in common with the former that our experience of them is heavily mind-dependent. (*See* SUBJECTIVE / OBJECTIVE.)

critical theory   Neo-MARXIST social theory originally associated with the FRANKFURT SCHOOL; it attempts to be at once explanatory of social phenomena, and NORMATIVE: morally critical of certain societies, and interested in the practicalities of changing them.

Croce, Benedetto (1866-1952) Italian philosopher best known for his IDEALISTIC AESTHETICS. ['CROW-chay']

crucial experiment This is an experiment whose outcome would provide a central or conclusive test for the truth or falsity of some position or scientific HYPOTHESIS. Sometimes called, in Latin, "experimentum crucis". ['ex-pair-uh-MEN-tum CROO-chis']

cube, reversing *See* NECKER CUBE.

cultural relativism / absolutism *See* RELATIVISM / ABSO-LUTISM.

curl *See* TILDE.

cybernetics The science of systems of control and communication in animals and machines. *See also* ARTIFICIAL INTEL-LIGENCE. ['sigh-bur-NET-iks']

cynics / cynicism In ordinary talk, a cynic (someone who is cynical, who practices cynicism) is one who doubts the existence of human goodness and offers unpleasant reinterpretations of apparent examples of this, in which people are seen as less virtuous and more self-interested. The philosophical source for this word is the Cynics, ancient Greek philosophers who denounced the conventional methods of seeking happiness (possessions, family, religion, reputation, etc.), and advocated self-control, self-knowledge and ASCETICISM. The best-known Greek Cynic was DIOGENES of Synope.

Cyrenaics The school of philosophy founded by ARISTIPPUS (in Cyrenaica), which held that pleasure was the only good in life.

D

Dante   *See* WRITERS.

Darwin,   Charles *See* SCIENTISTS.

Darwinism   *See* EVOLUTION.

Dasein   (German: "being-there") The word used by HEIDEG-GER for human existence. ['DAH-sign']

datum   (Latin: "the given") Something GIVEN—an ASSUMP-TION or premise (*see* ARGUMENT) from which other claims may be DERIVED, or a starting point for knowledge; *see* SENSE-DATA. ['Datum' is singular; plural 'data']

Davidson,   Donald (b. 1917) American contemporary META-PHYSICIAN and philosopher of mind and of language.

de Beauvoir,   Simone *See* BEAUVOIR.

decision matrix   A table designed to display the features involved in various options and outcomes of a decision. For example, the decision matrix for the PRISONER'S DILEMMA is shown here:

	Other Confesses	Other doesn't confess
You confess	3 years in jail	1 year in jail
You don't confess	4 years in jail	2 years in jail

Inside the four boxes are listed the consequences for you, given your action and that of the other prisoner.

decision procedure   An ALGORITHM which gives a result in a finite number of clearly defined steps; for instance, in logic, to the question whether a statement is a LOGICAL TRUTH, and whether an ARGUMENT is valid. The TRUTH TABLE is a decision procedure in SENTENTIAL LOGIC. VENN DIAGRAMS are a decision procedure for CATEGORIAL LOGIC, but there is no decision procedure for QUANTIFIER LOGIC.

decision theory   The largely mathematical theory of decision-making. Generally includes some way of evaluating desirability of outcomes and their probabilities when not certain.

deconstructionism   A sceptical and frequently anti-intellectual POST-MODERN movement which seeks to interpret texts and the positions held in them by "deconstructing" them—showing their incoherence, the hidden and often contradictory presuppositions, prejudices, motives, and political aims behind them. DERRIDA is perhaps the best-known deconstructionist.

de dicto / de re   (Latin: "about what's said" / "about a thing") A *de re* belief is a belief considered with respect to the actual thing that it's about. Thus, if someone mistakenly thinks that the moving thing in the sky he's looking at is a satellite, whereas it's actually a meteor, then he has the *de re* belief that a meteor is moving in the sky—more clearly: about that meteor, he believes it's moving in the sky above him. But he has the *de dicto* belief that a satellite is moving in the sky above him. Philosophers speak also of a distinction between *de dicto* and *de re* necessity. (*See* NECESSARY / CONTINGENT TRUTH.) It is *de re* necessary of the number of planets that it is larger than five (because nine is necessarily larger than five); but it is *de dicto* contingent, because there might have been only three planets. ['day DIK-tow', 'day ray']

deduction / induction   **1.** In an outdated way of speaking, deduction is reasoning from the general to the particular, and induction is reasoning from the particular to the general. **2.** Nowadays, this distinction between kinds of reasoning is made as follows: correct ("valid") deductive reasoning is reasoning of the sort that if the premises (*see* ARGUMENT) are true, the conclusion must be true; whereas correct inductive reasoning supports the conclusion by showing only that it's more probably true. Examples:

> Deduction: No pigs fly; Porky is a pig; therefore, Porky doesn't fly.

> Induction: Porky, Petunia, and all the other pigs observed in a wide variety of circumstances don't fly; therefore no pigs fly.

These examples in fact fit definition 1; but here are examples of deduction according to definition 2 that do not fit definition 1:

> No pigs fly; therefore all pigs are non-flying things.

> Porky doesn't fly; Porky is a pig; therefore not all pigs fly.

The two main sorts of deductive logic are SENTENTIAL and QUANTIFIER LOGIC. A common form of induction works by enumeration: as support for the conclusion that all A's are B's, one lists many examples of A's that are B's. (*See also* NATURAL DEDUCTION.)

deductive-nomological model   *See* COVERING LAW.

deductive validity   *See* DEDUCTION.

deep / surface structure   The deep structure (or depth grammar) of a sentence is what linguists take to be its underlying structure at the basic level; this is contrasted with its surface structure (or surface grammar), which includes the characteristics that English teachers call 'grammar'. Thus, for example, the sentence 'Fred loves Zelda' has the same deep structure as 'Zelda is loved by Fred', though they have different surface structures. The study of deep structure is associated with Noam CHOMSKY, who is also known for his position that the same deep structure is common to every natural language (*see* ARTIFICIAL / NATURAL LANGUAGES) and is INNATE.

de facto / de jure   (Latin: "from fact / from law") "*De facto*" means "as a matter of fact"; "*de jure*" means "as a matter of law". When segregation was enshrined in the law of some U.S. states, it held *de jure*; but it hasn't gone away now that the laws have been removed from the books; it holds *de facto*.

defeasible   Means 'defeatible', in the sense of 'capable of being overruled'. A driver's license confers a defeasible right to drive, for example, because under certain circumstances (e.g., when he is drunk) the holder of a valid license would nevertheless not be allowed to drive. A defeasible PROPOSITION is one that can be overturned by future evidence.

defection / cooperation   *See* PRISONER'S DILEMMA.

definiens / definiendum   A *definiendum* (Latin: "to be defined") is a word or phrase to be defined, and the definition is the *definiens* (Latin: "defining thing"). ['duh-fin-ee-ENS', 'duh-fin-ee-EN-dum']

definite / indefinite description   A definite description is a term of the form 'the **X**', for example, 'the tallest man in Brazil'. A definite description can apply to at most one thing. An indefinite description, by contrast, can apply to any one of a number of things: 'a tall man'. A famous controversy involving definite descriptions concerns whether or not statements containing them have EXISTENTIAL IMPORT: that is, whether a sentence whose subject is a definite description that refers to nothing is therefore false. Consider the sentence 'The present king of France is bald'; does the fact that there is no present king of France make the sentence false? On RUSSELL's account of the definite description it does. STRAWSON, however, argues that the existence of the present king of France is merely PRESUPPOSED by this sentence, as the statement 'Fred has stopped beating his wife' presupposes that Fred had been beating her. If what the statement presupposes is not true, then the statement itself is neither true nor false.

definition   A procedure for giving the meaning of a word or phrase. Philosophers have categorized definitions in many (sometimes overlapping) ways. Here are the ones you'll find in this dictionary:

analytical, Aristotelian, *per genus et differentiam* definitions—*see* GENUS / SPECIES

circular definition *see* CIRCULAR REASONING / DEFINITION

connotative / denotative definition *see* DENOTATION / CONNOTATION

EMOTIVE DEFINITION

FUNCTIONAL DEFINITION

NOMINAL / REAL DEFINITION / ESSENCE

OPERATIONAL DEFINITION

PERSUASIVE DEFINITION

RECURSIVE definition

STIPULATIVE / PRECISING / LEXICAL DEFINITION

VERBAL / OSTENSIVE DEFINITION

deflationary theory of truth   *see* REDUNDANCY THEORY OF TRUTH.

degrees of perfection argument for God's existence   This argument has been proposed in many different forms. Here's one:

Comparative terms describe degrees of approximation to superlative terms. Nothing would count as falling short of the superlative unless the superlative thing existed. Ordinary things are less than perfect, so there must be something completely perfect; and what is completely perfect is God.

An objection to this argument is that comparative terms do not imply the existence of a superlative instance. For example, the existence of people who are more or less stupid does not imply that someone exists who is maximally, completely, perfectly stupid.

de gustibus non disputandum   (Latin: "there's no disputing about tastes") If I like chocolate ice cream and you hate it, argument about who is right is silly: nobody is right or wrong about the matter. The relativism this slogan advocates is clearly appropriate for taste in ice-cream; but is it appropriate for taste in art or literature? How about when it comes to differences in moral attitudes? (*See* RELATIVISM / ABSOLUTISM.)

deism   A form of religious belief especially popular during the ENLIGHTENMENT. Deists practise "NATURAL RELIGION"— that is, they rely on reason, distrusting faith, REVELATION, and the institutional churches. They believe that God produced the universe with its LAWS[3] of nature, but then left it alone to operate solely by these laws. This form of religious belief seems incompatible with some aspects of conventional religion, for example, with the notion of a loving God, or with the practice of prayer. VOLTAIRE, ROUSSEAU, and (in a way) KANT were deists.

de jure   *See DE FACTO / DE JURE.*

delusion   *See* ILLUSION / HALLUCINATION / DELUSION.

demiurge   (Anglicised version of '*dēmiourgos*', Greek for 'craftsman'.) In PLATO's *Timaeus* the demiurge is a deity (perhaps just as a symbol or personification) seen as creating the universe, in conformity, as far as physical limitations allowed, with rationality and goodness.

democracy   That form of government whose actions are determined by the governed (or by their elected representatives). Often the meaning of this word is extended in a rather imprecise way to imply that democratic societies are EGALITARIAN, and respect individual RIGHTS.

Democritus   (c. 460-370 B.C.) Greek philosopher, known for advocating the theory of ATOMISM. He conceived of the world as consisting only of tiny indestructible atoms in motion, and empty space; the properties of these atoms determine their combinations and interactions, and explain the visible world of change. ['duh-MOCK-ruh-tus']

demonstrative   *See* INDEXICAL / DEMONSTRATIVE.

demonstrative definition   *See* VERBAL / OSTENSIVE DEFINITION.

De Morgan,   Augustus (1806-1871) British mathematician and logician, known for his work on LOGIC, the foundations of algebra, and the philosophy of mathematics.

De Morgan's laws, named for him, are rules of INFERENCE which assert the equivalence and interchangability of:

(~P & ~Q) and ~(P v Q)
(~P v ~Q) and ~(P & Q).

['duh MORE-gan']

Dennett,   Daniel C[lement] (b. 1942) American philosopher of mind, with several influential books about minds, brains, and intentions.

denotation / connotation   The denotation or REFERENCE of a word is what that word refers to—the thing in the world that it "names". The connotation or sense of a word is, by contrast, its meaning. Synonymous with 'EXTENSION / INTENSION'. At least close to this is FREGE's distinction between the 'sense' (in German, '*Sinn*') of a word—the thought it expresses—and the 'reference' (in German, '*Bedeutung*' ['buh-DOY-tung']) of a word—the object it represents. A word can have connotation but no denotation: 'unicorn' has meaning but no reference. Note that the philosophical use of 'connotation' is different from the ordinary one, in which it refers not to what a word means, but to more or less distant associations it has; for example, the word 'roses' may carry the connotation of romance to many people.

A connotative definition is one that gives the characteristics shared by all and only the objects to which the term refers; often a definition by GENUS / SPECIES. A denotative definition defines by identifying the denotation—for example, by pointing out or listing several things to which the word applies. (*See* list of other sorts of DEFINITION.)

denotative definition   *See* DENOTATION / CONNOTATION.

denying the antecedent   An incorrect form of reasoning involving the CONDITIONAL, in which one derives the denial of the consequent from a conditional plus the denial of its antecedent. Example:

>   If it rained this morning, the pavement would be wet now.
>   It didn't rain this morning.
>   Therefore the pavement must not be wet now.

AFFIRMING THE CONSEQUENT is a similar form of incorrect reasoning. And compare the correct forms: AFFIRMING THE ANTECEDENT, and DENYING THE CONSEQUENT.

denying the consequent   A correct form of reasoning involving the CONDITIONAL, in which one derives the denial of the antecedent from a conditional plus the denial of its consequent. Example:

>   If it rained this morning, the pavement would be wet now.
>   The pavement isn't wet now.
>   Therefore it must not have rained this morning.

AFFIRMING THE ANTECEDENT is a similar form of correct reasoning. And compare the incorrect forms: AFFIRMING THE CONSEQUENT, and DENYING THE ANTECEDENT.

deontic   Means 'having to do with OBLIGATION'. Deontic logic is that branch of MODAL LOGIC dealing with connections of sentences saying what one ought to do, must do, is permitted to do, etc.

deontology   *See* CONSEQUENTIALISM.

depth grammar   *See* DEEP / SURFACE STRUCTURE.

de re   *See* DE DICTO / DE RE.

derivation   A method for proving deductive validity, in which one writes down the premises, then moves to succeeding steps using accepted rules of INFERENCE, eventuating at the conclusion (*see* ARGUMENT). There are other methods of proof, for example, in SENTENTIAL LOGIC, the TRUTH TABLE.

Derrida,   Jacques (b. 1930) Algerian-born French philosopher, best-known of the post-STRUCTURALISTS. He sees his project as the "DECONSTRUCTION" of our ideas and other cultural products to reveal their underlying ASSUMPTIONS[1], PRESUPPOSITIONS, and meanings. ['deh-ree-dah']

Descartes,   René (1596-1650) French philosopher and mathematician, the founder of MODERN PHILOSOPHY. Earlier SCHOLASTICISM saw the job of philosophy as analyzing and proving truths revealed by religion; Descartes' revolutionary view (which got him into trouble with the Church) was that philosophy can discover truth. His famous recipe for doing this is the method of systematic doubt (*see* CARTESIAN DOUBT); this is necessary to begin the search for the INDUBITABLE FOUNDATIONS for knowledge, the first of which is the truth of his own existence as a thinking (not a material) thing (*see* COGITO ERGO SUM). Although he was a champion of MECHANISTIC thinking about the external material world, and in fact contributed substantially to the new science and mathematics, he was a DUALIST, and believed that minds are nonmaterial. ['day-kart']

description, definite / indefinite   *See* DEFINITE / INDEFINITE DESCRIPTION.

description, knowledge by   *See* KNOWLEDGE BY ACQUAINTANCE / BY DESCRIPTION.

descriptive ethics   *See* ETHICS.

descriptive meaning   *See* EMOTIVISM.

descriptivism   *See* EMOTIVISM.

design, argument from   *See*   TELEOLOGICAL ARGUMENT FOR GOD'S EXISTENCE.

designator, rigid / flaccid   *See*   RIGID / FLACCID DESIGNATOR.

destructive dilemma   *See* DILEMMA.

determinables / determinates   A relation between more general and less general kinds, but different from the GENUS / SPECIES relation. The DENOTATION of a species is marked off from the denotation of the more general genus by differentia: for example, 'man' has been defined as an animal differentiated by being rational. But consider the relation between the general kind 'colour', and the more specific kind 'red'. Red is a colour differentiated by being…what? Well, all we can say is, by being red. Other examples: scarlet is a determinate of the determinable red. Other determinables are size, weight, age, number, texture.

determinism   The view that every event is necessitated by its previous causes, so that given its causes, each event must have existed in the form it does. There is some debate about how (and whether) this view can be JUSTIFIED[1]. The view that at least some events are not fully caused is called 'indeterminism'. Determinism is often taken to be a PRESUPPOSITION of science; KANT thought it was NECESSARY; but quantum physics says that it is false. One of the main areas of concern about determinism arises when it is considered in connection with FREE WILL; for 'hard determinism' and 'soft determinism' see that entry.

deterrence   A motive for PUNISHMENT: that threatening punishment can prevent future occurrences of undesirable acts. (Other competing theories of punishment are RETRIBUTIVISM and REHABILITATION.) So one may try to justify jailing criminals by claiming that the threat of similar jailing will discourage them and others from future crime. One may even successfully deter crime by framing the innocent (so-called 'telishment', short for TELEOLOGICAL punishment'). Deterrence as a national defence policy attempts to prevent other nations' agression by threatening them with massive (perhaps nuclear) retaliation. The moral status of deterrence is controversial. Preventing war is of course a good thing, but is threatening deterrence justified when it involves the willingness to go through with really horrible retaliation? Imagine that you are president of the US, and your enemies have just bombed Pittsburgh. Should you go ahead with the massive nuclear retaliation you threatened, and destroy a city of theirs? This would be useless. But if this doesn't make sense now, no wonder they didn't take your threat seriously earlier. This is the 'paradox of deterrence'. For a further problem regarding deterrence, *see* INNOCENCE AND GUILT.

devil's advocate   In earlier times, one who urges the "devil's plea" against the canonization of a saint. So, by extension, one who advocates the wrong side, or (as the phrase is used most frequently in contemporary philosophical circles) one who argues in favour of a position one does not necessarily believe, just in order to further consideration of the arguments involved. (In Latin: '*advocatus diaboli*'.)

Dewey, John (1859-1952) American philosopher associated with PRAGMATISM and INSTRUMENTALISM, with the notion of WARRANTED ASSERTIBILITY in the explanation of truth, and with educational theory and reform.

diachronic *See* SYNCHRONIC / DIACHRONIC.

dialectic   This word stems from a Greek root meaning 'conversation', but it has come to have many meanings in philosophy. Some of the more important of these are: **1.** The method of philosophical argument used by the PRE-SOCRATICS and SOCRATES, typically refuting opponents' positions by drawing out unacceptable consequences of those positions (*see* "Socratic method" in entry for SOCRATES). **2.** For PLATO and others, dialectic is a process of question-and-answer discussion; perhaps (as Plato held) with the aim of discovering general and unchanging truths. **3.** ARISTOTELIAN dialectic is reasoning from probable premises. **4.** In KANT, the TRANSCENDENTAL Dialectic tries to show the futility of metaphysical speculation; but **5.** HEGEL disagreed. HEGELIAN dialectic is a process of reasoning starting with disagreement and argument, proceeding through revision toward greater sophistication and adequacy, and aiming at agreement. Hegel thought that this also described the processes of nature and history; his view is often described as holding that change takes place when some thing (the thesis) leads into its opposite (the antithesis); they then interact to produce a new unity (the synthesis), which becomes the thesis of another change. Hegelian dialectical logic emphasizes the processes of rational thought, rather than the LOGICAL FORM of sentences, and denies the universal validity of the so-called LAWS OF THOUGHT.

dialectical materialism / idealism   These theories of historical change combine a DIALECTICAL[5] theory of change with HISTORICAL MATERIALISM AND IDEALISM[2], respectively. Dialectical materialism is closely associated with MARXIST thought, in which the historical process is understood in terms of a process of conflict and resolution between opposing material (i.e., economic) forces and entities in society. This term is also more broadly used to refer to Marxist-LENINIST philosophy and political IDEOLOGY in general. Dialectical idealism, associated with HEGEL, thinks of history in terms of dialectical processes involving the ABSOLUTE Spirit.

dianoia   *See NOŪS / DIANOIA / DOXA / THEORIA / TECHNE / PHRONESIS.*

Diderot,   Denis (1713-1784) French literary and philosophical writer. An important figure in the French ENLIGHTENMENT, one of the ENCYCLOPEDISTS, known for his NATURALISTIC views and his MATERIALISM and DETERMINISM. ['dee-der-oh']

difference, method of   *See* MILL'S METHODS.

difference principle   The second principle in RAWLS'S theory of justice. It says that in a just society, goods are to be distributed equally unless unequal distribution is to the benefit of the worst off group. *See also* PRINCIPLE OF LIBERTY.

differentia   *See* GENUS / SPECIES.

dilemma   People often use this word loosely to mean any sort of problem. More precisely it refers to that sort of problem in which one has a choice between two undesirable alternatives (called 'horns of the dilemma'). A moral dilemma is a forced choice between two incompatible OBLIGATIONS, or between two morally unacceptable alternatives—for example, when telling the truth would hurt someone, but lying would also be wrong. Philosophers sometimes use this word to refer to a kind of ARGUMENT that forces the opponent to choose between two possibilities. A constructive dilemma is an argument with this form:
>Either A or B.
>If A then C; if B then D.
>Therefore C or D.

A simpler, special case of constructive dilemma is:
>Either A or B.
>If A then C; if B then C.
>Therefore C.

A destructive dilemma has the form:
>Not C or not D
>If A then C; if B then D
>Therefore either not-A or not-B.

Dilthey, Wilhelm (1833-1911) German philosopher, known for his analyses of nature and of the methodology of human studies, and his contributions to the development of HERMENEUTICS.

diminished responsibility   A condition of reduced mental ability that provides a legal excuse for a bad action (*see* MENS REA).

Ding an sich   *See* THING-IN-ITSELF.

Diogenes   of Sinope (Sometimes called 'Diogenes the Cynic') (c. 412-323 B.C.) Greek philosopher associated with the CYNICS. Known for his advocacy of a self-contained unconventional life. ['dy-AH-jen-eez']

Dionysian   *See* APOLLONIAN / DIONYSIAN.

direct / indirect discourse   *See* INDIRECT / DIRECT DISCOURSE.

direct realism   *See* NAÏVE REALISM.

direct reference theory of proper names   *See* PROPER NAMES.

disanalogy   *See* ANALOGY.

disappearance theory   In general, any theory which argues that some commonly-applied concept is empty and should disappear. ELIMINATIVE MATERIALISM is an example of disappearance theory.

disconfirmation   *See* CONFIRMATION / DISCONFIRMATION.

discourse, indirect / direct   *See* INDIRECT / DIRECT DISCOURSE.

disjunction   A sentence constructed out of two (or more) sentences connected by 'or'. The sentence 'It's raining or it's snowing' can be seen to be composed of the disjunction of the two sentences 'It's raining' and 'It's snowing'. Two sentences connected in this way are called 'disjuncts'. It is often thought that there are two sorts of disjunction ambiguously expressed by 'or' in English:
> (1) The exclusive disjunction is true when one of the disjuncts is true and the other false, and false otherwise (when both are true, or when both are false).

(2) The inclusive disjunction is true when one or both of the disjuncts are true, and false only when both of the disjuncts are false.

Suppose, then, that both snow and rain are coming down at once. Is the sentence 'It's snowing or it's raining' true? If this 'or' is taken to be inclusive, it's true; if exclusive, it's false. Standardly in SENTENTIAL LOGIC, the wedge, also called the vee (v) symbolizes the inclusive disjunction (*see* SYMBOLS OF SENTENTIAL LOGIC).

disjunctive syllogism   A rule of INFERENCE which allows:
(P v Q) , ~P therefore Q
(P v Q) , ~Q therefore P.

disposition   A property whose presence or absence would be manifested—would make an observable difference—only under certain conditions. Brittleness is a dispositional property: to say that something is brittle is to say that it will shatter if struck with sufficient force. Two pieces of metal, only one of which is brittle, may seem identical. The difference will be revealed only if both are struck.

disquotational theory of truth   *See* TRUTH.

distributed / undistributed term / middle   In traditional logic, a TERM is distributed when the sentence says something about everything the term designates. So 'pigs' is distributed in 'Pigs are sloppy eaters' but undistributed in 'Farmer Fred owns pigs'. No SYLLOGISM is VALID in which both MIDDLE terms are undistributed; thus the "fallacy of the undistributed middle".

distribution   **1.** (of terms)—see DISTRIBUTED / UNDISTRIBUTED / TERM / MIDDLE. **2.** A rule of INFERENCE which asserts the equivalence and interchangability of:
P & (Q v R) and (P & Q) v (P & R)
P v (Q & R) and (P v Q) & (P v R).

distributive justice   *See* JUSTICE.

distributively   *See* COLLECTIVELY / DISTRIBUTIVELY.

disvalue   The opposite of 'value'. Something has disvalue not when it merely lacks value, but rather when it is positively bad. Pain has disvalue. So do Brussels sprouts.

divine attributes   The characteristics traditionally thought to be true of God. These include OMNIPOTENCE, OMNISCIENCE, and maximum BENEVOLENCE.

divine command theory   The ethical theory which explains morality as what is commanded by God. It is often argued that this has things backwards: God commands it because it is right, not vice versa.

division, fallacy of   *See* COMPOSITION / DIVISION (FALLACIES OF).

D-N model   *See* COVERING LAW.

doctrine of acts and omissions   *See* ACTS / OMISSIONS.

dogma   A particular belief or system of beliefs proclaimed by authority (especially religious authority) to be true. Thus, this word has also come to mean anything someone believes merely on authority, without reason, especially when stated arrogantly and intolerantly.

doing / allowing harm   *See* ACTS / OMISSIONS.

dominance   **1.** The ordinary meaning of this word is 'exercising the most influence or control', and in this sense, dominance is a concern of ethics of personal relations, and of political philosophy. **2.** In a technical sense used in decision theory, one choice is said to be dominant if it has better features or consequences than the alternatives, whatever happens. The dominance principle tells you to pick the alternative that dominates. Of course, sometimes there is no such alternative, so this is of limited applicability. Other principles of DECISION THEORY are the MAXIMIN principle, and the principle that one should maximize EXPECTED UTILITY.

Dostoyevsky, Fyodor Mikhailovich *See* WRITERS.

dot The symbol '·', meaning 'and' (*see* SYMBOLS OF SENTENTIAL LOGIC).

double aspect theory *See* DUAL ASPECT THEORY.

double effect The doctrine of double effect holds that, although it is always wrong to use a bad means to a good end (*see* END / MEANS), one may act to bring about a good result when also knowingly bringing about bad results, under the following conditions:

(1) The bad result is not caused by the good result—both are caused by the action (thus 'double effect');

(2) there's no way of getting the good result without the bad;

(3) the good result is so good that it's worth accepting the bad one.

For example, a dentist is allowed to drill, and thus cause some pain (the bad result) for the sake of dental improvements (the good result), since these conditions hold—most notably (1): the pain doesn't cause the improvement—both are results of the drilling. This principle is associated with Catholic morality, and has been applied most frequently in contexts of medical ethics. It is disputed by some philosophers, who sometimes argue that the distinction between double effect and bad means / good end is artificial and not morally relevant.

double negation NEGATING something twice appears to get you back to where you started: it seems that to deny not-p is just to affirm p. So 'double negation' is a rule of INFERENCE which asserts the equivalence and interchangability of ~ ~P and P. But some logics work out what happens when you don't include this principle.

doubt   To doubt something can mean either to be uncertain or undecided about it, or to believe that it is false. When philosophical SCEPTICS present arguments for doubting ordinarily accepted statements, they may attempt to show that one should be uncertain or undecided about them, or should actually think they are false. But often the sceptic merely wants to show that the ordinarily accepted statement can't be justified—that it is without foundation—but does not want to get anyone to stop believing it.

doubt, Cartesian   *See* CARTESIAN DOUBT.

doxa   *See* NOŪS / DIANOIA / DOXA / THEORIA / TECHNE / PHRONESIS.

doxastic   Means 'pertaining to belief', as in 'doxastic state', 'doxastic principle' (for justifying beliefs).

Dretske,   Fred I[rwin] (b. 1932) Influential American EPISTE-MOLOGIST; important work on perception, knowledge, reasons and behaviour. [DRET-skee]

dual aspect theory   A theory (associated with SPINOZA and others) that mind and body are just different aspects of, different ways of looking at, the same SUBSTANCE or thing; so it's a form of monism (*see* DUALISM / MONISM / PLURALISM). Also called the 'double aspect theory'.

dualism / monism / pluralism   All three are views on the basic kind(s) of things that exist. Dualists hold that there are two sorts of things, neither of which can be understood in terms of the other. Often 'dualism' refers particularly to the view in philosophy of mind in which the two are the mental and the physical (*see* INTERACTIONISM, OCCASIONALISM, and PARALLELISM for particular varieties). Contemporary dualists sometimes don't insist that there are two sorts of things; their dualism is instead the claim that mental phenomena can't be explained solely in physical terms. Other sorts of dualism distinguish the visible and invisible, the actual and the possible, God and the universe, etc. Monists believe in only one

97

ultimate kind of thing, and pluralists in many. To be a plural-
ist about value is to believe that there are many incompatible,
but equally valid, value systems.

dubitability   *See* INDUBITABILITY / DUBITABILITY.

duck-rabbit   An ambiguous drawing used by WITTGENSTEIN in
the course of his discussion of "seeing-as". It can be seen as
a duck or rabbit.

See also MÜLLER-LYER ILLUSION, and NECKER CUBE.

Duhem,   Pierre *See* SCIENTISTS.

Dummett,   Michael [Anthony Eardley] (b. 1925) British
philosopher of language, logic, and mathematics; influential
defender of certain forms of antiREALISM.

dunce   Not a philosophical term, but you might be amused to
know that it's derived from the name of DUNS SCOTUS (his
followers were called 'dunces' by their opponents).

Duns Scotus,   John (c. 1265-1308) Scottish theologian and
philosopher; interests in THEOLOGY and METAPHYSICS.

Durkheim,   Emile *See* SCIENTISTS.

Dutch book   A set of beliefs with attached degrees of confidence constitute a Dutch book when betting on the basis of
this set will result in losing whatever happens. For example,
suppose that someone thought that the probability of heads
on a coin flip was a little over 3/5, and so was the probabili-

ty of tails. That person would be willing to bet $3 on a coin flip coming up heads, and $3 on the flip coming up tails, when $5 was to be collected for a winning bet. Having made both bets, the person will pay $6 and collect $5 whatever happens. A set like this fails a condition for rationality.

duty   *See* OBLIGATION.

Dworkin,   Ronald [Miles] (b. 1931) American philosopher of law; influential defender of LEGAL POSITIVISM.

dyadic predicates   *See* PREDICATES.

dyadic relation   *See* RELATIONS.

dystopia   *See* UTOPIA.

E

Eckhart, Johannes (c. 1260-1328), known as Meister Eckhart. German mystic and theologian. His work, considered at times heretical, was influential on later mystics and on philosophers including HEGEL, FICHTE, and HEIDEGGER.

ecofeminism The view that our mistreatment of the environment should be thought of as a consequence of PATRIARCHY.

Eddington, Arthur *See* SCIENTISTS.

Edwards, Jonathan (1703-1758) American Puritan Calvinist THEOLOGIAN.

effect, double *See* DOUBLE EFFECT.

effective procedure *See* ALGORITHM.

efficient cause *See* FOUR CAUSES.

egalitarianism The view that people are equal—that they are entitled to equal rights and treatment in society.

egocentric particular *See* INDEXICAL / DEMONSTRATIVE.

egocentric predicament The problem faced by theories that claim that the objects we directly perceive are our own SENSE-DATA: how can we ever know anything about what is outside our own minds—about real external objects, or others' experiences of them?

ego, empirical / transcendental *See* EMPIRICAL / TRANSCENDENTAL EGO.

egoism, ethical / psychological Psychological egoism is the position that people in fact act only in their own INTERESTS. If you think this is true, be careful that your belief is not merely an empty thought. It's sometimes argued that even the most generous act is done for the doer's own satisfaction; but this might simply be a way of saying that even the most generous act is motivated—something nobody would deny. If someone is motivated to act for others' benefit, and gets satisfaction from those actions, this shows that psychological egoism is not universally true. Ethical egoism is the position that I (or people in general) *ought* to act only in my (their) own interests. 'Egotism' (see that 't'?) is sometimes used synonymously, but precise speakers tend to use 'egotism' to mean the tendency to speak or write of oneself too much, or too boastfully. ['EE-go-ism' or 'EH-go-ism'] *See also*: SELF-ISHNESS, RATIONAL SELF-INTEREST.

eidos *See* FORM[1].

Einstein, Albert *See* SCIENTISTS.

élan vital *See* VITALISM.

Eleatics School started with PARMENIDES of Elea in the sixth century, including ZENO. The Eleatic stranger (or visitor) in PLATO'S *Sophist* and *Statesman* presents the problems the Eleatics had with non-being and false belief.

elements The elements of something are its basic components. Some ancient Greeks believed that all physical things were composed of four basic elements: earth, air, fire, and water. Nowadays, of course, we believe in different elements, and there are many more of them; neither are they basic (they have sub-atomic components).

eliminativism *See* MATERIALISM.

emergent properties *See* SUPERVENIENCE.

Emerson, Ralph Waldo *See* WRITERS.

emotion, appeal to *See AD POPULUM.*

emotive definition The sort of definition appropriate for a word that has evaluative as well as descriptive implications. The definition of 'courage', for example, must say more than 'steadfastness in the face of danger', for this defines 'fool-hardiness' as well. 'Courage' is *good* steadfastness in the face of danger. (*See* list of other sorts of DEFINITION.)

emotivism A position in meta-ETHICS that holds that ethical utterances are to be understood not as statements of fact that are either true or false, but rather as expressions of approval or disapproval, and invitations to the listener to have the same reactions and to act accordingly. Expressions of approval don't state facts: when I express my liking of ice cream by saying "Yum!" what I'm saying is neither true nor false. ("Expressivism" is a form of emotivism that emphasizes this expressive function in its ANALYSIS of ethical statements.) Neither is what I say when I urge you to try some. ("Prescriptivism" is a form of emotivism that emphasizes this ordering or requesting or inviting function in its analysis.) Thus emotivists emphasize the "emotive meaning" of ethical utterances, denying that they have cognitive meaning (*See* COGNITIVISM / NONCOGNITIVISM). Emotivists can nevertheless be "descriptivists" in that they can agree that evaluative utterances have some "descriptive content": when I say this is a good apple, I express my approval, but also describe it as having certain characteristics on which my approval rests: that it is, for example, not worm-infested. HUME might be construed as holding a form of emotivism; in this century, the position is associated with A. J. AYER and the American philosopher C(harles) L(eslie) Stevenson (1908-1975).

empathy *See* SYMPATHY / EMPATHY / BENEVOLENCE.

Empedocles (c. 490-430 B.C.) Greek philosopher; his poem

"On Nature" contains elaborate theories of the origin and constitution of the universe, in which the four ELEMENTS are joined and divided by the two basic principles: love and strife. ['em-PED-oh-kleez']

empirical   This means having to do with sense-experience and experiment. Empirical knowledge is knowledge we get through experience of the world; thus it is *a posteriori* (*see A PRIORI / A POSTERIORI*). An empirical CONCEPT is one that is not INNATE; it can be developed only through experience.

empirical / transcendental ego   The ego is the "I" —the self. This distinction is KANT'S. The EMPIRICAL ego is the collection of characteristics and mental events that one can sense in one's self, perhaps by INTROSPECTION; the TRANSCENDENTAL ego is what unifies—what *has*—these characteristics and is that in which the events happen; perhaps it's a mental SUBSTANCE one can't sense (*see also* BUNDLE THEORY).

empiricism   The position (usually contrasted with RATIONALISM) that all our CONCEPTS and substantive knowledge come from sense experience. Empiricists deny that there are INNATE concepts. While they grant that certain kinds of trivial knowledge (of CONCEPTUAL, analytic (*see* ANALYTIC / SYNTHETIC), and LOGICAL TRUTHS) can be gained by reason alone, independently of experience, they deny the existence of the synthetic (*see* ANALYTIC / SYNTHETIC) *A PRIORI*. ARISTOTLE is perhaps the founder of empiricism; the position is most strongly associated with EPICURUS among the Greeks. The classical MODERN empiricists were LOCKE, BERKELEY, and HUME. MILL was a strong empiricist. The view has been an important influence on contemporary ANALYTIC PHILOSOPHY. 'Logical empiricism' was another name for LOGICAL POSITIVISM. ['em-PEER-uh-sism', 'em-PEER-uh-kl']

empty set   *See* SET.

Encyclopedists   A group of French thinkers including CONDIL-

LAC, DIDEROT, ROUSSEAU, Montesquieu and Voltaire (*See* WRITERS). They were associated with the *Encyclopedia*, (in French, *Encyclopédie*) a massive, hugely influential work published in stages between 1751 and 1772, central to the French ENLIGHTENMENT.

end in itself   **1.** Something sought for its own sake; an INTRINSIC good. **2.** Someone is seen as an end in him / herself when that person's aims are seen as having value just because they are that person's aims. Treating people as ends in themselves is respecting their aims, and refraining from thinking of, or using, that person merely as a means to your aims. A central principle of KANT's ethics is the necessity of treating others as ends in themselves, and not as means only.

ends / means   A long-standing controversy in ethics is whether one might be permitted to use bad means to a good end: does the end justify the means? For example, is it permitted to lie to someone if everyone will be better off in the long run as a result? Sometimes the slogan "The end does not justify the means" expresses the radical position that no action that is bad in itself is ever permitted no matter how good the consequences. This position is taken by the more extreme opponents of CONSEQUENTIALISM. Notice that this means that telling a little lie would not be justified even if it would prevent the destruction of the earth. A more reasonable interpretation of this slogan thinks of it as warning against actions which are so bad in themselves that the good consequences do not overwhelm this badness. The distinction between ends and means parallels the distinction between intrinsic and extrinsic goods—*see* INTRINSIC / INHERENT / INSTRUMENTAL / EXTRINSIC. *See also*: DOUBLE EFFECT *and* CATEGORICAL / HYPOTHETICAL IMPERATIVE.

Enlightenment   The Enlightenment was a cultural and philosophical movement of the seventeenth and eighteenth centuries whose chief features were a belief in rationality and scientific method, and a tendency to reject conventional religion and other traditions. The Age of Enlightenment is also known as the 'Age of Reason'.

en soi   *See* IN-ITSELF / FOR-ITSELF.

entailment   *See* INFERENCE / IMPLICATION / ENTAILMENT[1].

entelechy   In ARISTOTLE, the state of achieved potential that things aim at (*see* 'final cause' in FOUR CAUSES). In Leibniz, the active force in each MONAD. In VITALISTS, a non-material force or purpose that is supposed to bring about organic processes. ['en-TEL-uh-kee']

entertain   To entertain a PROPOSITION is to consider it without necessarily believing it.

enthymeme   An argument with some steps left unstated but understood. 'All pigs are sloppy eaters, so Porky is a sloppy eater' is an enthymeme, leaving unsaid 'Porky is a pig'. ['EN-thuh-meem']

entities, hypothetical / theoretical   *See* THEORETICAL ENTITIES.

entity   A thing, an existent being.

entrenchment   A PREDICATE[3] is entrenched when it has been used in successful past science. GOODMAN argues that the only difference between GRUE and green is that the latter is entrenched. This does not, however, provide justification for continuing to prefer it.

enumerative inductive inference   *See* DEDUCTION / INDUCTION.

Epictetus   (c. 55-135) Greek STOIC; his views emphasized duty and inner freedom. ['ep-ik-TEE-tus']

epicureanism   The ordinary use of the word 'epicurean', meaning devoted to pleasure, especially from eating fine food, has distant connections to its philosophical use, in which it refers to the philosophy of EPICURUS and his followers. Chief tenets are an emphasis on the visible world (as opposed to the world imagined by religion or many philosophies), and the advocacy of calmness of mind. ['ep-uh-kew-REE-an-ism']

Epicurus   (of Samos) (c. 341-271 B.C.) Greek philosopher, founder of EPICUREANISM, known for his MATERIALIST and ATOMIST views, and for his position that the good life was one based on pleasure. ['ep-uh-CURE-us']

Epimenides' paradox   *See* LIAR'S PARADOX.

epiphenomenalism   A variety of DUALISM in which mental events are just "by-products" of physical ones: physical events cause mental ones, but not vice versa. As an analogy, think of the noise your car makes: it's caused by the mechanical goings-on inside, but it has no effect on them. ['ep-ee-feh-NOM-in-al-ism']

epistemic   Having to do with knowledge. Epistemic logic is that branch of MODAL LOGIC dealing with relations between sentences involving 'knows', 'believes', etc. ['ep-is-TEE-mik' or 'ep-is-TEH-mik']

epistemic basic relation   *See* BASING RELATION.

epistemic closure principle   *See* CLOSURE.

epistemology   Theory of knowledge: one of the main branches of philosophy. Among the central questions studied here are: What is the difference between knowledge and mere belief? Is all (or any) knowledge based on sense-perception? How, in general, are our knowledge-claims justified? ['eh-piss-teh-MOL-uh-jee']

E proposition   *See* A / E / I / O PROPOSITIONS.

equilibrium, reflective   *See* REFLECTIVE EQUILIBRIUM.

equiprobable   (or 'equipossible'): having the same probability.

equivalence   *See* BICONDITIONAL.

equivocation   An ambiguous word, or a shift in the course of speaking or reasoning from one meaning of a word to another. Equivocation is sometimes used to mislead; and sometimes it results in faulty reasoning (the FALLACY of equivocation). An example, which equivocates on the word 'law':
> The existence of any law shows that there is a lawmaker.
> The law of gravity was not made by humans.
> Therefore there must be a non-human lawmaker—God.

['ih-kwiv-uh-KAY-shun']

Erasmus,   Desiderius *See* WRITERS.

erasure   In DECONSTRUCTIONISM, a word is used "under erasure" when it is doubtful that it really means anything. Words used under erasure are sometimes enclosed in inverted commas.

eros   *See* AGAPE / PHILIA / EROS.

erotetic   Means having to do with questions. Erotetic logic is the logic of questions.

error theory   A theory which claims to find a philosophical error in some general way of thinking, and urges that this be corrected. J. L. MACKIE popularized this term in connection with his view that ordinary talk and thought about ethics reflected the philosophical error of thinking that ethical properties were objective. (*See* SUBJECTIVE / OBJECTIVE.)

eschatological   Having to do with "the last matters"—especially, in Christian thought, with death, the end of the world, the Last Judgment, Heaven, Hell, and the significance of these for our present lives. Don't confuse this word with 'scatological', which means something quite different. ['es-kat-uh-LODGE-i-cal']

ESP *See* EXTRASENSORY PERCEPTION.

esse est percipi (Latin: "to be is to be perceived") This slogan expresses Berkeley's IDEALISTIC view that the only things there are in the world are perceived qualities and "spirits"— minds that do the perceiving. ['essay est pur-KIP-ee']

essence / accident The essential characteristics of something are the ones that it must have in order to be what it is, or the kind of thing it is. It is essential, for example, for a tree to be a plant—if something was not a plant, it could not be a tree. By contrast, a tree that in fact is thirty-three meters high could still be a tree if it weren't thirty-three meters high; thus this characteristic is accidental. (Note that 'accident' and 'accidental' don't have their ordinary meanings in this philo-sophical use.) Some philosophers think that the essence / accident distinction does not concern the real characteristics of something, but is only a consequence of the words we apply to them: being a plant is said to be an essential charac-teristic of a tree only because it's part of the definition of 'tree'. But essentialist philosophers believe in real, objective essences.

essential / accidental quality / property / characteristic *See* ESSENCE / ACCIDENT.

essentialism **1**. *See* ESSENCE / ACCIDENT. **2**. *See* EXISTEN-TIALISM / ESSENTIALISM.

E statement *See* A / E / I / O PROPOSITIONS.

esthetics *See* AESTHETICS.

eternal return The doctrine that every event and series of events has occurred, and will occur, identically in every detail, an infinite number of times. This was held by a number of ANCIENT, MEDIEVAL, and nineteenth-century philosophers. Also known as 'eternal recurrence'.

ether   The invisible "stuff" formerly thought to permeate everything, including apparently empty space, supposed to be the medium for apparent ACTION AT A DISTANCE, especially as the medium for electromagnetic waves which, it was thought, must be waves *in* something. ['EE-thur'; sometimes spelled 'aether']

ethical absolutism   *See* RELATIVISM / ABSOLUTISM.

ethical cognitivism   *See* COGNITIVISM / NONCOGNITIVISM.

ethical Darwinism   *See* EVOLUTION.

ethical egoism   *See* EGOISM.

ethical externalism   *See* EXTERNALISM / INTERNALISM.

ethical internalism   *See* EXTERNALISM / INTERNALISM.

ethical naturalism / supernaturalism / nonnaturalism   Those who think that the ethical words like 'good' and 'right' may be defined in terms of natural properties (the ordinary properties of the physical world) are ethical naturalists. For example, some ethical naturalists think that 'the right act' means 'the act that produces the most happiness'. Ethical supernaturalism is the view that ethical properties really are properties having to do with the supernatural or divine: for example, the view that calling an action good is the same as saying that it conforms to the will of God. (*See* DIVINE COMMAND THEORY.) Nonnaturalists deny that ethical words are equivalent in meaning to words that name the natural (or supernatural) world, though good things may as a matter of fact share some physical properties. They claim that ethical properties are basic properties on their own, not really properties in some other realm. For G. E. MOORE's argument against ethical naturalism, see the OPEN QUESTION ARGUMENT. Moore thought that any reasoning that was based on the false assumption that ethical properties were actually natural properties committed what he called the "naturalistic fallacy". *See also:* IS / OUGHT PROBLEM.

ethical noncognitivism   *See* COGNITIVISM / NONCOGNITIVISM.

ethical objectivism   *See* RELATIVISM / ABSOLUTISM *and* SUBJECTIVE / OBJECTIVE.

ethical relativism   *See* RELATIVISM / ABSOLUTISM.

ethics   The general philosophical study of what makes things good or bad, right or wrong. Often the following areas of study are distinguished within ethics:

1. Descriptive ethics: the discovery of what ethical views particular societies in fact have; and speculative anthropological theorizing about the origin and function of these views.
2. NORMATIVE ethics: theorizing about what the basic principles are that might serve systematically to distinguish right from wrong, etc.
3. Applied ethics: the normative ethics of particular areas or disciplines: medical ethics, business ethics, computer ethics … .
4. Meta-ethics: the study of the meaning of moral language and the possibility of ethical knowledge. (Sometimes unhyphenated: 'metaethics'.)

'Morality' and 'ethics' (and 'moral' and 'ethical') are usually used as synonyms, though 'ethics' is more frequently generally used as the name of the philosophical study of these matters. Philosophers usually avoid the tendency in ordinary talk to restrict the word 'ethics' to an official code of acceptable behaviour in some area (as in 'professional ethics'). There are very many entries in this dictionary relevant to ethics—far too many for me to give a complete list here, but here's a partial one:

ACT / AGENT MORALITIES

CONSEQUENTIALISM

contractarianism—*see* SOCIAL CONTRACT

deontological ethics—*see* CONSEQUENTIALISM

deontology—*see* CONSEQUENTIALISM

DIVINE COMMAND THEORY

EGOISM, ETHICAL / PSYCHOLOGICAL

EMOTIVISM

'ETHICAL — '

ethical COGNITIVISM / NONCOGNITIVISM

ETHICAL NATURALISM / SUPERNATURALISM / NONNATU-
RALISM

EXTERNALISM / INTERNALISM

HEDONISM

INTUITIONISM

'MORAL —'

REFLECTIVE EQUILIBRIUM

RELATIVISM / ABSOLUTISM

SUBJECTIVE / OBJECTIVE

TELEOLOGY

VIRTUE ETHICS.

ethics, descriptive   *See* ETHICS.

ethics, evolutionary   *See* EVOLUTION.

ethics, normative   *See* ETHICS.

ethics, teleological   *See* TELEOLOGY.

ethnocentric   Someone is ethnocentric who regards the views or characteristics of his / her own race or culture as the only correct or important ones. Other "-centric" words have arisen by analogy: EUROCENTRIC, LOGOCENTRIC, PHALLOCENTRIC for example.

etiology   *See* AETIOLOGY.

eudaimonia   (Greek: "living well") Since ARISTOTLE thought that the happy life was the good life, this word might be taken to mean 'happiness', particularly the complex and long-lasting kind of happiness that Aristotle had in mind. His position can be called "eudaemonism"—the view that this is the real aim of life. ['you-duh-MO-nee-ah' or 'you-DIE-mo-NEE-ah'; sometimes spelled 'eudemonia' or 'eudaemonia']

Euler diagram   *See* VENN DIAGRAM.

eurocentrism   Narrowminded exclusion or ignorance of non-European culture and ways of thought. Coined by analogy with ETHNOCENTRISM.

euthanasia   Euthanasia is mercy-killing, the intentional bringing-about or hastening the death of someone, presumably for his own good, when his life is judged not to be worth continuing, typically when that person is suffering from an untreatable, fatal illness causing horrible unavoidable pain or suffering. Voluntary euthanasia is done at the expressed wish of that person; this wish is not expressed in the case of involuntary euthanasia (for example, when the person has mentally deteriorated beyond the point of being able to express, or perhaps even to have, coherent wishes). Passive euthanasia involves refraining from providing life-prolonging treatment to someone suffering from a fatal condition; active euthanasia is killing, for example, by administering a fatal injection. Ethical opinion is deeply divided concerning euthanasia. Some who argue in favour of its permissibility would accept it only when voluntary, and/or only when passive. ['you-tha-NAY-zee-ah' or 'you-tha-NAY-zha']

Evans,   Gareth (1946-1980) English philosopher with influential work on mind and language.

event causation   *See* AGENT / EVENT CAUSATION.

evil genius As part of his technique of CARTESIAN DOUBT, DESCARTES imagined that a powerful but evil spirit could be systematically fooling us about everything we thought we knew. Sometimes also called 'evil genie' or 'evil demon'. (Descartes' term, in French, was '*malin génie*', roughly, 'ma-LAN zhay-nee'.)

evil, problem of *See* PROBLEM OF EVIL.

evolution Broadly speaking, any process by which something gradually changes into a different, usually more complex, form. Most often used to refer to theories of change of kinds of living things, especially to the view nowadays held by almost all biologists that living creatures owe their present state of complex adaptation to their environment to a long natural process in which inherited characteristics varied at random; the characteristics that were more adaptive in the bearers' environment allowed those bearers to survive and reproduce, passing those characteristics on. This scientific THEORY is associated with Darwin (*see* SCIENTISTS), so it is sometimes called Darwinism; his name is also associated with some moral and social theories (ethical and social Darwinism) that hold that the good can be identified with the more evolved, and that social policies ought to be based on the furthering of evolution (for example, by refraining from interfering with "natural" processes, and allowing those with less "fit" genetic endowment to die off). Darwin was not a social or ethical Darwinist.

examination paradox *See* SURPRISE QUIZ PARADOX.

excluded middle, law of the *See* 'law of the excluded middle', in LAWS OF THOUGHT.

exclusive or / disjunction *See* DISJUNCTION.

executioner's paradox *See* SURPRISE QUIZ PARADOX.

exhaustive   *See* MUTUALLY EXCLUSIVE / JOINTLY EXHAUSTIVE.

existence   The subject of many different philosophical problems, for example: Is all that exists mental in nature (*see* IDEALISM[2]) or physical (*see* MATERIALISM)? Are we justified in believing in things—for example, THEORETICAL ENTITIES or UNIVERSALS—that we don't perceive (*see* REALISM)? This word is sometimes misspelled 'existance'. Please don't do that.

existential   The adjectival form of the word 'existence' and the root of the term 'EXISTENTIALISM'. For some of its uses *see* the following entries. ['eggs-iss-TEN-shul']

existential anguish   The horrible feeling the EXISTENTIALISTS suppose we have when confronted with our own complete and irremovable FREEDOM[1] and RESPONSIBILITY. Also called 'anxiety', (German) '*Angst*', (French) '*angoisse*'.

existential generalization   A rule of INFERENCE which allows inferring that there exists something that has property P (*see* QUALITY / ATTRIBUTE / PROPERTY) from the statement that INDIVIDUAL a has property P.

existential import   Said to be true of a sentence when it ASSERTS or IMPLIES or PRESUPPOSES the existence of something. If we take the sentence, 'All unicorns have horns' to have existential import, it implies that unicorns exist, so it is false. In TRADITIONAL logic, but not in modern logic, 'All S is P' is taken to have existential import.

existential instantiation   A rule of INFERENCE which allows inferring certain conclusions from the statement that there exists something that has property P (*see* QUALITY / ATTRIBUTE / PROPERTY). It's obviously incorrect to infer that a particular individual has P, so this rule needs qualification and restrictions.

existentialism / essentialism   Existentialism is a school of philosophy developed largely in twentieth-century France and Germany, closely associated with KIERKEGAARD, HEIDEGGER, JASPERS, SARTRE, BEAUVOIR, CAMUS, among others. Although existentialists have had things to say about many areas of philosophy, they are best known for their views on FREEDOM[1] and RESPONSIBILITY. They tend to believe that we are totally free—that we are never caused to act by environment, heredity, or personality; and thus that we individually create all our decisions and values (the only source for ethical obligation) and are responsible for all our actions. They criticise the BAD FAITH "essentialist" view that we have a pre-existing essence which causes us to be some way, or gives us objective standards (*see* SUBJECTIVE / OBJECTIVE). A view is called "essentialist" in general when it holds that individuals in a group of things (or especially people) have certain characteristics by virtue of belonging to that group. For example, contemporary essentialists might argue that there are biologically rooted characteristics associated with gender or race. ['eggs-iss-TEN-shul-ism']

existential proposition / quantifier   *See* SYMBOLS OF QUANTIFIER LOGIC.

expected utility / value   The expected utility (or value) of an ACTION is calculated by multiplying the UTILITY (or value) of each possible result of that action by its PROBABILITY, and adding up the results. For example, consider this betting game: you get \$10 if a random draw from a deck of cards is a spade; and you pay \$4 if it's any other suit. Assuming the utility of each dollar is 1, to calculate the expected utility of this game we add:

.25 (probability of a spade) x 10 (the utility if it's a spade)
.75 (the probability of a non-spade) x -4 (the utility of a non-spade).

Since $(.25 \times 10) + (.75 \times -4) = 2.5 - 3 = -.5$, the game thus has an expected utility of -.5; not playing at all has an expected utility of 0. One (controversial) theory for rational decision-making advocates maximizing expected utility, so you should not play this game. (But if you enjoy gambling, this has to be figured in too, and might make it worthwhile.) *See also* MINIMAX, DOMINANCE.

experience, mystical / religious   *See* MYSTICAL EXPERIENCE ARGUMENT FOR GOD'S EXISTENCE *and* MYSTICISM.

experiment, thought   *See* THOUGHT EXPERIMENT.

experimentum crucis   *See* CRUCIAL EXPERIMENT.

explanans / explanandum   An *explanandum* (Latin: "to be explained") is something that is being explained: what does the explaining is the *explanans* (Latin: "explaining thing"). ['ex-pluh-NANS', 'ex-pluh-NAN-dum']

explanation   An explanation answers the question 'Why?' and provides understanding; sometimes it also provides us with the abilities to control, and to predict (and RETRODICT) the world. This is fairly vague, and philosophers have tried to provide theories of explanation—to give a general account of how explanations work, and what makes some good and some bad. One important account is the COVERING LAW model. One (but only one) sort of explanation is CAUSAL: we explain something by saying what its causes are. Sometimes, instead, we explain by telling what something is made of, or by giving reasons for human ACTIONS (*but see* REASONS / CAUSES), as in some explanations in history.

explication   Explanation, but sometimes in particular explanation of the meaning of a term in ways other than by providing an explicit definition—for example, by showing its use.

exploitation   Making use of selfishly or unfairly. There's a good deal of contemporary concern about the exploitation of women, workers, various groups not of European origin.

exportation   A rule of INFERENCE which allows the mutual inference and interchangeability of the equivalent expressions (P & Q) ⊃ R and P ⊃ (Q ⊃ R).

expressivism   *See* EMOTIVISM.

extension / intension   [Note the 's' in 'intension'; be careful not to confuse 'intensional' with 'INTENTIONAL'.] **1a.** Sometimes 'extension' is used synonymously with 'denotation' and 'intension' with 'connotation' (*see* DENOTATION / CONNOTATION). Thus the extension of a term or a PREDICATE is the SET of things to which that term or predicate applies (*see* COEXTENSIVE). **1b.** An extensional CONTEXT is one in which COEXTENSIVE PREDICATES cannot be inter-substituted *SALVA VERITATE*. Contexts which are non-extensional are called intensional or MODAL. Some philosophers have argued that any referentially transparent (*see* OPAQUE / TRANSPARENT) CONTEXT must be extensional. If so then all referentially opaque or INTEN*T*IONAL (notice that '*t*') contexts are also inten*s*ional. Note however that this needs argument, and 'inten*t*ional' and 'inten*s*ional' should not be used as bare synonyms. An extensional logic is a TRUTH-FUNCTIONAL logic. **2.** The extension of something is its dimensions in space. Having extension is characteristic of things composed of extended SUBSTANCE, also known as 'physical substance'. Mental substance is unextended—it has no spatial dimensions. (In this sense, 'extension' does not contrast with a corresponding sense of 'intension'.)

externalism / internalism   A variety of related doctrines. Meta-ETHICAL externalism holds that the fact that something is good does not by itself automatically supply the motivation for someone to do it; in addition, motivation ("external" to the mere belief about goodness) must be supplied. Internalism is the view that the judgment that something is good itself guarantees or includes the motivation to do it. As a theory of mind, externalism is the view that to specify the "content" of a belief one must refer to the external facts or objects that the belief is about. For an internalist contrast here, *see*

METHODOLOGICAL SOLIPSISM. Externalism about meaning similarly insist on connections with externals. CAUSAL THEORIES are externalist.

external relations   *See* INTERNAL / EXTERNAL RELATIONS.

extrasensory perception   The supposed ability to know facts not perceived by the ordinary senses. A PARANORMAL PHENOMENON about whose existence mainstream science is sceptical. Abbreviated 'ESP'.

extrinsic   *See*   INTRINSIC / INHERENT / INSTRUMENTAL / EXTRINSIC.

F

facticity An EXISTENTIALIST term meaning the sum of facts true of a person and his/her world. For HEIDEGGER and SARTRE, facticity is our world seen as not of our creation, the sometimes burdensome or recalcitrant surroundings we find ourselves involuntarily inserted into.

fact-value gap *See* IS / OUGHT PROBLEM.

faith Belief in something (usually God) despite lack of adequate evidence, or even in the face of contrary evidence; generally thought of as an act of will (in contrast to usual belief, which develops in one unintentionally). In religious circles, 'faith' also often refers to love of and trust in God, and other attitudes thought religiously appropriate.

faith, bad / good *See* BAD FAITH / GOOD FAITH / AUTHENTICITY / INAUTHENTICITY.

fallacy A fallacy is an ARGUMENT of a type that may seem correct but in fact is not. (Thus, not just any mistaken argument should be called 'fallacious'.) Formal fallacies are mistakes in reasoning that spring from mistakes in LOGICAL FORM; their persuasiveness springs from their similarity, on first glance, to valid forms. An example is an argument involving AFFIRMING THE CONSEQUENT. Informal fallacies spring instead from ambiguities in meaning or grammar, or from psychological tendencies to be convinced by reasons that are not good reasons. Fallacies defined in this dictionary are:
ACCIDENT
AD BACULUM
AD HOC reasoning
AD HOMINEM

AD IGNORANTIAM
AD MISERACORDIAM
AD POPULUM
AD VERECUNDIAM
AFFIRMING THE CONSEQUENT
AMBIGUOUS MIDDLE
AMPHIBOLE
COMPOSITION
converse ACCIDENT
DENYING THE ANTECEDENT
division—*see* COMPOSITION / DIVISION
misplaced CONCRETENESS
EQUIVOCATION
FALSE CAUSE
GAMBLER'S FALLACY
GENETIC FALLACY
hasty generalization—*see* ACCIDENT
IGNORATIO ELENCHI
MODAL FALLACY
Monte Carlo fallacy—*see* GAMBLER'S FALLACY
NATURALISTIC FALLACY
PATHETIC FALLACY
post hoc ergo propter hoc—*see* FALSE CAUSE
undistributed middle—*see* DISTRIBUTED / UNDISTRIBUTED
     / TERM / MIDDLE.

fallibilism   The view that our beliefs in general (or of a certain sort) are never CERTAIN—always possibly mistaken, subject to being overturned by future evidence. Fallible beliefs may be acceptable however.

false cause   Drawing the mistaken conclusion that **x** caused **y** from the fact that **y** followed **x**; also called '*post hoc ergo propter hoc*' (Latin: "after that, therefore because of that", ['post hock AIR-go PROP-tur hock']. It may be that their conjunction is just a coincidence, or that something else caused both **x** and **y**.

false, logically   *See* LOGICAL TRUTH / FALSEHOOD.

falsidical   *See* VERIDICAL / FALSIDICAL.

falsifiability   *See* VERIFIABILITY.

falsification   *See* CONFIRMATION / DISCONFIRMATION / VERIFICATION / FALSIFICATION.

family resemblance   By ANALOGY with the ways members of a family resemble each other, this is the sort of similarity shared by things classified into certain groups: each shares characteristics with many but not all of the others, and there are no NECESSARY OR SUFFICIENT CONDITIONS for belonging in that classification. WITTGENSTEIN argued that many of our CONCEPTS are family-resemblance concepts. His best-known example is the concept of a game.

Fārābī   al- *See* AL-FĀRĀBĪ.

Faraday,   Michael *See* SCIENTISTS.

fascism   A twentieth-century form of state characterized by an extremely strong and AUTHORITARIAN right-wing, nationalistic, and often racist COMMUNITARIAN government in which the INTERESTS of the state supersede any individual's interests. **2**. With a capital 'F', it refers to the government of Mussolini's Italy; with a lower-case 'f', it characterizes Nazi Germany and some other governments. Most of the philosophers of that century were hostile to fascism; one exception was HEIDEGGER. ['FASH-ism']

fatalism   The position that our futures are inevitable, whatever we do—that events are "fated" to happen. It's important to distinguish this from DETERMINISM, which claims merely that our futures are determined. A determinist who is not a fatalist thinks that our futures are not inevitable—they depend on what we do.

feel   Some philosophy students express their philosophical positions by saying, "I feel that..." This suggests that they regard their positions as mere feelings—vague attitudes that can't be defended and shouldn't be trusted. Don't be so modest. Philosophers are supposed to make clear claims and argue for them, so it's better to say "I think that..." or "I believe that...", or just to make an ASSERTION unmodified by any of these phrases.

Feigl, Herbert (1902-1988) Austrian-American LOGICAL POSITIVIST; member of the VIENNA CIRCLE; a well-known work defends a MATERIALISTIC view of mind. [FIE-gul]

Feinberg, Joel (b. 1926) American philosopher with influential work on ethics, ACTION THEORY, philosophy of law, and political philosophy.

felicific calculus BENTHAM thought that the best ACTION was the one that produced the greatest happiness for the greatest number of people (*see* UTILITARIANISM), so he proposed that we determine what was right by quantifying the amounts of happiness produced by each result of an action, adding them up, and comparing this sum to the sum for other possible actions. 'Felicific' means 'having to do with happiness', so this process is called the 'felicific CALCULUS'; also sometimes called the 'felicity', 'pleasure-pain', 'HEDONIC', or 'happiness calculus'. ['fel-uh-SIF-ik']

feminism The name of various philosophical—especially ethical, social, and political—THEORIES and movements that see elements of our society as unjust to and EXPLOITATIVE of women, and which advocate their change. Feminists often advocate equality under the law and equal economic status, especially in employment opportunity, for women; but many go further, arguing in favour of preferential treatment for women to counteract past injustices. Sometimes they find male bias and male patterns of thought in many areas of our personal, social, and intellectual lives. Recent developments are feminist theories of the self, of knowledge, and of science.

Fermat's Last Theorem / Goldbach's conjecture   Pierre de Fermat (French mathematician, 1601-1665, ['fair-ma']) wrote in the margin of a book that he had a proof that there are no solutions for the formula $x^n + y^n = z^n$, where x, y, z, and n are integers, and n is greater than 2; but added that unfortunately the margin didn't have enough room to write it down. It wasn't until the 1990s that a (generally accepted) proof was provided.

But there is still no proof for the suggestion made by Christian Goldbach (Russian mathematician, 1690-1754), that every even number larger than 2 is the sum of two primes. Could it be that this is true but unprovable? Interesting issues are raised for the philosophy of mathematics.

Feuerbach,   Ludwig Andreas (1804-1872) German philosopher, theologian, and moralist. Known mainly for his critiques of HEGEL and of religion, and his defense of MATERIALISTIC, HUMANISTIC, and scientific views. ['FOY-er-baCH']

Feyerabend,   Paul [Karl] (1924-1994) Austrian-American philosopher of science who argued that there is no single scientific methodology, and that scientific objectivity was impossible. ['FIRE-abend']

Fichte,   Johann Gottlieb (1762-1814) German philosopher, student of KANT. Knowledge for him is the product of a free self-determining creative intellect; a central notion is the "ABSOLUTE"—identified with God, and containing the moral order of the universe. ['FICH-tuh']

fideism   The position that knowledge, especially of a religious sort, depends on FAITH or REVELATION.

Field,   Hartry H[amlin] (b. 1946) American METAPHYSICIAN, philosopher of language, mathematics, science; best known for his work on TARSKIAN theory of truth, and NOMINALIST theory of mathematics.

figure of a syllogism   In TRADITIONAL logic, the form of a SYL-
LOGISM categorized with respect to the position of the middle
term. The four figures are those in which the middle term has
these positions:

(1) subject of major premise; predicate of minor.
(2) predicate of both premises
(3) subject of both premises
(4) predicate of the major premise and subject of minor
(*See* MAJOR / MIDDLE / MINOR TERM / PREMISE.)

final cause   *See* FOUR CAUSES.

first cause argument for God's existence   Here's one version
of this argument:

> Every natural event has a preceding cause; tracing this
> CAUSAL CHAIN back in time would lead to an infinite series,
> without any start, if there were no first, supernatural cause.
> But an infinite series of this sort is impossible—something
> without a start doesn't exist. So there must have been a
> first, supernatural cause (an "UNMOVED MOVER"): God.

> This argument is often criticized by questioning its
> ASSUMPTION that an infinite series is impossible. It is some-
> times thought that the ancient Greeks, for whom the notion
> of infinity was unthinkable, found this assumption plausible;
> but we now are able to think about infinity, and need not
> accept it.

first mover   *See* UNMOVED MOVER.

first-order logic   *See* QUANTIFIER LOGIC.

first principles   The INDUBITABLE assumptions from which
other truths are derived; ASSUMPTIONS, AXIOMS, POSITS. Some
philosophers think these must be the starting point for any
reliable system of belief. *See also* FOUNDATIONALISM.

five ways   THOMAS AQUINAS'S five arguments for God's existence:

(1) Things are moving and changing; thus there must have been a FIRST CAUSE.

(2) Things need causes to exist; thus there must have been a first cause.

(3) Things are contingent (*see* NECESSARY / CONTINGENT), so there must be something that's necessary.

(4) Things fall short of perfection; therefore something perfect exists. (*See* DEGREES OF PERFECTION ARGUMENT.)

(5) Things are orderly and collectively tend toward a universal aim; thus there must be an intelligent Orderer (*see* TELEOLOGICAL ARGUMENT).

flaccid designator   *See* RIGID / FLACCID DESIGNATOR.

Flew,   Anthony [Garrard Newton] (b. 1923) English philosopher best known for his criticisms of Christian doctrine.

flux   The world conceived of as flowing, constantly changing. Some ancient Greek philosophers (for example, HERACLITUS) identified flux as the basic principle of the universe, whereas others (for example, PLATO) thought that the eternal and unchanging must be the really real.

Fodor,   Jerry A[lan] (b. 1935) American philosopher identified with the views that mind can be understood as a computational system, and that there is a "LANGUAGE OF THOUGHT".

folk psychology   The name given by some philosophers of mind to our ordinary everyday ways of thinking about people and their minds, seen as a THEORY committed to the existence of beliefs, desires, personality traits, etc. Some philosophers argue that folk psychology fails various tests for good scientific theories (not merely because there is not much of the sort of observation and experiment we would expect in good science), and so, like other primitive belief-systems (e.g., astrology, belief in witches) it should be replaced by a more rigorous science of the mind not committed to the existence of beliefs, etc. (*see* eliminative MATERIALISM).

follow   The conclusion of a valid ARGUMENT is said to follow from its premises.

foole, the   *See* HOBBES'S FOOLE.

Foot, Philippa R[uth] (b. 1920) English philosopher best known for her work in naturalistic ethics (*see* ETHICAL NATURALISM), on VIRTUE theory and against UTILITARIANISM.

force   *See* SPEECH ACTS.

force, appeal to   *See* AD BACULUM.

foreknowledge   Knowledge of the future. It is often assumed that God has perfect foreknowledge. This raises the problems of FUTURE CONTINGENTS and FREE WILL.

form   **1**. For PLATO, what things of one sort have in common is that they "participate" in a "form" or "idea" (in Greek, '*eidos*' ['EYE-dos' or 'AY-dos'], or 'archetype'. Thus this, that, and the other green thing are all green because of their relation to the form, greenness. Forms are eternal and unchanging, and exist necessarily and independently of the earthly things for which they serve as patterns. True knowledge is of the forms, not of their earthly representations. **2**. ARISTOTLE agreed that the form of something is its essence and the object of real knowledge, but denied that the forms have independent existence; greenness is (somehow) *in* each green thing. **3**. KANT thought of form as the organizing principles the mind imposes on what we perceive as a precondition of its INTELLIGIBILITY. *See* UNIVERSALS *and* ABSTRACT / CONCRETE ENTITIES / IDEAS.

formal   As philosophers use this term, it doesn't have the ordinary implications of stiff and ceremonious. It means pertaining to structure (as opposed to content); or rigorous and rule-governed. *See* INFORMAL / FORMAL LOGIC, LOGICAL FORM, FORMAL SYSTEM, *and* FALLACY.

formalism   The idea that mathematics is an uninterpreted CACULUS: syntax without SEMANTICS.

formal cause   *See* FOUR CAUSES.

formal fallacy   *See* FALLACY.

formal logic   *See* INFORMAL / FORMAL LOGIC, LOGICAL FORM.

formal system   A systematic and rigorous set of statements, rules, etc., whose total structure and procedures are specified—like SYMBOLIC LOGIC, but unlike ordinary language, which doesn't state (and perhaps doesn't even have) rigorous rules.

formation rules   *See* WELL-FORMED FORMULA.

form, logical   *See* LOGICAL FORM.

forms, Platonic   *See* FORM[1].

formula   Any series of symbols in SYMBOLIC LOGIC. *See also* WELL-FORMED FORMULA.

formula, well-formed   *See* WELL-FORMED FORMULA.

Foucault,   Michel (1926-1984) French philosopher, historian, author, associated with the STRUCTURALISTS. Best known for his works attempting to uncover the underlying structure and PRESUPPOSITIONS of the ideas of madness and sexuality in Western civilization. ['foo-ko']

foundationalism   The position that there is a particular sort of statement (sometimes thought to be INDUBITABLE) from which all other statements comprising a system of belief should be derived. There are foundationalist theories of knowledge, of ethics, etc.

four causes   ARISTOTLE's distinction:
  (1) The efficient cause of something: what brings it into existence
  (2) The formal cause: its abstract structure—its "blueprint"
  (3) The material cause: what it's made of
  (4) The final cause: its purpose or aim

Aristotle did not mean by 'cause' exactly what we do, though the sorts of explanation we give when we say "because..." can correspond with his four "causes": perhaps his four causes should be understood as the four basic kinds of characteristics that things have, which are useful in categorizing them and explaining what they're like and how they work.

Frankfurt,   Harry [Gordon] (b. 1929) American philosopher with influential works on FREEDOM and VOLITION.

Frankfurt School   An association of German philosophers (and others) during the first half of the twentieth century, including Max Horkheimer (1895-1973), Theodor Adorno (1903-1969), MARCUSE, and HABERMAS. Associated with the development of CRITICAL THEORY.

freedom   1. Personal (METAPHYSICAL) freedom—FREE WILL. **2.** Political freedom is what people have insofar as they are unrestricted by laws, or insofar as they have RIGHTS. What constitutes political freedom, and to what extent it is a good thing, is a central concern of political philosophy.

free logic   Makes no PRESUPPOSITION that anything in its formulas refers; so Fa does not IMPLY (∃x)Fx.

free-rider problem   Since public goods can be enjoyed even by those who do not participate in paying for them, it seems rational for each person to avoid contributing to a public good (if possible) but to free-ride on the contributions of others. But if everyone did this, the public good would not be provided. This is a general problem in social philosophy which has the form of the PRISONER'S DILEMMA.

free / bound variable   *See* SYMBOLS OF QUANTIFIED LOGIC.

free will   To say that we have free will (or FREEDOM[1]) is to say that our decisions and actions are sometimes entirely (or at least partially) "up to us"—not forced or DETERMINED by anything internal or external to us. We can then either do or not do—we have alternatives. It seems that only if we have free will can we be RESPONSIBLE for what we do. But if determinism is true, then our actions and "decisions" are determined by previous causes, themselves determined by still earlier causes, and ultimately whatever we decide or do is determined by events that happened a long time ago, and that are not up to us. Thus, it seems that determinism is incompatible with free will. There are three main responses to this apparent problem:

(1) Hard determinists accept determinism, which they take to rule out free will.

(2) LIBERTARIANS[1] accept free will. They think that this means determinism is false, at least for some human events (*see* CONTRA-CAUSAL FREEDOM). Both libertarianism and hard determinism are incompatibilist (*see* COMPATIBILISM); that is, they hold that the freedom of an act is incompatible with its being determined.

(3) Soft Determinists are compatibilists, in that they attack the reasoning above, and argue that our actions might be determined, but also free in some sense— that a determined action might nevertheless be up to the doer, and one that the doer is morally responsible for—when it's determined but not compelled (*see* COMPULSION).

Frege,   [Friedrich Ludwig] Gottlob (1848-1925) German logician and philosopher of language, the founder of modern mathematical logic. He is best known for inventing quantification in logic (*see* SYMBOLS OF QUANTIFIER LOGIC), for his arguments that mathematics should be understood as an extension of logic, and for his investigations into the relation between sense and reference (*see* DENOTATION / CONNOTATION) in philosophy of language. ['FRAY-guh')

frequency theory of probability   *See* PROBABILITY.

Freud,   Sigmund *See* SCIENTISTS.

function   **1.** Loosely speaking, a correspondence between one group of things and another. The notion has its home in arithmetic, where, for example, y is said to be a function of x in the formula $y = x^2$. Thus, each value of x corresponds to a value of y: if x is 1 then y is 1, if x is 2 then y is 4, and so on. The value you stick in (in place of x, in this case) is called the 'argument' of the function, and what you get out (the corresponding value of y, in this case) is called the 'value' of the function for that argument. Given the argument 3, the value is 9. *See also* TRUTH-FUNCTIONALITY. **2.** The function of something is its use, goal, proper or characteristic activity, the way it normally fits into CAUSAL relations with other things (*see* FUNCTIONALISM and FUNCTIONAL KIND).

functional definition   Defines by giving the typical use of the kind of thing, or its typical cause-and-effect relations with other things (*see* FUNCTIONAL KIND; *see also* list of other sorts of DEFINITION).

functional explanation   EXPLANATION by FUNCTION[2]— thought to be appropriate, for example, in physiology (explaining the pancreas, for example, by telling what use it is to the organism), and in sociology and anthropology: (explaining a social ritual, for example, by showing what it does for the society).

functionalism   The view that a certain sort of thing is actually a FUNCTIONAL KIND. A widely discussed view is functionalism about mental states: that each sort of mental state is a functional kind, definable in terms of its typical causes and effects. Functionalists tend to be token (*see* TYPE / TOKEN) MATERIALISTS, because they think that a particular internal state described functionally would be a particular physical state of the person's brain, though each type of mental state need not correspond to a type of physical state (*see*, by analogy, the can-opener example, in FUNCTIONAL KIND).

functional kind   A functional kind is a categorization in terms of what things can do—what their cause-and-effect relations with the world are—and not in terms of what they are made of, or how they are constructed. 'Can opener', for example, names a functional kind, because a can opener is anything whose operations result in a can being opened; this kind admits a wide variety of different physical kinds of things (compare an old-fashioned lever-tool, the can opener you turn, the electric can opener). (*See also* FUNCTIONAL DEFIN-ITION.)

function, truth   *See* TRUTH-FUNCTION.

future contingents   The problem here, first discussed by ARIS-TOTLE, is how future events can be (METAPHYSICALLY) con-tingent, given that statements about them can now be true. Aristotle asks us to consider the proposition that there will be a sea battle tomorrow. If it is true *now* that there is a sea bat-tle tomorrow, how can that event fail to happen then? How could the admiral decide tomorrow morning not to have the battle, and prevent its happening? Similarly, if it's false now, it's impossible that it happen. Either way, it wouldn't be con-tingent. Maybe it's neither true nor false now.

fuzzy set / logic   Normally, we think of things as either inside or outside a SET: everything is, for example either an apple (inside the set of apples) or a non-apple (outside the set). But sometimes it seems that the boundaries of a set are not sharp, and that some things are neither definitely in nor definitely out. A fuzzy set, then, allows for degrees of membership; fuzzy logic results when set membership, or applicability of a predicate, admits of such degrees.

G

Gadamer, Hans-Georg (1900-2002) German philosopher, known for his work on philosophical HERMENEUTICS, the "reader response" theory of interpretation of a text.

Galileo Galilei *See* SCIENTISTS.

gambler's fallacy The mistake of thinking (as many people, not only gamblers, do) that, for example, the fact that a fair coin has been flipped five times and has come up heads every time means it's much more likely to come up tails the next (to "try" to even out the frequency). If it's really a fair coin, the PROBABILITY that it will come up tails is .5 for the sixth flip, as it is for each flip. (Also called the 'Monte Carlo fallacy'.)

game In philosophical usage, this term includes but is not limited to contests and sports. To play a game is to attempt to achieve a certain state of affairs using only those means permitted by the rules; a game is a choice situation where more than one individual is choosing and where the choices made by the participating individuals determine how well the other individuals' choice turns out. Game theory is a systematic mathematical theory of human interaction that sees it as a rule-governed, sometimes competitive, group activity with certain aims and strategies. Most centrally a theory of economic behaviour, but also applied to other sorts of human interactions, such as political and moral ones.

Gassendi, Pierre (1592-1655) French philosopher and mathematician. Known for his SCEPTICISM, MECHANISTIC theories, and objections to DESCARTES.

Gauthier, David [Peter] (b. 1932) Canadian moral philosopher; responsible for a version of the contractarian (*see* SOCIAL CONTRACT) derivation of morality from rationality. ['GO-tee-ay']

Geach, Peter [Thomas] (b. 1919) British philosopher, known for his work in logic, and METAPHYSICS, and for his defense of Christian dogma and morality. ['geech']

Gedankenexperiment *See* THOUGHT EXPERIMENT.

Gemeinschaft / Gesellschaft The first of these German terms refers to 'community'—social entities constituted by tradition, giving members IDENTITY[1]—the family, rural peasant villages; the second to mere 'society'—social entities which are merely collections of autonomous individuals: the modern city. (*See* HOLISM / INDIVIDUALISM.)

gender / sex A distinction in some contemporary FEMINIST theory. The former is the male / female distinction as socially constructed and as psychologically and politically significant; the second is merely a matter of biology.

general idea *See* CONCEPT.

generalization A statement about a group of things, or about everything in a particular category, contrasted with a 'PARTICULAR STATEMENT / PROPOSITION'; or the process of reasoning that arrives at one of these. Inductive logic (*see* DEDUCTION / INDUCTION) studies the principles of deriving them from particular instances; in deductive logic, the rules for deriving quantified statements are called EXISTENTIAL GENERALIZATION and UNIVERSAL GENERALIZATION. An ethical generalization is a rule everyone should follow; KANT argued that the right action was the one whose MAXIM could be generalized.

general will What is desired by, or desirable for, society as a whole; sometimes taken to be the appropriate JUSTIFICATION for government policy. This notion can be problematic when it is taken (in its classical formulation by ROUSSEAU, for instance) to mean something other than what's revealed by majority vote or unanimity. *See also:* SOCIAL CHOICE THEORY.

generative grammar   Noam CHOMSKY is a central figure in the development of this approach to linguistics, which attempts to discover a general "DEEP STRUCTURE"—a "universal GRAMMAR"—common to all natural languages (*see* ARTIFICIAL / NATURAL LANGUAGES), which are generated from this plus surface grammar and vocabulary peculiar to the language. Contrary to the EMPIRICIST position that the mind is born a *TABULA RASA*, Chomsky argues that the universality of this grammar, and the speed with which children learn their first language on the basis of very little experience, show that this deep structure must be INNATE.

genetic fallacy   The mistaken argument that the origins of something are the thing itself, or that its origins prove something about it. One form of this is the *AD HOMINEM* argument.

genius, evil   *See* EVIL GENIUS.

genus / species   For philosophers, not just biological hierarchical divisions, but divisions anywhere. A genus is a general classification; a species subdivides the genus. This nomenclature is especially associated with ARISTOTLE, who thought that a species ought to be defined by giving the ESSENTIAL characteristics of its genus, plus the *differentia* (Latin: "differences") that distinguish that species from others in the genus. So an 'Aristotelian definition' gives genus and differentia. (This sort of definition is also called 'by genus and species', in Latin, '*per genus et differentia*', and 'analytic definition'.) For an argument against the universal applicability of this sort of definition, *see* FAMILY RESEMBLANCE.

Gesellschaft   *See* GEMEINSCHAFT / GESELLSCHAFT.

Gettier,   Edmund (b. 1927) American philosopher whose counter-examples to the view that knowledge is justified true belief have immortalized his name by coming to be called 'Gettier examples'. Imagine, for example, that you see a clock which says that it's noon, and you believe it's noon as a result. It is in fact noon, so your belief is true. The clock is normally reliable, so your belief is justified. But in fact the clock stopped at noon yesterday, so it's just lucky that the information it gave you is true, and you don't know that it's noon, despite having justified true belief. *See also* TRACKING THE TRUTH.

Ghazālī,   al- *See* AL-GHAZĀLĪ.

ghost in the machine   RYLE'S disparaging term for how mind / body DUALISTS see a person: as a physical, mechanical body containing a ghostly, non-material mind. He argued that minds are, like ghosts, thought to exist because of philosophically mistaken reasoning. (*See   also* CATEGORY MISTAKE).

Gilson,   Étienne (1884-1978) Eminent French Catholic MEDIEVALIST, NEO-THOMIST philosopher. ['zheel-SON']

given   The given is the sort of thing that is the ground floor of our knowledge: that for which there is no evidence, but which counts as evidence for anything else. For example, perception is often supposed to provide the given. Some philosophers doubt that there is anything that is given in this sense. (*See also* MYTH OF THE GIVEN, DATUM, FOUNDATIONALISM, BASING RELATION.)

Glover,   Jonathan (b. 1941) British philosopher, important in the rebirth of applied ethics.

gnosticism   The doctrine of the Gnostics, an early marginally

Christian sect which offered salvation through otherwise hidden knowledge of spiritual truths (rather than through faith), and advocated transcending the evil material world. ['NOS-ti-sizm']

God   Among traditional Christians and Jews, God is the supernatural creator of the universe, who provides the source for morality, answers our prayers, is all-powerful and all-knowing, cares for us, and provides for immortality and salvation. With a lower-case 'g', 'god' refers to any other supernatural being believed in by other religions. There has been frequent philosophical debate about whether God's existence can be proven rationally. For a list of many classical attempts to do this, *see* ARGUMENTS FOR GOD'S EXISTENCE.

Gödel,   Kurt (1906-1978) American (born in Austria-Hungary) mathematician and LOGICIAN, widely known for Gödel's theorem: his proof of the INCOMPLETENESS of any CONSISTENT logic strong enough to include elementary number theory. A common version of this proof involves "Gödel numbering"–a scheme for assigning a number to every proposition in the language. [The closest many English-speakers can get to pronouncing his name is 'girdle'—that's closer than 'go-del', anyway]

Goldbach's conjecture   *See* FERMAT'S LAST THEOREM / GOLDBACH'S CONJECTURE.

golden mean   *See* MEAN.

Golden Rule   A principle of morality associated with Christianity: "Do unto others as you would have them do unto you."

Goldman,   Alvin I[ra] (b. 1938) American philosopher, producer of NATURALIZED theories of knowledge and mind.

Goldman,   Emma (1869-1940) Lithuanian-American political activist and social theorist. Red Emma was outspoken in her advocacy of SOCIALISM, free speech, women's rights, and trade unionism.

good, intrinsic / extrinsic / instrumental   *See*   INTRINSIC / EXTRINSIC / INSTRUMENTAL GOOD.

good faith   *See*   BAD FAITH / GOOD FAITH / AUTHENTICITY / INAUTHENTICITY.

Goodman,   (Henry) Nelson (1906-1998) American philosopher associated (together with QUINE) with contemporary PRAGMATISM; influential writings in theory of knowledge, philosophy of language and of science (for Goodman's paradox, *see* GRUE), and METAPHYSICS.

good / right   Both terms of moral approval. The distinction between them isn't very strict, but sometimes 'good' is taken to apply to people or things, and 'right' to actions. (*See also* ACT / AGENT MORALITIES.)

good will   KANT wrote that the foundation of ethics was the good will: the motivation to do what is right not because of its consequences, nor because of any natural feeling of benevolence, but because of the knowledge of what is good.

grammar   Philosophers use this word in a wider way than English teachers do. It means the form, that is, the general structure, of a sentence. This can include its LOGICAL FORM as well as its syntax (*see* SEMANTICS / SYNTAX / PRAGMATICS). Linguists sometimes include in grammar the semantics and PHONETICS of a sentence as well. For the distinction between depth and surface grammar, *see* DEEP / SURFACE STRUCTURE.

grammar, depth / surface / generative / universal   *See* GENERATIVE GRAMMAR.

Great Chain of Being   The MEDIEVAL notion (named by the historian A. O. Lovejoy (1873-1962)) that the universe contained every possible being (the 'principle of plenitude'), with everything ordered in a hierarchy from the highest to the lowest. Also called the "Chain of Being".

greatest happiness principle   *See* UTILITARIANISM.

Greek Academy   *See* ACADEMY.

Grelling's paradox   Named for the German logician Kurt Grelling (1886-1942). Some adjectives apply to themselves, for example, 'English', 'short', 'polysyllabic'. Call these 'autological' adjectives. Some adjectives do not apply to themselves, for example, 'French', 'long', 'monosyllabic'. Call these 'heterological' adjectives. Now consider the adjective 'heterological'. Is this a heterological adjective? This, like the LIAR'S PARADOX, is a paradox of SELF-REFERENCE.

Grice,   H[erbert] Paul (1913-88) English philosopher, developed an AUSTINian theory of meaning based on speakers' intentions.

Grotius,   Hugo (1583-1645). (Name in Dutch: Huigh de Groot.) Dutch thinker, with early influential work on the foundation of international law. [groshs]

grue   A colour name invented by Nelson GOODMAN, defined as follows:
> **x** is grue if and only if:
> (1) It is before time **t** and **x** is green; or
> (2) It is **t** or after and **x** is blue.

Let **t** be some future time, say midnight tonight. All emeralds observed so far have been green, so they have also been grue. Using the usual inductive reasoning process (*see* DEDUCTION / INDUCTION), you conclude that they will be green tomorrow. But all those emeralds have also been grue; the same reasoning shows that they will be grue tomorrow; but that means they will be blue tomorrow. Both predictions can't be correct; why do you think only the first is? Goodman raised what he called the "new riddle of induction" (*see* PROBLEM OF INDUCTION for the "old riddle"): we all think that green is a PROJECTIBLE property and grue isn't, but Goodman argued there's no JUSTIFICATION for this. The only difference is that green is ENTRENCHED; but this doesn't justify its use. And the same sort of reasoning can be extended to every intuitively acceptable inductive argument. The grue paradox is also known as 'Goodman's paradox'.

Grünbaum, Adolf (b. 1923) German/American philosopher of science, important especially in the philosophies of physics and psychiatry.

Gyges, ring of *See* HOBBES'S FOOLE.

H

Habermas, Jürgen (b. 1929) German social philosopher, member of the FRANKFURT SCHOOL, known for his rejection of POSITIVISM and EMPIRICISM in favour of an ANALYSIS of knowledge in terms of social theory.

haecceity This penny looks a lot like every other penny, and exactly like some. Is there some characteristic that only this penny has, and only this one could have—for example, the characteristic of *being this penny*? This is a peculiar sort of characteristic, but some MEDIEVAL and contemporary philosophers argue that it's necessary to distinguish any particular thing from every other actual and possible thing. This sort of characteristic is called in Latin a '*haecceitas*' (a 'this-ness'), in English a 'haecceity'. The belief that such characteristics exist is haecceitism. ['hex-EYE-ih-tee' or 'hex-AY-ih-tee'; 'HEX-ee-a-tizm']

hallucination *See* ILLUSION / HALLUCINATION / DELUSION.

Hampshire, Stuart Newton (b. 1914) English philosopher, best known for his contributions to the philosophy of mind and action.

hangman's paradox *See* SURPRISE QUIZ PARADOX.

happiness HEDONISTS sometimes count happiness as one, or the only, basic element in a good life, but they often think of happiness not as merely feeling jolly, but as a more complex sort of state; for example, as characterizing a life that achieves its highest goal.

happiness calculus *See* FELICIFIC CALCULUS.

happiness paradox   It's sometimes supposed that happiness is best achieved by those who do not seek it (but who go after other goals). Thus the pursuit of happiness is self-defeating. (*See* SELF-FULFILLING / SELF-DEFEATING.)

hard determinism   *See* FREE WILL.

Harding,   Sandra (b. 1935) American philosopher of science; known for her critiques of traditional conceptualizations of science, and her suggestions for revision in terms of FEMINIST theory.

Hare,   R(ichard) M. (1919-2002) British philosopher, best known for his prescriptivist EMOTIVIST ethics.

Harman,   Gilbert (b. 1938) American philosopher best known for his contributions in philosophy of mind, ethics, and EPIS-TEMOLOGY.

harmony of the spheres   *See* MUSIC OF THE SPHERES.

harmony, pre-established   *See* PRE-ESTABLISHED HARMONY.

Harré,   Rom[ano Horace] (b. 1927) New Zealand-born philosopher of physical and social science. ['HAR-ray']

Hart,   H[erbert] L[ionel] A[dolphus] (1907-1992) English philosopher of law influential for his work on LEGAL POSI-TIVISM.

hasty generalization (fallacy of)   *See* ACCIDENT.

heap, paradox of the   *See* SORITES.

hedonic calculus   *See* FELICIFIC CALCULUS.

hedonism   In ordinary talk, this is seeking or desiring what some call the "lower" pleasures—wine, persons of the opposite sex, and song. In philosophical talk, this term also has to do with pleasure. Philosophical hedonists, however, often distinguish between the "higher" and "lower" pleasures, making the former more important. As in the case of EGOISM, we may distinguish psychological hedonism, the claim that people in fact seek only pleasure, from ethical hedonism, the claim that people ought to seek pleasure (or only pleasure). The philosophical hedonists include EPICURUS, LOCKE, HOBBES, HUME, BENTHAM, and MILL. ['HEE-dun-izm'. 'Hedonic' means 'pertaining to pleasure'; pronounced 'heh-DON-ik' or 'hee-DON-ik']

Hegel, Georg Wilhelm Friedrich (1770-1831) Foremost of the German IDEALISTS, still an enormous influence on CONTINENTAL philosophy; at the end of the nineteenth century, most English-speaking philosophers were Hegelians. Known for his "DIALECTICAL^5" philosophy of history, of thought, and of the universe as a whole, which he sees as the progressive unfolding of reason—of the "Absolute Idea". ['HAY-gul']

hegemony The preponderant influence of one group or country. ['heh-JEM-uh-nee']

Heidegger, Martin (1899-1976) German founder of EXISTEN-TIALIST PHENOMENOLOGY. He attempted to provide a theory of the "authentic self" based on the feeling of dread and the awareness of death. ['HIGH-digger']

Heisenberg, Werner *See* SCIENTISTS.

Heisenberg uncertainty principle *See* UNCERTAINTY PRINCI-PLE.

Held, Virginia (b. 1929) American FEMINIST moral and politi-cal theorist.

Helmholtz, Hermann Ludwig von *See* SCIENTISTS.

Hempel, Carl (Gustav) (1905-1997) German-born American philosopher, member of the VIENNA CIRCLE, important in philosophy of science and contemporary EMPIRICISM. For "Hempel's paradox" *see* RAVEN PARADOX. ['HEM-pl']

Heraclitus of Ephesus (540-475 B.C.) PRE-SOCRATIC philosopher who taught that all things were composed of fire and in constant flux. ['hair-uh-KLY-tus']

heresy An opinion rejected as contrary to the official doctrine of a religious group and officially prohibited by them.

hermeneutics The practice of interpretation or EXPLANATION; once closely associated with interpretation of the Bible, but now used (especially in CONTINENTAL circles) to mean a general science or methodology of interpretation. Influential philosophers in this area of study include HEIDEGGER, DILTHEY, GADAMER, and RICOEUR. [English speakers usually say 'her-man-OO-ticks' or 'her-man-YOU-ticks']

hermeneutic circle One can understand **x** only once one has understood **y**; but one can understand **y** only once one has understood **x**. Now what?

heterodox *See* ORTHODOX / HETERODOX.

heterogeneous *See* HOMOGENEOUS / HETEROGENEOUS.

heterological *See* SELF-REFERENCE; *see also* GRELLING'S PARADOX.

heteronomy *See* AUTONOMY / HETERONOMY.

Hick, John (b. 1922) Widely-read English defender of the truth of religious doctrine.

Hildegard of Bingen (1098-1179) (in German: '*van Bingen*')

One of a very rare breed: female MEDIEVAL philosophers. German writer on COSMOLOGY, METAPHYSICS, MYSTICISM, medicine.

Hintikka, Jaakko (b. 1929) Finnish-American logician; his work has been specially important in the formulation and application of various MODAL LOGICS.

historical materialism / idealism Philosophers of history sometimes argue about what sorts of things are the most basic items at work in the process of history. We ordinarily think that these factors are people, economic conditions, countries, etc., but some philosophers have speculated that there is some sort of invisible "idea" or "spirit" whose operations underlie, at the most basic level, the most general historical processes. These philosophers are called 'historical IDEALISTS'. Those who insist that history gets its structure from more mundane physical or economic states and events are the historical MATERIALISTS; this view is especially strongly associated with MARX. *See also* DIALECTICAL MATERIALISM / IDEALISM.

historicism **1.** A view that emphasizes the variability of belief among historical periods; thus it tends to relativism (*see* RELATIVISM / ABSOLUTISM). **2.** The view that certain human phenomena cannot be understood in isolation from their historical development and from their significance to the particular historical period in which they existed and to the people in this period. **3.** The view that there are laws of, or some sort of necessity to, large-scale historical development.

Hobbes, Thomas (1588-1679) English philosopher, a central figure in the birth of MODERN PHILOSOPHY. Hobbes was instrumental in replacing the earlier ARISTOTELIAN view of change as motion from potentiality to actuality with a modern MATERIALISTIC, MECHANISTIC view: atoms in motion, interacting because of their physical properties, not purposes, explain the world. Hobbes is also associated with the

view that strong government is justified by a SOCIAL CON-
TRACT in which naturally selfish citizens bind themselves for
their mutual protection and well-being. ['hobz']

Hobbes's Foole   A character, created by HOBBES, who decides
that it would be more rational for him to pretend to be just
than actually to be just. (Is he right?) Other philosophers
have created similar characters to raise similar philosophical
questions. HUME's Sensible Knave pretends to be just but
really is not. In PLATO's *Republic*, Glaucon tells the story of
a Lydian shepherd who finds the Ring Of Gyges which
allows him to become invisible. Glaucon asks why the shepherd, who could commit immoral acts without detection or
punishment, should act morally.

holism / individualism   **1.** The chief use of 'holistic' outside of
philosophy nowadays is in 'holistic medicine'—a mixture of
pseudo-science and fraud that preys on the ill and ignorant;
but in philosophical use: **2.** It is the position that certain sorts
of things are more than merely the sum of their parts—that
they can be understood only by examining them as a whole;
contrasted with 'individualism'. In social science and history, for example, holists argue that one can't explain what's
going on on the basis of individual people's ACTIONS,
because these get their significance only by virtue of facts
about the whole society. Voting, for example, is not just the
sum of the individual actions of marking on a piece of paper
or pushing down a lever: its significance can be explained
only by thinking about it *as* voting—that is, by appealing to
characteristics applying only to the society as a whole.
SEMANTIC holism (associated with QUINE) insists that words
and sentences get their meaning only through their relationships with all other words and sentences. Holism about living things refuses to see them merely as the sum of their non-
living parts. 'Methodological individualism' is the method in
sociology of investigating social facts by discovering facts
about individual people. Individualism in social theory
emphasizes individual rights and freedoms, contrasting with

COMMUNITARIANISM. *See also* SUPERVENIENCE, REDUCTION-ISM, VITALISM[3].

homogeneous / heterogeneous   An object or collection that's homogeneous is the same throughout; otherwise heterogeneous. ['HET-er-oh' or 'HO-mo' + '-JE-nee-us'] (Alternatively, 'homogenous' ['ho-MOJ-uh-nus'])

homological   *See* SELF-REFERENCE.

homunculus   (Latin: "little man") Homuncular theories of mind postulate sub-mechanisms that do some aspect of mental processing. Sometimes this is attributed desparagingly, as when, for example, a theory of perception imagines that visual images are "projected"—represented—somehow in the brain, where they are "seen"—perceived somehow—by a "homuncular" visualizer. This only moves the problems of perception one step down.

honourific   An honourific term is one that carries, as part of its meaning, an IMPLICATION of praise. To call someone 'brave', for example, is not just to say that that person is steadfast in the presence of danger—it's also to praise that person. 'Brave' and 'rash' are applied to someone depending entirely on whether you want to praise or disparage that person's steadfastness in the face of danger. If you refuse to call someone who runs from battlefield danger a 'soldier', you are using that word as an honourific, in a way not central to its basic sense in English: some soldiers are faint-hearted. *See also* PERSUASIVE DEFINITION. [Spelled 'honorific' in the US]

horns of a dilemma   *See* DILEMMA.

horseshoe   A SYMBOL OF SENTENTIAL LOGIC, '⊃', used to form a material CONDITIONAL. 'P ⊃ Q' is roughly equivalent to 'If P then Q'.

hot ziggety!   According to MALCOLM'S memoirs, WITTGEN-

STEIN would utter this exclamation when offered a plate of bread and cheese by Mrs. Malcolm.

humanism   Any view that centres on the value and dignity of humans, or that makes actual human values and relevance for humans the central starting points. Associated with the Renaissance movement, which turned away from MEDIEVAL supernaturalism and other-worldliness and emphasized human worth and FREEDOM[2], and the effectiveness of human action. 'LIBERAL' (or 'secular') 'humanism' has come to characterize any position that de-emphasizes religion and advocates LIBERTY[2], tolerance, and human welfare seen in terms of "earthly" values. It's sometimes a derogatory term, when used by right-wing believers to characterize political leftists and liberals, atheists, agnostics, and religious non-fundamentalists.

Hume,   David (1711-1776) Scottish philosopher and historian, among the greatest philosophers of all time. A thoroughgoing EMPIRICIST, he believed that all our ideas were copies of sense impressions (*see* IDEA / IMPRESSION); he argued that many of our notions (such as the continuing "self", and the necessary connection we suppose exists between CAUSE and effect), since unsupported by perception, are mistaken, and that *A PRIORI* knowledge must derive merely from logical relations between ideas. He is famous also for SCEPTICAL conclusions regarding moral "knowledge": our ethical reactions, he argued, come merely from the psychological tendency to feel SYMPATHY with others. His scepticism and empiricism were enormously influential in the ANALYTIC PHILOSOPHICAL tradition.

Husserl,   Edmund (1859-1938) German-Czech philosopher and mathematician, founder of PHENOMENOLOGY; influenced by BRENTANO, and greatly influential on EXISTENTIALISM. His method involved "BRACKETING" experience—considering limited aspects of it so that the ESSENCES of things are revealed.

Hutcheson, Francis (1694-1746) Irish-born philosopher who worked in Ireland and Scotland; known for the theory of the "MORAL SENSE", a kind of perception whereby feelings of approval or disapproval are raised in us.

Huxley, Thomas *See* SCIENTISTS.

hyle (Greek: "wood", hence "matter") ARISTOTLE used this term to refer to the underlying matter that he thought the characteristics (FORM) of something applied to. It's one of the FOUR CAUSES. We know about matter not through our senses, since we sense the characteristics, not the underlying matter, but rather as a consequence of our ANALYSIS of change. ['HOO-lay']

hylomorphism The view that a thing is FORM² plus matter. (*See* HYLE.)

Hypatia of Alexandria (370-415) Greek mathematician, astronomer, and neoplatonic (*see* PLATONISM) philosopher, she was tortured and killed by Christians.

hypostatization *See* REIFICATION.

hypothesis A tentative suggestion that may be merely a guess or a hunch, or may be based on some sort of reasoning; in any case it needs further evidence to be rationally acceptable as true. Some philosophers think that all scientific enquiry begins with hypotheses. [*Note*: singular 'hypothesis'; plural 'hypotheses']

hypothetical entities *See* THEORETICAL ENTITIES.

hypothetical imperative *See* CATEGORICAL / HYPOTHETICAL IMPERATIVE.

hypothetical proposition *See* CATEGORICAL / HYPOTHETICAL PROPOSITION.

hypothetical syllogism   A rule of INFERENCE:
If P then Q.
If Q then R.
Therefore, if P then R.

hypothetico-deductive model   The view of the structure of science that sees it as the process in which: first a HYPOTHESIS is formed; then statements about particular, observable facts are DERIVED from this hypothesis; and then the hypothesis is tested by CONFIRMATION of these statements. *See also* COVERING LAW.

I

Ibn Rushd   Abù al-Walìd Muhammad (1126-1198) Spanish-born Islamic philosopher. Influenced by PLATO and ARISTOTLE; his commentaries on the latter earned him the nickname 'The Commentator'. His defence of philosophical reason against AL-GHAZĀLĪ'S attacks was influential on THOMAS AQUINAS. The Latinized version of his name is 'Averroës'.

Ibn Sīnā   Abù'Alì al-Husayn (980-1037) Persian Islamic philosopher and physician. NEO-PLATONIST commentator on ARISTOTLE. The Latinized version of his name is 'Avicenna'.

idea, general / abstract   *See*   CONCEPT *and* ABSTRACT / CONCRETE ENTITIES / IDEAS.

idea / impression   An "idea" is, in general, any thought or perception in the mind. Platonic FORMS[1] are sometimes called 'ideas'. In HUME, ideas are the faint imprint left on the mind by impressions, which are the mental events one has as the immediate result of, and while, using one's senses (= SENSE-DATA). Ideas may be called up later in the absence of sensation. EMPIRICISTS believe that all ideas are copies of impressions.

idealism   **1.** In the ordinary sense of the word, an idealist is one who adheres to moral principle, or who is an impractical dreamer. This has little to do with its philosophical sense. **2.** in which idealism is the view that only minds and their contents really or basically exist (*see* DUALISM / MONISM / PLURALISM).

idealism, historical   *See*   HISTORICAL MATERIALISM / IDEALISM.

ideal language   An artificial language (*see* ARTIFICIAL / NAT-

URAL LANGUAGE) constructed in such a way that it contains all the ASSERTIONS we'd want to make in a certain area, in unambiguous and simplest form, and only these assertions; and so that the logical relations between these assertions are clear and unambiguous. Natural languages are clearly far from ideal languages. Some philosophers think that the construction of an ideal language is an important step in producing a THEORY. An aim of SYMBOLIC LOGIC is to produce an ideal language.

ideal limit theory of truth   To say that a proposition is true is to say that it would be agreed on at the ideal limit of enquiry—that is to say, when maximally intelligent and observant people had all the evidence it is possible to get. (For competing theories, *see* TRUTH.)

ideal observer theory   A theory of ethics that attempts to explain what is really good as what would be chosen by an ideal observer—that is, someone who would have all the relevant information, and who would not be misled by particular INTERESTS or biases.

ideas, abstract   *See* CONCEPT *and* ABSTRACT / CONCRETE ENTITIES / IDEAS.

ideas, clear and distinct   *See* CLEAR AND DISTINCT IDEAS.

ideas, innate   *See* INNATENESS.

ideas, Platonic   *See* FORM[1].

ideas, simple / complex   *See* SIMPLE / COMPLEX IDEAS.

idea theory of meaning   The meaning of a word is the idea it is associated with. Also known as the 'ideational' theory.

identity   **1.** Your identity is what you are—what's important about you, or what makes you different from everyone else. **2.** In an ordinary way of talking, two different things might be said to be 'identical' when they are exactly alike in some characteristics; this is sometimes called 'qualitative identity'—i.e., identity of qualities or characteristics. **3.** Object **a** and object **b** are said to be ('strictly' or 'numerically' or 'quantitatively') identical when **a** and **b** are in fact the same thing—when '**a**' and '**b**' are two different names or ways of REFERRING to exactly the same object. This is symbolized using the equals sign: **a** = **b** (*see* SYMBOLS OF QUANTIFIER LOGIC). **4.** Identity (over time) is the relation between something at one time and that same thing at another time: they are said to be two 'temporal stages' (or 'time-slices') of the same continuing thing. Note that two stages of the same thing are not quantitatively identical (they're different stages), and need not even be qualitatively identical: you're now taller than when you were an infant. On what basis do we judge that two stages of things (or people) are identical in this sense? This is the "problem of identity". *See also:*

PERSONAL IDENTITY
"BALL OF WAX" EXAMPLE
RELATIVE IDENTITY
SYNCHRONIC / DIACHRONIC
'principle of identity' in LAWS OF THOUGHT.

identity of indiscernibles   *See* LAW OF THE INDISCERNABILITY OF IDENTICALS.

identity, law of   *See* LAWS OF THOUGHT.

identity, personal   *See* PERSONAL IDENTITY.

identity, relative   *See* RELATIVE IDENTITY.

identity theory of mind   The view that each mental state is really a physical state, probably of the brain. Often identity theorists believe in addition in the TYPE-identity of mental and physical states (*see* IDENTITY[3]).

ideology   A system of values and beliefs, especially one concerning social and political matters. MARX thought of official ideological systems as delusions resulting from the false consciousness of the class societies in which they developed. Even in the mouths of non-Marxists, the word 'ideology' may suggest this sort of falsity. ['eye-' or 'ih-' + '-dee-OL-o-jee']

idiolect   A language or variant on a language used by only one person. ['ID-ee-o-lect']

if and only if   *See* BICONDITIONAL.

iff   An abbreviation for 'if and only if'. *See* BICONDITIONAL.

ignorance, appeal to   *See* AD IGNORANTIAM.

ignoratio elenchi   (Latin: "by ignoring the issues") The sort of reasoning that is faulty because the premises are irrelevant to the conclusion, or because it misses the point, refutes something which is not at issue, or ignores a well-known and obvious ARGUMENT to the contrary. Also called the 'fallacy of irrelevant conclusion'. ['ig-no' + '-RAHT-' or '-RAHTZ' + '-ee-o eh-LENK-ee']

illocutionary act / intention   *See* SPEECH ACTS.

illusion / hallucination / delusion   **1.** Illusions and hallucinations are "false" perceptual experiences—ones that lead, or could lead, to mistakes about what is out there. A hallucination is the apparent perception of something that does not exist at all (as in dreaming, mirages, drug-induced states). An illusion is the incorrect perception of something that does exist (examples are the MÜLLER-LYER ILLUSION, and the familiar way a straight stick half-immersed in water looks bent). A delusion is a perception that actually results in a false belief; illusions and hallucinations can delude, but often do not. The ARGUMENT FROM ILLUSION draws EPISTEMOLOG-

ICAL conclusions from the existence of these things. **2.** 'Illusion' and 'delusion' are sometimes used to refer to any false belief: Freud (*see* SCIENTISTS) and MARX called religious beliefs "illusions".

imagination   In the ordinary sense, this is our faculty for thinking things up, especially unreal things. Some philosophers have used this word to refer to the faculty of having images—mental pictures.

imitation game   *See* TURING.

immanent   *See* TRANSCENDENT / IMMANENT.

immaterialism   **1.** The view that some things exist that are not material: that are not made of ordinary physical stuff, but of mental or spiritual—immaterial (synonym: 'incorporeal')—stuff instead. This is the denial of MATERIALISM. The most extreme form of immaterialism is the view that no material things exist: this is IDEALISM[2]. (*See also* SUBSTANCE.) **2.** The view that objects are merely collections of qualities, without a SUBSTRATUM to hold them together. (*See* BUNDLE THEORY.) If one thinks of qualities as essentially mental perceptions, then this is a species of immaterialism in sense **1.**

immaterial substance   *See* SUBSTANCE.

immediate / mediate   **1.** In the ordinary sense, 'immediate' means 'without delay' but **2.** in its more technical philosophical sense it means 'without mediation'—that is, 'directly', as opposed to 'mediate'. In this sense, for example, philosophers ask whether external things are sensed immediately, or mediated by the sensing of internal images. An immediate inference is one performed in one step, needing only a single use of only one rule, for example, when **Q** is inferred from (**P** and **Q**).

immorality / amorality   The first means 'contrary to morality';

the second, 'without morality'. Someone who knows about moral rules but intentionally disobeys them or rejects them is immoral; someone who doesn't know or think about morality is amoral. Amorality is typical of small children; immorality of adults.

immortality   The supposed continuation of the soul or spirit or mind or person forever, after the death of the body. It is, of course, a central feature of the beliefs of most religions, but philosophers have sometimes been sceptics about the possibility and even the desirability of immortality.

imperative   A statement telling you to do something.

imperative, categorical / hypothetical   *See*   CATEGORICAL / HYPOTHETICAL IMPERATIVE.

implicans / implicate   Old-fashioned terms for the antecedent / consequent of a CONDITIONAL.

implication   *See* INFERENCE / IMPLICATION / ENTAILMENT[1].

implicature   *See* INFERENCE / IMPLICATION / ENTAILMENT.

imply / infer   *See* INFERENCE / IMPLICATION / ENTAILMENT[1].

import, existential   *See* EXISTENTIAL IMPORT.

impression   *See* IDEA / IMPRESSION.

inalienable right   *See* RIGHTS.

inauthenticity   *See* BAD FAITH / GOOD FAITH / AUTHENTICITY / INAUTHENTICITY.

inclination   Any desire, or pro or con feeling. Some philosophers (KANT is a good example) think that acting from inclination cannot be moral action; the only right actions are those motivated by an understanding of duty, and are often contrary to inclination.

inclusive 'or' / disjunction   *See* DISJUNCTION.

incoherent   *See* COHERENT.

incommensurability   *See* COMMENSURABILITY / INCOMMENSURABILITY.

incompatiblism   *See* FREE WILL.

incompleteness   *See* COMPLETENESS / INCOMPLETENESS.

inconsistency   *See* CONSISTENCY.

incorrigibility / corrigibility   'Corrigibility' means 'correctibility'. Something is incorrigible when it is impossible to correct it, or when it is guaranteed correct. Some philosophers have thought that our beliefs about our own mental states are incorrigible. For example, if you sincerely believe that you are now feeling a pain, how could you be wrong?

incorporeality   *See* SUBSTANCE *and* IMMATERIALISM[1].

indefinite description   *See* DEFINITE / INDEFINITE DESCRIPTION.

indeterminacy of translation / reference   The view, associated with QUINE, that there are many possible ways to translate another language into your own, and that there may not be conclusive reasons to prefer one translation to another. Quine argued that there is no fact of the matter about what someone means by what he / she says; there is only a preferred translation. Because there may be several equally likely hypotheses about what object someone's words refer to, there is indeterminacy (or "inscrutability") of reference. *See also* RADICAL TRANSLATION.

indeterminacy, principle of   *See* PRINCIPLE OF INDETERMINA-
CY.

indeterminism   *See* DETERMINISM.

indexical / demonstrative   The REFERENCE of indexical terms
is partly determined by the context of utterance. 'I', 'it',
'there', 'now', 'tomorrow' for example. Demonstrative terms
are "pointing" indexicals—for example, 'this' in 'This is
mine'. Also called 'egocentric particulars'.

indifference principle   The idea that if there is no information
at all about whether or not **x** is more likely than **y**, then **x** and
y should each be assigned probabilities of .5. It's easy to
show that this is not a good principle.

indirect / direct discourse   Direct discourse (also called, in
Latin, *oratio recta*) reports what someone said by direct quotation: "Fred said, 'We're gonna have rain.'" Indirect discourse (Latin, *oratio obliqua*) does so without quoting: 'Fred
said that it was going to rain.' Similarly one reports someone's beliefs in indirect discourse: 'Fred believed it was
going to rain.'

indirect proof   Proof of a statement accomplished by ASSUM-
ING[2] its denial and deriving a SELF-CONTRADICTION or
ABSURDITY from that. Also known as *reductio ad absurdum*
(Latin: "reduction to the absurd").

indiscernibles   *See* LAW OF THE INDISCERNABILITY OF IDENTI-
CALS.

individual constant   *See* SYMBOLS OF QUANTIFIER LOGIC.

individual essence   *See* ESSENCE.

individual / individuation   **1.** In ordinary talk, the word 'individual' can be used correctly as a contrast to 'group', 'orga-
nization', etc., but is frequently misused as a pompous syn-

onym for 'person'. **2.** In philosophical talk, an individual is a single thing (not necessarily a person) that is basic in the sense of not being ANALYZABLE into parts. Individuation is distinguishing between one thing and another: philosophers sometimes try to discover criteria for individuation of some sort of thing, that is, the tests we use to tell things of that sort from one another, and to count how many of them there are in a group of them. 'Particulars' is a synonym for 'individuals'.

individualism   *See* HOLISM / INDIVIDUALISM.

individual variable   *See* SYMBOLS OF QUANTIFIER LOGIC.

individuation   *See* INDIVIDUAL / INDIVIDUATION.

indubitability / dubitability   'Dubitable' means 'doubtable'. Dubitable statements are not just ones we are psychologically capable of doubting, but ones about which even highly fanciful and unlikely doubts might be raised, doubts that no one in his/her right mind would seriously have. Thus DESCARTES thought that because our senses might be fooled, information from them was dubitable. He then went on to try to discover what sort of belief was really indubitable: about which it could be proven that no doubt can be raised. *See also* CERTAINTY.

induction   *See* DEDUCTION / INDUCTION.

induction, problem / principle of   *See* PROBLEM OF INDUCTION.

ineffable   Indescribable, not communicable. Some religious or mystical experiences are said to be ineffable.

inference / implication / entailment **1.** Implication (also known as entailment) is a logical relation that holds between two statements when the second follows DEDUCTIVELY from the first. The first is then said to 'imply' (or 'entail') the second. Be careful not to confuse these with 'inference', which is something that people do, when they reason from one statement to another (which the first statement implies/ entails). A rule of inference is an acceptable procedure for reasoning from one set of statements of a particular form to another statement. **2**. Sometimes a sentence 'implies' what it doesn't literally state. For example, if I said "Fred is now not robbing banks", I imply that at one time he was robbing banks. This sort of implicature is sometimes called 'conversational' or 'contextual' implicature, or 'pragmatic' implication, to distinguish it from 'logical' implicature. (This should be distinguished from PRESUPPOSITION.) **3**. Sometimes a material or strict CONDITIONAL is called an 'implication'. **4**. 'Implication' is the name of rule that permits inference[1] between, and replacement of, the equivalent forms (P ⊃ Q) and (~P v Q).

infinite regress   A sequence (often of DEFINITION, EXPLANATION, or JUSTIFICATION) that must continue backwards endlessly. For example, if every event must have a cause, then a present event must be caused by some past event; and this event by another still earlier, and so on infinitely. Sometimes the fact that reasoning leads to an infinite regress shows that it is faulty. One then calls it a 'vicious' regress.

infinitesimals   These are infinitely small things, for example, points on a line. Philosophers have been worried, from time to time, about the possibility of their existence. The branch of mathematics now called 'calculus' had the original full name of 'calculus of infinitesimals', because its object is (in a sense) these things.

informal fallacies   *See* FALLACY.

informal / formal logic   The latter is that kind of logic that relies heavily on SYMBOLS and rigorous procedures much like those in mathematics; it concentrates on reasoning that is correct because of syntax. (*See* SEMANTICS / SYNTAX / PRAG-

MATICS.) Only a small fraction of the ordinary sorts of reasoning we do can be explained this way, and there is a vast scope for informal logic, which analyzes good and bad arguments semantically, and relies less heavily on symbols and mathematics-style procedures.

informed consent   Agreement based on sufficient knowledge of relevant information; relevant especially to medical ethics. It's widely agreed that informed consent by the patient is necessary for all medical procedures, but problems arise here: how much information is enough? what should be done when the patient is unable to understand the information or to make a rational choice?

inherent   *See*   INTRINSIC / INHERENT / INSTRUMENTAL / EXTRINSIC.

in-itself / for-itself   1. These are the two fundamental categories SARTRE thought the world was divided into. The realm of the for-itself (in French, '*pour-soi*', ['poor swa']) includes free things—things that are conscious, create their own characteristics, and are RESPONSIBLE for everything they do. This realm is often thought to include only PERSONS. The realm of the in-itself (French: '*en-soi*', ['AN-swa']) includes everything else. **2.** For a different sense of 'in-itself', *see* THING-IN-ITSELF.

innateness   A belief, CONCEPT, or characteristic is innate when it is inborn—when it doesn't come from experience or education—though experience may be thought necessary to make conscious or actualize something that is given innately. An argument for the innateness of something is that experience is not sufficient to produce it in us. Well-known innateness views are PLATO'S (for the innateness of concepts) and CHOMSKY'S (for the innateness of concepts and of the DEEP STRUCTURE of language).

innocence and guilt   The DETERRENCE theory of PUNISHMENT claims that inflicting punishment is JUSTIFIED if this prevents future undesirable acts. But suppose that punishing someone who was in fact innocent prevented a great deal of future crime (by others); it seems that this would be justified by the deterrence theory. Does this show that the theory is wrong? A second way innocence and guilt enter into a philosophical argument is in the theory of the "JUST WAR". Many people are willing to allow that going to war under some circumstances is morally justified; but in every war innocent people are hurt and killed. Does this show that it's acceptable to harm innocent people? Or that there's something wrong with "just war" theory?

in principle   Contrasted with 'in fact' or 'in practice'. Philosophers talk about things we can do in principle, meaning that we could do them if we had the time or technology, or if other merely practical difficulties did not stand in the way. For example, we can VERIFY the statement 'There is a red pebble lying on the north pole of Mars' in principle, though at the moment we can't test this by observation. We might forever be unable to test statements about extremely distant stars, but these are verifiable in principle. In principle, we can count to one trillion, because we know the rules for doing it, though in fact we lack the patience and wouldn't live long enough anyway.

instantiation   The name of the process or the product of substituting an individual constant for a quantified variable; the result is also called a 'substitution instance'. (*See* SYMBOLS OF QUANTIFIER LOGIC.)

instrumental   *See*   INTRINSIC / INHERENT / INSTRUMENTAL / EXTRINSIC.

instrumentalism   *See* OPERATIONALISM / INSTRUMENTALISM.

intelligence, artificial   *See* ARTIFICIAL INTELLIGENCE.

intelligibility / unintelligibility   Something is intelligible when it is possible to understand it; otherwise, unintelligible.

intension / intensional   *See* EXTENSION / INTENSION.

intentional   Note the second 't' in this word; be careful not to confuse it with 'intensional' (*see* EXTENSION / INTENSION). **1.** Sometimes 'intentional' means 'on purpose', or 'having to do with intentions' (i.e., plans or desires about ACTIONS). **2.** Intentionality is the idea that mental events have objects which they "point to" or are "about"; thus, if you think that Venus is a planet your thought has intentionality or *aboutness*: it is about Venus. BRENTANO held that intentionality was the distinguishing feature of the mental. Intentionality is problematic because some of the items we think about do not exist. Thus if you think Santa Claus lives at the north pole, your thought is about Santa—it has Santa as its intentional object—even though (bad news) there is no Santa. (*See also* SUBSISTENT ENTITY.) Likewise it seems that there is a difference between thinking about the Morning Star and thinking about the Evening Star—you might think something about one that you didn't think about the other—even though the Morning Star is IDENTICAL[2] with the Evening Star (they are just different names for Venus). So there seem to be two intentional objects even though there is only one planet. **3.** A sentence is said to provide an intentional (or oblique) CONTEXT if CO-REFERRING TERMS cannot be substituted within it *SALVA VERITATE*, that is, if it is referentially OPAQUE.

intentional fallacy   The (supposed) mistake of identifying the meaning of a work of art with what the artist intended it to mean. It is a mistake if a work of art can mean something different from what its creator intended.

interactionism   A form of mind / body DUALISM. It holds that mind and body can interact—that is, that mental events can cause physical events (e.g., when your decision to touch something causes your physical hand movement) and that physical events can cause mental events (e.g., when a physical stimulation to your body causes a mental feeling of pain). A standard objection to this commonsense position is that it's hard to see how this sort of causal interaction could take place, since the mental and the physical work according to their own laws: how could an electrical impulse in a (physical) nerve cell cause a non-physical pain in a mind? Perhaps this even violates the law of conservation of energy. DESCARTES was a classical interactionist.

interests   Not, as in an ordinary sense, those things about which you are curious or fascinated; rather, that which is of value to you. Something may be thought to be a (real) interest of yours even though you don't think you want it—it's an objective, not a subjective, interest. (*See* SUBJECTIVE / OBJECTIVE.) Sometimes interests are distinguished from needs: you can't do without the latter. Thus food is a need, but watching TV is only an interest.

internalism   *See* EXTERNALISM / INTERNALISM.

internal / external relations   An internal relation is a RELATIONAL PROPERTY which is ESSENTIAL to its bearer. (ABSOLUTE IDEALISTS thought there were such things.) Relational properties which are not essential are external.

interpretation, radical   *See* RADICAL TRANSLATION / INTERPRETATION.

interpreted calculus   *See* CALCULUS.

intersection / union of sets   The intersection of two SETS (also known as the 'product' of the two) is the set of things these two sets hold in common; the union (also known as the 'sum' of the two) is the set of things in either or both of them. Thus the intersection of the set of dogs and the set of brown things is the set of brown dogs; the intersection of the set of dogs and the set of cats is empty (i.e., there is no thing that is both a dog and a cat); the union of the set of dogs and the set of cats is the set of dogs and cats (that group of things consisting of all dogs plus all cats).

intransitive   *See* TRANSITIVE / INTRANSITIVE / NONTRANSITIVE.

intrinsic / inherent / instrumental / extrinsic   Something has intrinsic value when it is valuable for its own sake and not merely as a means to something else. Pleasure, for example, is intrinsically valuable. The contrast is with instrumental value. Something has instrumental value when it is valuable as a means to some other end. The value of money is primarily instrumental (though some people also value it intrinsically—they like having it just in itself). An intrinsic or inherent or natural RIGHT is one people have permanently or essentially, because of the very nature of a person. An extrinsic right is one people have only temporarily, or one they don't have unless they are granted it. *See also* RELATIONAL / INTRINSIC PROPERTIES.

intrinsic properties   *See* RELATIONAL / INTRINSIC PROPERTIES.

introspection   The capacity for finding things out about oneself by "looking inward"—by direct awareness of one's own mental states. You might find out that you have a headache, for example, by introspection. This is contrasted with the way someone else might find this out, by observing your outward behaviour—your groaning, holding your head, etc. Sometimes called 'reflection'. [a chiefly British alternative spelling is 'reflexion']

intuition   A belief that comes IMMEDIATELY[2], without reasoning, argument, evidence; before ANALYSIS (thus 'preanalytic'). Some philosophers think that certain intuitions are the reliable, rational basis for knowledge of certain sorts. Some beliefs that arise immediately when we perceive are the basis of our knowledge of the outside world (though perceptual intuitions are not always reliable). Our ethical intuitions are sometimes taken to be the basis and the test of ethical theories. *See also* INTUITIONISM.

intuition pump   A THOUGHT-EXPERIMENT designed to produce INTUITIONS; calling it an intuition-pump often carries the implication that the intuitions generated are not reliable indicators of ordinary conceptualization, but are fraudulently generated by the thought-experiment.

intuitionism   Intuitionism is any theory that holds that INTUITION is a valid source of knowledge. DESCARTES, SPINOZA, and LOCKE are associated with intuitionism about certain kinds of knowledge. Ethical intuitionism is the position that ethical truths are intuited. MOORE, for example, held that there is a special sort of facility for intuiting ethical truths. Nowadays, ethical theorists mostly doubt this, but many rely on what they call 'ethical intuitions' (i.e., ethical reactions not based on theory or reasoning) as data to CONFIRM ethical theories. Intuitionism in mathematics has a rather special meaning: it holds that any sort of mathematical entity exists only if it is possible to give a CONSTRUCTIVE EXISTENCE PROOF of it.

INUS condition   'INUS' is an acronym; an INUS condition is an **I**nsufficient but **N**ecessary part of an **U**nnecessary but **S**ufficient condition. (*See* NECESSARY / SUFFICIENT CONDITION.) For example, lightning striking a house is an INUS condition for the house's burning down: it's a necessary part of a complex of conditions for one way (not the only way) the house might burn down. J. L. Mackie (English philosopher, 1917-1981) coined this term while proposing this complex sort of condition as part of an ANALYSIS of CAUSATION. ['EYE-nus']

invalid argument   *See* ARGUMENT.

invalidity   *See* ARGUMENT.

inverted spectrum   Suppose the visual images someone gets when seeing coloured things are "inverted" from the normal ones, so that when she sees something red, she gets a violet visual image, and when she sees something yellow, she gets a blue image, and so on. She uses colour words just the way everyone else does. This supposition is part of an argument for the existence of QUALIA, and against any FUNCTIONALIST or BEHAVIOURIST theory of mind.

invisible hand   Adam Smith (see SCIENTISTS) wrote that individuals who seek to further their own economic interests frequently thereby unintentionally promote the public interest – as if by an "invisible hand". Social theorists of a *LAISSEZ-FAIRE* bent argue against centralized economic and political control by referring to such alleged "invisible hand" phenomena.

involuntary euthanasia   *See* EUTHANASIA.

iota operator   *See* SYMBOLS OF QUANTIFIER LOGIC.

I proposition   *See* A / E / I / O PROPOSITIONS.

Irigary,   Luce (b. 1939) Belgian-born French FEMINIST philosopher. She has theorized about the differences between male and female outlooks, and has claimed that a "PHALLOCENTRIC" society subordinates the latter. ['ear-ee-ga-ree']

irrational / irrationality   *See* RATIONAL / IRRATIONAL.

irreflexive   *See* REFLEXIVE / IRREFLEXIVE / NONREFLEXIVE.

irrelevant conclusion (fallacy of)   *See IGNORATIO ELENCHI.*

is / ought problem   Clearly what is is sometimes different from what ought to be; but can one INFER the latter from the former? HUME and MOORE (*see* the OPEN QUESTION ARGUMENT) argued that you can't: no matter how detailed an account you have of how things are, they don't imply how things ought to be. But ETHICAL NATURALISTS and other objectivists (*see* SUBJECTIVE / OBJECTIVE) typically claim that they do, because ethical facts are facts too. The supposed is / ought gap is also known as the "fact-value gap".

I statement   *See*   A / E / I / O PROPOSITIONS.

J

Jackson, Frank [Cameron] (b. 1943) Australian philosopher, with work on the REPRESENTATIONAL theory of perception and on CONDITIONALS.

James, William (1842-1910) American philosopher and psychologist, the founder of modern psychology; brought PEIRCE'S PRAGMATISM to a wide audience; argued influentially in favour of religious belief on the grounds of its good practical effect on our lives.

Jaspers, Karl (1883-1969) German EXISTENTIALIST philosopher/psychiatrist, known for his analyses of the "authentic" and "inauthentic" self. ['YAS-purs']

Jeffrey, Richard (b. 1926) American logician, with important work in probability and DECISION THEORY.

jointly exhaustive *See* MUTUALLY EXCLUSIVE / JOINTLY EXHAUSTIVE.

joint method of agreement and difference *See* MILL'S METHODS.

judgment Thinking that something is the case or not the case. Sometimes this word is also used as a synonym for 'PROPOSITION' or for 'ASSERTION'. [may also be spelled 'judgement']

Jung, Carl Gustav *See* SCIENTISTS.

justice Fair or correct treatment or social arrangements. A legal system is just to the extent that it treats those under it fairly, or with equal concern and respect, or as free and equal moral AGENTS. Distributive justice is fairness of distribution of goods and benefits in a society. There is a good deal of philosophical controversy about what the principles of justice are. John RAWLS has presented an influential contemporary theory of justice.

justice, retributive   *See* RETRIBUTIVISM.

justification   **1.** An argument to show that some statement is true, or that some act is morally acceptable. **2.** The explanation required for each step in a DERIVATION, which tells which preceding steps and which rule of INFERENCE were used to derive that step.

just war   The morality of war has worried philosophers; some claim that, under certain conditions, activities ordinarily quite immoral might be justified in a "just war". This has historically been a special concern within Christian ethics; AUGUSTINE and THOMAS AQUINAS have written about it.

K

Kant, Immanuel (1724-1804) German philosopher, one of the most important figures in the history of philosophy. His EPISTEMOLOGICAL concern was with the "truths of reason" (for example, that everything has a cause) that HUME seemed to have shown cannot be supported by experience, and are not analytic (*see* ANALYTIC / SYNTHETIC) consequences of the relations between ideas. Kant thought that such knowledge was *A PRIORI* and synthetic (*see* ANALYTIC / SYNTHETIC), and that it could be accounted for by the way that any rational mind necessarily thinks. Similarly, he argued that the basis of ethics is not EMPIRICAL or psychological (for example, it cannot be based upon our actual felt desires). Ethical knowledge can be derived merely from the *a priori* form any ethical ASSERTION must have: it must be UNIVERSALIZABLE—that is, rationally applicable to everyone. Kant took this to be equivalent to saying that the basic ethical truth was that everyone must be thought of as an end, never merely as a means (*see also* CATEGORICAL / HYPOTHETICAL IMPERATIVE).

Kaplan, David B. (b. 1933) American philosopher, known for his work in logic and philosophy of language.

karma In Hinduism and Buddhism, *karma* is the force which brings about one's destiny, punishment and reward in this life and in future REINCARNATIONS, as a result of one's actions.

katharsis *See* CATHARSIS.

Kenny, [Sir] Anthony [John Patrick] (b. 1931) British philosopher with work on the history of philosophy and the philosophies of religion and mind.

Kepler,   Johannes *See* SCIENTISTS.

Keynes,   John Maynard *See* SCIENTISTS.

Kierkegaard,   Søren (Aabye) (1813-1855) Danish philosopher and theologian; a Lutheran minister, though a critic of conventional religion. His views on pure choice in an ABSURD context were an important influence on ATHEISTIC EXISTENTIALISM; Kierkegaard, however, put these into a Christian framework. ['KEER-kuh-gard']

killing / letting die   *See* ACTS / OMISSIONS.

Kim,   Jaegwon (b. 1934) Korean-American philosopher, with influential work in METAPHYSICS and EPISTEMOLOGY.

kind, natural   *See* NATURAL KIND.

kings, philosopher   *See* PHILOSOPHER-KINGS.

knave, sensible   *See* HOBBES'S FOOLE.

knowing how / knowing that   Two sorts of knowing: one knows *how* to ride a bicycle; one knows *that* Saskatoon is in Saskatchewan.

knowledge / belief   Believing and knowing something both involve thinking that it's true. One can correctly be said to know something, however, only if it's true; but one can have a false belief. What else is different about knowledge is controversial. Must one be JUSTIFIED in thinking what one does in order to be said to know it? Must one be connected in some way with the fact one is said to know, for example, when that fact causes one's belief?

knowledge by acquaintance / by description   If you have never been to the top of Mount Everest, you know it only by description—by how others have described it, or only insofar as it's called 'the top of Mount Everest'. Knowledge by acquaintance comes from actual personal experience of the thing known. Though knowledge by acquaintance is a very small proportion of what you know, it is sometimes supposed to provide the FOUNDATION for the rest. This distinction is due to RUSSELL.

knowledge, pure / empirical   *See* PURE REASON.

kosmos   *See* COSMOS.

Kripke,   Saul A. (b. 1940) Contemporary American philosopher known for his work on philosophy of language and of psychology, and on the POSSIBLE WORLDS account of necessity and possibility. ['KRIP-kee']

Kuhn,   Thomas [Samuel] (1922-1996) American philosopher of science. His widely discussed claim was that, rather than being a gradual steady increase of knowledge, the course of science shows periods of stable "normal science" interspersed with intellectually violent "scientific revolutions" when old ways of seeing things are overturned in a "PARADIGM[2]-shift" in which one conceptual world-view is replaced by another.

L

labour theory of value   The theory of (economic) value associated with MARX, according to which the value of a commodity is a function of the amount of labour put into its production; but its selling price, adding the capitalist's profit, is above this. [American spelling is 'labor'.]

Lacan,   Jacques (1901-1981) French STRUCTURALIST philosopher, applied structural methodology to FREUDIAN psychology, exploring its philosophical and cultural implications. ['la-CAN']

laissez-faire   (French: "let [them] do") Pertaining to an economic policy of allowing free competition, without government interference or direction. A feature of what was formerly called 'LIBERAL', now (confusingly) called 'conservative', social policy. ['less-ay fair']

Lakatos,   Imre (1922-1974) (Earlier names: Imre Loposchitz, Imre Molnar) Hungarian-British philosopher of science and mathematics. ('IM-reh LAK-a-tosh')

Lamark,   Chevalier de *See* SCIENTISTS.

Langer,   Susanne K[atherina Knauth] (1895-1985). German/American neo-KANTIAN philosopher, writer on the philosophy of art and the emotions.

language-game   WITTGENSTEIN used this term for language and its uses, in a broad sense, including the way our language influences the way we think and act. The emphasis here is on the similarity of a language to a game: both are rule-governed systems of behaviour, and the rules vary over times and contexts.

language, ideal   *See* IDEAL LANGUAGE.

language, object / meta-language   *See* META-LANGUAGE.

language of thought hypothesis   The idea that our thoughts are structured in a way closely analogous to language, with a "grammar" and a "vocabulary" and rules for INFERENCE. This language is sometimes called "Mentalese". It is certainly not learned—never heard or spoken publicly; it must be INNATE. Learning a publicly spoken language, then, must be a process of learning how to translate it into and out of Mentalese.

language, ordinary   *See* ORDINARY LANGUAGE PHILOSOPHY.

languages, artificial / natural   *See* ARTIFICIAL / NATURAL LANGUAGES.

Laplace,   Pierre *See* SCIENTISTS.

large numbers, law of   *See* LAW OF LARGE NUMBERS.

lateral / linear thinking   The idea has attracted a certain degree of attention (in the popular mind, if not much among philosophers) that ordinary "linear" step-by-step logical modes of reasoning are insufficiently imaginative, and should be supplemented or even replaced by "lateral" thinking "outside the box"—thinking which makes creative and intuitive leaps instead. One hears the charge that a variety of society's problems come from our LOGOCENTRISM[2].

law   **1.** A RULE or principle established and enforced by government ('civil law'), or by society. **2.** A rule of morality ('moral law'). **3.** A law of nature—a formulation of the general regularities of the way things work ('NATURAL LAW'). A law of nature may be more than merely a correct description of regularities, however (*see* NOMIC).

law, covering   *See* COVERING LAW.

lawlike statements   Statements which have the LOGICAL FORM of LAWS[3] whether they are true or not. Part of the philosophy of science is the attempt to specify the logic of lawlike statements.

law, natural   *See* NATURAL LAW.

law of...   *See*   the following entries; or under what follows 'of'; or under 'PRINCIPLE OF...'.

law of contradiction   *See* LAWS OF THOUGHT.

law of excluded middle   *See* LAWS OF THOUGHT.

law of identity   *See* LAWS OF THOUGHT.

law of large numbers   Suppose you flip a fair coin four times. PROBABILITY theory tells you that you're most likely to get two heads, but you wouldn't be surprised to get three heads, or one, or four, or none. But if you flip a coin one thousand times, you'll very likely get very close to one-half heads. The law of large numbers says that it is more probable that the observed frequency will be close to the frequency predicted by theory as the number of observed events increases.

law of the indiscernibility of identicals   The supposed law of METAPHYSICS (associated with LEIBNIZ, thus also called 'Leibniz's law') that says that if **x** AND **y** are IDENTICAL[2]— that is, if **x** is **y**, then **x** and **y** are indiscernible (share all the same properties). Distinguish this from its reverse, the law of the identity of indiscernibles: if **x** and **y** are indiscernible, then they are identical. Imagine two things that are alike in every detail: they even occupy the same space at the same time. Why then think of them as two? Wouldn't there really be only one thing?

laws, De Morgan's   *See* DE MORGAN.

laws of thought   These 'laws' were sometimes taken to be the three basic principles of LOGIC and of all rational thought, clearly true and in need of no proof. They are:

The law of identity: If anything is **P** (i.e., has the property **P**), then it is **P**.

The law of contradiction: A sentence and its NEGATION (i.e., its denial) cannot both be true; alternatively, nothing can be both **P** and not-**P**. Also known as the law of noncontradiction.

The law of the excluded middle: Either **P** or not-**P**. This is sometimes distinguished from the principle of bivalence: Every statement is either true or false.

The notion that these are laws of thought went out of favour when it became widely doubted that all three (especially the second and third) must hold of all rational thought; certainly they are not all laws of all modern systems of logic. But the idea that logic should give us psychological laws of the way people actually think, rather than idealized norms of rationality, has become recently popular—*see* "naturalized epistemology" in NATURALISM.

learner paradox   PLATO argues that certain kinds of knowledge—mathematics, for example—cannot be learned from experience. When it is "taught" what is actually happening is that the pupil remembers it (*see* RECOLLECTION). (This may merely be a colourful way to say that the knowledge is INNATE.) The paradox here is that one cannot learn such things unless one already knows them. Also known as the learning or learner's or Meno paradox (because it is discussed in Plato's *Meno*).

left hand problem   If you're right-handed, you probably will accept the truth of this statement: "If you have to have one of your hands cut off, then you want to have your left hand cut off." Suppose that you have to have a hand cut off. It follows by *MODUS PONENS* that you want to have your left hand cut off. But this conclusion is clearly false: you wouldn't want to lose either of your hands. Where has this reasoning gone wrong? Is there something wrong with *modus ponens*?

legal positivism   The doctrine that the law is a set of rules each of which has the "law-making pedigree"—that is, which are made by whatever the law-making procedures are. (Perhaps this amounts to their having been enacted by the proper officials in the proper way.) Thus it holds that there is no necessary connection between law and morality. An immoral law which is enacted in the appropriate way is nevertheless a law.

legal realism   By analogy with other varieties of REALISM, you might expect 'legal realism' to mean the belief in legal principles that exist independently of any legislation or adjudication, but in fact, it names the reverse position: that law is not fixed by eternal principles or legislation, and is nothing but what actual courts decide (because that's when it has real practical upshot).

legitimacy   In general, legality or appropriateness. In political theory a legitimate ruler is one who has the right to rule; there are many different theories of what makes a ruler legitimate.

Lehrer,   Keith (b. 1936) American EPISTOMOLOGIST, known for his defense of the COHERENCE THEORY of knowledge.

Leibniz,   Gottfried Wilhelm (1646-1716) German scientist, mathematician, and philosopher. He and Newton (*see* SCIENTISTS) independently developed the differential and integral CALCULUS. Known for the views that all propositions are necessary (*see* NECESSARY / CONTINGENT TRUTH), and that this is the "BEST OF ALL POSSIBLE WORLDS". ['LIBE-nits']

Leibniz's law   *See* LAW OF THE INDISCERNABILITY OF IDENTICALS.

lemma   A sub-proof: something proved in the course of, and for the purpose of, proving something else.

Lenin, Vladimir Ilych (Original surname Ulyanov) (1870-1924) Russian thinker and political leader. He is best known for his establishment of the structure of the communist state; but he was also the author of more abstract philosophical work, in which he argued against antimetaphysical POSI-TIVISM.

Leonardo da Vinci *See* SCIENTISTS.

Leviathan Name of a terrible sea-monster in the Bible, and the title of HOBBES's major work; he saw the sea-monster as a metaphor for the powerful state he thought necessary for civilized life.

Lévi-Strauss, Claude (b. 1908) French STRUCTURALIST philosopher, known for his application of structuralism to anthropology, and for drawing philosophical conclusions from this application.

Lewis, C(larence) I(rving) (1883-1964) American philosopher, best-known for his work in MODAL logic and EPISTEMOLOGY.

Lewis, David K(ellogg) (1941-2001) American philosopher known for his work on COUNTERFACTUALS and CONVEN-TIONS.

lexical ambiguity *See* AMBIGUITY.

lexical definition *See* STIPULATIVE / PRECISING / LEXICAL DEF-INITION.

lexical ordering A method of ordering all finite sequences of symbols. For example, consider all finite-length combinations of letters, including 'g', 'zzyx', 'psdfeu' and so on. Lexical ordering begins with an alphabetical ordering of all sequences of length 1, then of length 2, etc. This ordering shows that the set of all "words" is denumerably infinite.

lexicon In general, a dictionary. In logic in particular, the list giving the INTERPRETATION of a set of symbols, translating them, as it were, into ordinary language. This may give us the sentences which sentence-letters stand for, the names of properties meant by PREDICATE[3] expressions, the names of INDIVIDUALS represented by individual constants, and so on. (*See* SYMBOLS OF QUANTIFIER LOGIC *and* SYMBOLS OF SENTENTIAL LOGIC.)

lex talionis   (Latin: 'law of retaliation') The idea that wrong-doers should suffer the same harm as they produced: "an eye for an eye". A RETRIBUTIVIST theory of PUNISHMENT.

liar's paradox   Consider this sentence:

> The sentence in the
> box is false

Is it true? If it is, then what it says—that it's not true—is correct, so it's not true. But if it's not true, then it's true. It seems that it can't be either true or false. This PARADOX arises from the SELF-REFERENCE of the statement. Logicians consider what to do with this, and what its implications are. Does it mean, for example, that some indicative sentences are neither true nor false? The name 'liar's paradox' comes from versions of this such as one in which someone says, "The statement I'm making right now is a lie."

liberalism   This refers to a confusingly large family of (sometimes incompatible) positions in political theory. Traditionally, liberals valued political LIBERTY—freedom—above all, and advocated less government restriction. LOCKE'S advocacy of individual RIGHTS and (limited) freedom from state constraint is a classical moderate form of liberalism in this sense. Nowadays, however, those who hold this view are more likely to be called 'conservatives'; liberals often advocate more government intervention, especially when that is thought necessary for what contemporary liberals value: for freeing people from ignorance and misery, or for solving other social problems such as poverty. Contemporary liberals also characteristically advocate DEMOCRACY, rule by all. Sometimes the word is used these days merely to designate any left-wing position (or any position left of the speaker's— thus possibly fairly far right). For a contemporary use, *see* 'liberal HUMANISM'.

libertarianism   **1.** The position that some of our actions are free in the sense of not being caused (*see* FREE WILL and CONTRA-CAUSAL FREEDOM). **2.** The political position that people have a strong right to political LIBERTY. Thus libertarians tend to object to restrictive laws, taxes, the welfare state, and state economic control. A more specific variety of (traditional) LIB-ERALISM, though nowadays this position tends to be espoused by some of those who are called "conservatives".

liberty   *See* FREEDOM[1] *and*[2]. *See also* PRINCIPLE OF LIBERTY.

linguistic analysis / philosophy   *See* ANALYTIC PHILOSOPHY.

life, meaning of   *See* MEANING OF LIFE.

Locke,   John (1632-1704) English philosopher and political theorist. None of our ideas is INNATE, he argued; our con-cepts and knowledge come from experience. This position makes him the first of the three great British EMPIRICISTS (the others are BERKELEY and HUME). Influential also in political theory, he is known for his advocacy of (traditional) LIBER-ALISM and natural rights (*see* INTRINSIC / INHERENT / INSTRU-MENTAL / EXTRINSIC).

Lockean proviso   The principle of property rights advocated by John LOCKE, that in legitimately acquiring previously unowned property one must leave as much and as good of the same for others.

locutionary act / intention   *See* SPEECH ACTS.

logic   Loosely speaking, logic is the process of correct reasoning, and something is logical when it makes sense. Philosophers often reserve this word for things having to do with various THEORIES of correct reasoning. TRADITIONAL LOGIC included categorizations of some types of correct and incorrect reasoning, centred around study of the SYLLOGISM. Nowadays, most of logic exhibits the types of sentences, and gives rules for reasoning correctly about them, in SYMBOLIC form (that is, with symbols taking the place of logically relevant words or connections); though INFORMAL logic is also important. For a description of the two main sorts of logic, *see* DEDUCTION / INDUCTION.

logical atomism   The position, associated with RUSSELL and (early) WITTGENSTEIN, that language might be analyzed into "atomic PROPOSITIONS", the smallest and simplest sentences, each of which corresponds to an "atomic fact", one of the simplest bits of reality.

logical behaviourism   *See* BEHAVIOURISM.

logical certainty   *See* CERTAINTY.

logical empiricism   *See* LOGICAL POSITIVISM.

logical equivalence   *See* BICONDITIONAL.

logic, alethic   *See* ALETHIC.

logical falsehood   *See* LOGICAL TRUTH / FALSITY.

logical form   The form of a sentence is its general structure, ignoring the particular content it has. Logical form is the structure a sentence has because of the logical words it contains. Thus, for example, 'If it's Tuesday, then I'm late for class' and 'If Peru is in Asia, then Porky is a frog' have the same overall logical form ('if P then Q'). The sort of LOGIC that works by exhibiting, often in SYMBOLIC notation, the logical form of sentences is called 'formal logic'. 'Formal' here may also refer to logic as a FORMAL SYSTEM. (*See also* INFORMAL / FORMAL LOGIC.)

logical impossibility *See* LOGICAL TRUTH / FALSITY.

logically proper names *See* PROPER NAMES.

logical necessity / contingency *See* LOGICAL TRUTH / FALSITY.

logical positivism A school of philosophy (also known as "logical empiricism"), subscribed to by many twentieth-century English-speaking philosophers. Its source was the VIENNA CIRCLE, whose best-known member was Rudolf CARNAP; its propagation in the English-speaking world is due largely to Carnap, who moved to America, and to A. J. AYER in England. Greatly impressed by EMPIRICISM and by the success and rigour of science, the logical positivists advocated that philosophers avoid speculation about matters only science and experience could settle; if a sentence was not scientifically VERIFIABLE or a matter of LOGICAL TRUTH or CONCEPTUAL TRUTH, it was nonsense and should be discarded: the VERIFIABILITY CRITERION. Ethical statements were thought not verifiable, so they didn't have any literal meaning: they were sometimes thought merely to be expressions of feelings of approval or disapproval (*see* EMOTIVISM). Arguments against the verifiability criterion resulted in the virtual demise of logical positivism, but its general influence among English-speaking philosophers who do ANALYTIC PHILOSOPHY is still strong.

logical possibility / impossibility *See* LOGICAL TRUTH / FALSITY.

logical symbol *See* SYMBOLS OF QUANTIFIER LOGIC *and* SYMBOLS OF SENTENTIAL LOGIC.

logical truth / falsity A sentence is logically true (or false) when it is true (or false) merely because of its logical structure. Examples: 'All pigs are pigs' or 'Either it's raining or it's not raining'. These should be distinguished from analytic truths / falsehoods (*see* ANALYTIC / SYNTHETIC), which are true / false merely because of the meaning of their words: for example, 'All fathers are male'. Logical truths / falsehoods are also called 'logically necessary / impossible' sentences, but these should also be distinguished from (METAPHYSICALLY) necessary truths / falsehoods (*see* NECESSARY / CONTINGENT TRUTH): those that *must* be true or false. All logical truths are necessarily true, but some philosophers think that there are necessary truths that are neither analytically nor logically true. KANT thought that 'All events have a cause' is necessarily true, but not logically true, or analytically true. 'Tautology' is sometimes used as a synonym for 'logical truth', though in ordinary talk a tautology is something that says the same thing twice. Thus, 'It's raining and it's raining' is a tautology in the ordinary sense, though not in the philosophers' sense. Sentences that are neither logically true nor logically false—that are merely true or false—are said to be logically contingent (or logically indeterminate) truths or falsehoods. *See also* TRUTH TABLE.

logic, classical   *See* TRADITIONAL LOGIC.

logic, deductive   *See* DEDUCTION / INDUCTION.

logic, deontic   *See* DEONTIC.

logic, dialectical   *See* DIALECTIC[5].

logic, epistemic   *See* EPISTEMIC.

logic, erotetic   *See* EROTETIC.

logic, formal   *See* INFORMAL / FORMAL LOGIC.

logic, free   *See* FREE LOGIC.

logic, fuzzy   *See* FUZZY SETS / LOGIC.

logic, inductive   *See* DEDUCTION / INDUCTION.

logic, informal   *See* INFORMAL / FORMAL LOGIC.

logic, intuitionistic   *See* INTUITIONISTISM.

logicism   **1.** The view that all NECESSARY TRUTHS are CONCEP-
TUAL or analytic (*see* ANALYTIC / SYNTHETIC) or LOGICAL
TRUTHS. HUME may be thought of as a champion of this
view; EMPIRICISTS tend to be logicists. Opposed to logicism
is the view that some necessity is not a matter of the way we
think or talk, but a feature of external reality. KANT argued
for this position. **2.** The view that mathematics can be
derived from LOGIC; associated with FREGE and RUSSELL.

logic, many-valued   *See* MANY-VALUED LOGIC.

logic, modal   *See* MODAL LOGIC.

logic, paraconsistent   *See* PARACONSISTENT LOGIC.

logic, predicate   *See* QUANTIFIER LOGIC.

logic, quantifier   *See* QUANTIFIER LOGIC.

logic, quantum   *See* QUANTUM LOGIC.

logic, sentential   *See* SENTENTIAL LOGIC.

logic, symbolic   *See* SYMBOLIC LOGIC.

logic, temporal   *See* TEMPORAL LOGIC.

logic, traditional   *See* TRADITIONAL LOGIC.

logic, truth-functional   *See* SENTENTIAL LOGIC.

logocentrism   1. DERRIDA's name for the view he opposed that our thoughts have necessary built-in DENOTATION and connotation that determine our METAPHYSICS. **2.** But this word has also come to mean narrow-minded reliance on logic or rationality (compare 'ETHNOCENTRISM')—a bad thing, according to some contemporary views.

logos   (Greek: "speech", "thought", "reason", "word", "meaning", "statement", "explanation") As you might expect, given its multiplicity of meanings in Greek, this word has been used in a great variety of ways; often it refers to the principle of rationality or law that some philosophers think is responsible for the way the universe works. ['LOW-gos']

lottery paradox   Consider a lottery with 1000 tickets. The chance of ticket #1 winning is 1/1000, so it is reasonable for you to believe that ticket #1 won't win. Similarly for ticket #2, #3, and each of the rest. If it is reasonable for you to believe each of these propositions, it (apparently) is reasonable for you to believe their CONJUNCTION[1]: "Ticket #1 won't win and ticket #2 won't win and ticket #3..." But this is equivalent to the proposition that none of the tickets will win, and this is clearly false, not reasonable to believe at all. What has gone wrong with this reasoning?

love, Platonic   *See* PLATONIC LOVE.

Lucretius   (full name: Titus Lucretius Carus) (c. 96-55 B.C.) Ancient Roman poet/philosopher, who popularized the scientific and ethical views of the EPICUREAN ATOMISTS. ['loo-KRE-shus']

Lukács,   Gyorgy (1885-1971) Hungarian MARXIST HEGELIAN philosopher. Known for his defense of Communism, and for his application of Marxism to literary theory. ('dyu-or-DYUH LOO-cutch')

Łukasiewicz,   Jan (1878-1956) Polish/Austrian/Ukrainian logician, responsible for much in the development of modern logic, including the MANY-VALUED LOGICS. ('yon woo-kah-SHEH-veech')

Lydian shepherd   *See* HOBBES'S FOOLE.

Lyotard,   Jean-François (1924-1998) French POSTMODERN philosopher; his work emphasized the INCOMMENSURABILITY of human "discourses", and urged us not to worry so much about truth. ['lee-oh-tar']

M

Mach, Ernst (1838-1916) Czech / Austrian physicist and philosopher. The father of contemporary philosophy of science, he argued for a POSITIVISTIC view that knowledge is propositions based on our sensations and gathered into economical theories. Known as well for his PHENOMENALISM, in which the "I" is unreal. ['maCH']

Machiavelli, Niccolo (1469-1527) Italian statesman and political theorist, famous (or infamous) for his power- and practicality-minded political theories and his de-emphasis of morality in politics. A "Machiavellian" politician is one who is Nixonian: unprincipled, deceitful, opportunistic. ['mack-ee-uh-VEL-lee']

MacIntyre, Alasdair C[halmers] (b. 1929) Scottish/English/ American philosopher best known for his work on morality, examined in a wide historical and social context.

Mackie, J[ohn] L[eslie] (1917-1981). Australian-born philosopher influential in a number of areas, but especially for his moral SUBJECTIVISM.

MacKinnon, Catharine A. (b. 1946) American professor of law, feminist scholar; widely known for her strong and influential arguments for the suppression of pornography.

Maimonides (or Moses ben Maimon) (1135-1204) Spanish-born Jewish philosopher and theologian; codifier of the Talmud; synthesizer of MEDIEVAL Jewish thought with Aristotelianism.

major / middle / minor term / premise Distinctions made in

TRADITIONAL LOGIC to talk about SYLLOGISMS. The major TERM[2] is the term that is the PREDICATE[2] of the conclusion. The major premise is the premise (*see* ARGUMENT) containing the major term. The minor term is the term that is the subject of the conclusion. The minor premise is the premise containing the minor term. The middle term is the term that is in both of the premises but not in the conclusion. So, for example, in the syllogism

All pigs are sloppy eaters.
Nothing that is a sloppy eater is a friendly thing.
Therefore no pigs are friendly things.

The major term is 'friendly thing'. The minor term is 'pig'. The middle term is 'sloppy eater'. The first premise is the minor premise, and the second premise the major.

Malcolm, Norman [Adrian] (1911-1990) American philosopher, best known for his writings on philosophy of mind, and for having brought his teacher WITTGENSTEIN'S ideas to wide attention in the US.

Malebranche, Nicolas (1638-1715) French philosopher, influenced by DESCARTES; known now mostly for his OCCASIONALISM. ['mal-brANsh']

malin génie *See* EVIL GENIUS.

Malthus, Thomas *See* SCIENTISTS.

Mannheim, Karl (1893-1947) Hungarian/German/British philosopher, closely associated with the birth of the sociology-of-knowledge movement.

Manichaeism An influential religion of the ancient world, of Persian origin. Its best-known feature is its view that evil is a separate and basic feature of the world, along with good, and not (as some Christians held) to be seen as merely the absence of good. ['man-uh-KEE-ism'; alternative spellings 'manicheism', 'manichaeanism' 'manicheanism']

manifest / scientific image   Terms due to Wilfrid SELLARS. The first is the common way of thinking about oneself and one's world, the second is the very different scientific way.

manifold   In KANT, the diverse, changing, unorganized DATA presented by the senses; these must be structured by our CONCEPTS in order to become experiences.

many questions, fallacy of   *See* COMPLEX QUESTION.

many-valued logic   It is commonly thought that each indicative sentence must be either true or false (*see* 'law of the excluded middle' in LAWS OF THOUGHT). But the possibility that a sentence might be neither true nor false, and that there might be a third possibility, or many, or an infinite number, has led to two-, three-, infinite- (etc.) valued logics ('valued' here refers to TRUTH VALUE), which work out the laws, systems, and techniques such many-valued logics might include. Also known as 'multi-valued logic'.

Mao   Zedong (1893-1976) (Name earlier transliterated as Mao Tse-Tung) Known, of course, as long-time leader of China, but also as a Marxist social and political thinker. ['mow' (rhymes with 'now') + 'tsi-TOONG' or 'Dzu-Doong']

Marcel,   Gabriel (1889-1973) French philosopher and dramatist; a theistic (see ATHEISM / THEISM / AGNOSTICISM) EXISTENTIALIST.

Marcus,   Ruth Barcan (b. 1921) American philosopher, best known for her substantial contributions to MODAL LOGIC.

Marcus Aurelius   (or Marcus Aurelius Antoninus) (121-180) Roman Emperor, STOIC philosopher.

Marcuse,   Herbert (1898-1979) German-born American philosopher, associated with the FRANKFURT SCHOOL. His blend of MARX, Freud (see SCIENTISTS), and EXISTENTIALISM had a great influence on revolutionary American youth in the 1960s and 1970s.

Maritain, Jacques (1882-1973) French Catholic philosopher, influential on contemporary THOMISM.

Marx, Karl [Heinrich] (1818-1883) German philosopher and social theorist who constructed the basis for socialist and communist IDEOLOGY (*see* SOCIALISM / COMMUNISM). He accepted HEGEL's idea of the DIALECTICAL[5] nature of change, but rejected Hegel's HISTORICAL IDEALISM. For Marx, it is material—economic—causes that interact, and understanding these leads to understanding the sources of past oppression and the goal to which historical progress is directed: the revolution of the working class, and the development of a classless society. Communist society based on Marx's thought as developed by LENIN and Stalin in the former Eastern Bloc states has almost disappeared; but Marxist thought is still influential among intellectuals.

mass noun *See* COUNT / MASS NOUN / SORTAL.

master morality *See* SLAVE / MASTER MORALITY.

material *See* MATERIALISM.

material biconditional *See* BICONDITIONAL.

material cause *See* FOUR CAUSES.

material conditional *See* CONDITIONAL.

material equivalence *See* EQUIVALENCE.

material implication *See* CONDITIONAL.

materialism The ordinary meaning of this term is the desire for consumer goods, comfort and money rather than for more "spiritual" goods. But as a philosophical term, it means something quite different: it is the philosophical position that all that exists is physical. LUCRETIUS and HOBBES are two of the many philosophers associated with this position. Materialists about mind sometimes argue that apparently non-physical things like the soul or mind or thoughts are actually material things (*see* IDENTITY THEORY). Central-state materialists identify mental events with physical events central in the body (i.e., in the nervous system). Some materialists, however, think that categorizing things as mental is altogether a mistake (like believing in ghosts), and that mental events do not exist and this sort of talk ought to be eliminated as science progresses. They are called 'eliminative materialists'. The terms 'materialism' and 'physicalism' are usually used as synonyms, though 'physicalism' sometimes means the position that everything is explainable by physics. For the distinction between type and token materialism, *see* TYPE / TOKEN. *See also* DIALECTICAL MATERIALISM *and* HISTORICAL MATERIALISM / IDEALISM.

materialism, dialectical   *See* DIALECTICAL MATERIALISM.

materialism, historical   *See* HISTORICAL MATERIALISM / IDEALISM.

material substance   *See* SUBSTANCE.

material supposition   *See* SUPPOSITION.

matter of fact / relation of ideas   HUME's distinction. It's not completely clear exactly what he meant, but roughly speaking, a matter of fact is a CONTINGENT state of affairs, to be discovered *a posteriori* (*see* A PRIORI / A POSTERIORI); a relation of ideas is a CONCEPTUAL or analytic (*see* ANALYTIC / SYNTHETIC) or LOGICAL TRUTH, which can be known *a priori*.

mauvaise foi   *See* BAD FAITH / GOOD FAITH / AUTHENTICITY / INAUTHENTICITY.

maxim   In KANT, a rule for action.

maximin   A rule for choice among alternatives, telling you to *maxi*mize the *mini*mum—that is, to choose the alternative whose worst features or consequences are better than the worst features or consequences of any of the alternatives. (Also known as 'minimax': perhaps the emphasis here is *mini*mizing the *maxi*mum harm.) Clearly this rule is not suitable for every choice situation; sometimes we might want to choose an alternative which has consequences that are worse than those of other alternatives, but highly unlikely. Other rules talked about in DECISION THEORY are the principle of DOMINANCE and the principle that one should maximize EXPECTED UTILITY.

Maxwell,   James Clerk *See* SCIENTISTS.

McDowell,   John (b. 1942) English/American WITTGENSTEIN-IAN philosopher of mind and language.

McTaggart,   John (McTaggart Ellis) (1866-1925) English METAPHYSICIAN, known for his IDEALIST views and his denial of the reality of time.

Mead,   George Herbert (1863-1931) American PRAGMATIST philosopher of sociology.

mean   ARISTOTLE thought that a general principle of the good was that it was a mean (i.e., a point in between extremes). Courage, for example, is a good thing, between rash foolhardiness and cowardliness. Sometimes called the 'golden mean'. Students sometimes automatically argue for a compromise between opposing positions, thinking that the mean position is always the best; but this doesn't always make for good philosophy.

meaningful / meaningless   *See* VERIFIABILITY CRITERION[1].

meaning holism   *See* HOLISM / INDIVIDUALISM.

meaning of life   Life is a grilled-cheese sandwich.

means / end   *See* INTRINSIC / INHERENT / INSTRUMENTAL / EXTRINSIC.

mechanistic   Having to do with the sorts of causes and effects we suppose operate in merely physical processes. A mechanistic explanation would avoid talk of aims, desires, purposes, and FUNCTIONS.

mediate inference   *See* IMMEDIATE / MEDIATE.

medieval philosophy   The dividing lines between ANCIENT, medieval, and MODERN PHILOSOPHY are rough, but it's often said that medieval philosophy starts with AUGUSTINE (about 400), and ends just before DESCARTES (about 1600). Some of the best-known medieval philosophers are BOETHIUS, ANSELM, ABELARD, THOMAS AQUINAS, DUNS SCOTUS, and OCKHAM. [sometimes spelled 'mediaeval']

Meinong,   Alexius (1853-1920) Austrian philosopher; developed BRENTANO'S views on the different sorts of "existence" of the objects of thought. Known for the view that the "*So-sein*" (character) of objects is independent of their "*Da-sein*" (existence), thus opening the way for two kinds of objects: the existing and the non-existing. ['MY-nong']

members of a set   *See* SET.

meme   Memes are contagious ideas or other social phenomenon, e.g., rumours, children's games, patterns of thought. ['meem']

Meno paradox / puzzle   *See* LEARNER PARADOX.

mens rea   (Latin: "guilty mind") Commonly, a prerequisite for criminal punishment: the wrongdoer must either intend the action, or know that it will result from another action, or be negligent in not preventing it.

Mentalese   *See* LANGUAGE OF THOUGHT HYPOTHESIS.

mention / use   If you heard someone say "The pig is short", you might be unsure whether he meant that a pig is not tall, or that the phrase 'the pig' is a short phrase. If he was saying the first, then he was *using* the term 'the pig'; if the second, then he was *mentioning* it. Had he said "The phrase 'the pig' is short" then it would have been unambiguous that he was mentioning that phrase, not using it. In written English, ambiguity can be eliminated by putting the mentioned part in quotes: 'The pig' is short. One sometimes sees philosophers wiggling fingers in the air to indicate quotation marks in what they speak. A frequent philosophical custom is to put mentioned bits of language into single quotes—that has been done in this dictionary. Double quotes are used for reporting what someone said (and for other uses).

mereology   The logic of the relationships of part to whole. A mereological sum is something thought of as nothing but the sum of its parts.

Merleau-Ponty,   Maurice (1908-1961) French PHENOMENOLO-GIST and EXISTENTIALIST, follower of HUSSERL. Applied phenomenological methods to perception and language. ['mur-low-pon-tee']

meta-   This prefix often means 'beyond', or 'about', so thinking about meta-**x** is (sometimes) thinking about the structure or nature of **x**. Examples of its use are 'META-LANGUAGE' and 'meta-ETHICS'; it is used differently, however, in 'META-PHYSICS'.

meta-ethics   *See* ETHICS.

meta-language / object language   A meta-language is a language used in talking about another language. In LOGIC, one distinguishes between the object language and the meta-language. Thus, for example, particular inferences are symbolized in the object language, but general forms of valid inference are symbolized in the meta-language. [sometimes unhyphenated: 'metalanguage']

metanarrative   This (according to certain POST-MODERN philosophers) is a mythology about human nature told in a society to justify its social control mechanisms; and those philosophers take it to be their job to subvert these stories.

metaphysical behaviourism   *See* BEHAVIOURISM.

metaphysical certainty   *See* CERTAINTY.

metaphysical realism   Belief in the mind-independent existence of various controversial sorts of things, but especially UNIVERSALS. (*See* REALISM.)

metaphysics   One of the main branches of philosophy, having to do with the ultimate components of reality, the types of things that exist, the nature of CAUSATION, change, time, GOD, FREE WILL, etc. It is said that this word derives from the fact that later editors called one of Aristotle's books *The Metaphysics*, merely because '*meta*' in Greek means 'next' or 'beyond', and the editors placed it after Aristotle's book on "physics"—i.e., nature. In this case the etymology suggested in the definition of 'META-', above, does not work: metaphysics is not only the study of the structure or of the ultimate components of physics or nature.

metempsychosis   *See* REINCARNATION.

method of agreement / disagreement / residues / concomitant variation   *See* MILL'S METHODS.

method of doubt   *See* CARTESIAN DOUBT.

methodological behaviourism   *See* BEHAVIOURISM.

methodological individualism   *See* HOLISM / INDIVIDUALISM.

methodological solipsism   Jerry FODOR's term for what he claims is the method that is (or should be) used by psychologists and philosophers of psychology: one concentrates on what's going on "inside the head" only, ignoring its connection with the outside world. (*See* SOLIPSISM—though this is just an ANALOGY to solipsism, not a form of it.) This method thinks of mental items as having narrow content (*see* WIDE / NARROW CONTENT).

micro-reductionism   *See* REDUCTIONISM.

middle term / premise   *See* MAJOR / MIDDLE / MINOR TERM / PREMISE.

Mill,   John Stuart (1806-1873) The most influential English philosopher of his time. Known for his thoroughgoing EMPIRICISM, his work on the principles of scientific enquiry, his development of UTILITARIANISM, and his LIBERAL political views.

Millikan,   Ruth (b. 1933) American philosopher who attracted a good deal of attention for her application of evolutionary theory to philosophical problems, most notably the notions of representation and FUNCTION[2].

Mill's methods   Five rules proposed by John Stuart MILL for inductive reasoning (*see* DEDUCTIVE / INDUCTIVE). They are:
 (1) The Method of Agreement: If two (or more) instances of a **x** have only condition **C** in common, that **C** is the cause of **x**.
 (2) The Method of Difference: **x** occur one time, and doesn't another, and if these two cases are the same except for **C** when **x** occur, then **x** causes **C**.
 (3) The Joint Method of Agreement and Difference: Uses both the above methods.
 (4) The Method of Residues: Subtract from a phenomenon what's known to be the effect of certain conditions, and what's left is the effect of the other conditions.

> (5) The Method of Concomitant Variation: When two phenomena vary together, either one causes another, or they have a common cause.

mind-body problem What is the relation between mental and physical events? Is one sort of event REDUCIBLE to the other? Or are they distinct? Are mental events merely a sort of bodily event?

minimax *See* MAXIMIN.

minor term / premise *See* MAJOR / MIDDLE / MINOR TERM / PREMISE.

miracles In ordinary talk, a "miracle" is something wonderful, astounding. But theologians and philosophers think more particularly of a divine intervention contrary to the normal order of nature. But there are certain problems that arise with this notion. How can there be a genuine exception to a genuine law? If we discovered, for example, something that traveled faster than the speed of light, wouldn't we just say that we were wrong that it's a universal law that nothing does? And HUME'S famous treatment of miracles raises the question of evidence: isn't it always unreasonable to believe in something that is supposed to run counter to universal past experience?

misplaced concreteness *See* CONCRETE, REIFICATION.

modal A sentence or CONTEXT is said to be modal if COEXTENSIVE PREDICATES cannot be substituted within it *SALVA VERITATE*. Sentences traditionally regarded as modal include: sentences about cause and effect, about the PROPOSITIONAL ATTITUDES, about NOMIC and METAPHYSICAL NECESSITY and possibility, and COUNTERFACTUAL sentences. (*See* EXTENSION / INTENSION.)

modal fallacy A fallacy in modal reasoning (*see* MODAL LOGIC), for example:

It's necessary that: if P then Q
P
Therefore it's necessary that Q

modal logic   The LOGIC of MODAL sentences; often particularly the study of the logic of necessity and possibility (ALETHIC logic); but there are also modal logics of moral obligation and permission (DEONTIC logic), of knowledge and belief (EPISTEMIC logic), and of time (TEMPORAL logic).

modal realism   This position, associated with David LEWIS, asserts the real existence of merely POSSIBLE WORLDS. So the fact that there might have been an earthquake last night means that there really exists a parallel universe in which there was an earthquake last night. Some philosophers find modal realism puzzling: if every possible universe really exists, then what's the difference between the actual universe and one that's merely possible? (*See also* REALISM.)

model   A model, in the sense in which scientists and philosophers use the term, is a tool for studying something which shares some features in a simplified way with what is being studied. SYMBOLIC LOGIC, for example, is a model of ordinary language, in that it represents the basic logical connections in language. A scientific theory can explain some natural phenomenon by proposing a model for it: an ANALOGOUS structure, or a simple and abstract system of LAWS[3] and equations that represents its behaviour.

modern philosophy   The borderline between MEDIEVAL PHILOSOPHY and modern philosophy is rough, but it is usually said that DESCARTES was the first modern philosopher (around 1600). The era of modern philosophy can be said to extend through the present, though it's sometimes taken to end around the beginning of the nineteenth century, or later with the advent of POSTMODERNISM.

modes   Normally means kinds or manners of things; but this word has a bewildering variety of special uses, including: In

TRADITIONAL LOGIC, the possible arrangements of sorts of premises in a SYLLOGISM, or the NECESSITY or contingency of a proposition; in MEDIEVAL METAPHYSICS, what distinguishes one thing from another; in DESCARTES, particular EXTENSIONS (of body) or thoughts (of mind); in SPINOZA, accidental (*see* ESSENTIAL / ACCIDENTAL) properties or modifications of attributes; in LOCKE, ideas representing complex properties of things.

modus ponens   (Latin: "method of putting") A rule for correct DEDUCTION of the form: 'If **P** then **Q**; **P**; therefore **Q**'. Also called 'AFFIRMING THE ANTECEDENT' (*see also* CONDITIONAL).

modus tollens   (Latin: "method of taking [or removing]"; thus denying [the consequent]) A rule for correct DEDUCTION of the form: 'If **P** then **Q**; it's not the case that **Q**; therefore it's not the case that **P**'. Also called 'DENYING THE CONSEQUENT' (*see also* CONDITIONAL).

monad   A simple, basic, indivisible, impenetrable, self-determining thing, containing all its past, present, and future properties. The term is associated most closely with LEIBNIZ, who thought that the universe was to be understood as an infinite number of monads, in perfect harmony.

monadic predicates   *See* PREDICATES.

monism   *See* DUALISM / MONISM / PLURALISM.

monotheism / polytheism / pantheism   Monotheism is the belief in one (and only one) God. Polytheism is the belief in many gods. Pantheism is the belief that God somehow exists in everything, or that everything is God. Examples of this last view are SPINOZA's identification of God with nature, and HEGEL's finding the ABSOLUTE world-spirit in everything.

Montaigne,   Michel *See* WRITERS.

Monte Carlo fallacy   *See* GAMBLER'S FALLACY.

Montesquieu,   Charles de Secondat, Baron de. *See* WRITERS.

mood   **1.** In TRADITIONAL LOGIC, the moods are the forms of valid (and invalid) reasoning. Each SYLLOGISM has two PREMISES and a CONCLUSION, and each of these three statements can be an A, E, I, or O statement (*See* A / E / I / O PROPOSITIONS) so there are 64 moods: AAA, [that is, A major premise, A minor premise, A conclusion], AAE, AAI, AAO, AEA, and so on, down to OOO. **2.** In grammar, the moods include the indicative, the imperative, the subjunctive, etc., and are thought to indicate differences in illocutionary force (*see* SPEECH ACTS).

Moore,   G(eorge) E(dward) (1873-1958) English philosopher; led the revolt early in this century against IDEALISM[2]; a father of ANALYTIC PHILOSOPHY; his then-revolutionary philosophical methodology was based on COMMON SENSE[2] and on clarification and ANALYSIS of meanings.

Moorean beliefs   Some beliefs of COMMON SENSE[2] held so strongly that one is more inclined to doubt an argument against the belief (no matter how good the argument seems) than to abandon the belief. The term comes from G. E. MOORE, who used this notion to argue against certain SCEPTICAL conclusions.

moral argument for God's existence   Here is one version of this ARGUMENT:
> There is a real objective difference between right and wrong, but the only way to make sense of this is to think of it as arising from God's will. So the existence of morality shows that God exists.

Critics of this argument dispute its premise that morality is objective (*see* SUBJECTIVE / OBJECTIVE), or its premise that the only sense that can be made of objective morality is to think of it as God's will.

moral certainty   *See* CERTAINTY.

moral dilemma   *See* DILEMMA.

moralities, act / agent   *See* ACT / AGENT MORALITIES.

morality   *See* ETHICS.

morality, slave / master   *See* SLAVE / MASTER MORALITY.

moral [—]   *See also* ETHICAL [—].

moral realism   The view that there are real, objective, knowable moral facts. (*See also* REALISM.)

moral sense theory   The idea that we have a way of "sensing" the objective moral properties (*see* SUBJECTIVE / OBJECTIVE), on the analogy of the way we can sense the property redness using our eyes. The moral sense would clearly be a very different kind of sensation, however; what is the sense organ involved?

mover, unmoved   *See* UNMOVED MOVER.

Müller-Lyer illusion   An optical ILLUSION (named for the German philosopher Franz Müller-Lyer, 1857-1916) in which two lines of equal length appear different in length. A standard example of illusion sometimes showing up in discussions of the philosophy of perception.

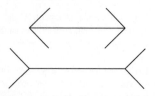

(*See also* NECKER CUBE, DUCK-RABBIT.)

multiplication theorem / rule The principle that the PROBABIL-
ITY that both of two independent events **x** and **y** will happen
is the probability of **x** times the probability of (**y** given **x**). If
the two events are not correlated, then the probability of both
happening is merely the probability of **x** times the probability of **y**. (Also called the 'product theorem'.) (*See also* ADDI-
TION THEOREM / RULE.)

multi-valued logic *See* MANY-VALUED LOGIC.

music of the spheres PYTHAGORAS appears to have been the
origin of the belief that the crystal spheres the planets and
stars were supposed to be embedded on had dimensions corresponding to harmonic divisions of the string of a musical
instrument; thus heavenly movement produces heavenly
music—the music (or harmony) of the spheres. A poetic
expression of his philosophical conviction that simple
numerical ratios were at the heart of the structure of the universe.

mutatis mutandis (Latin: "having changed the things that
were to be changed") Philosophers say things like "This case
is, mutatis mutandis, like the other", meaning that the two
cases are alike except for certain details—that one can derive
one case from the other by making the appropriate substitu-
tions or changes. ['myou-TAH-tis myou-TAN-dis']

mutually exclusive / jointly exhaustive Mutually exclusive
SETS do not overlap each other in membership. For example,
each of these sets: mammals, birds, fish, reptiles, amphib-
ians, is exclusive of the others, since nothing belongs to more
than one of them. The list is jointly exhaustive of vertebrates,
since every vertebrate is included in these categories. It is
mutually exclusive *and* jointly exhaustive because every vertebrate is included in *exactly one* of these categories. In
PROBABILITY theory, mutually exclusive events are events
that cannot both occur; if Fred's allowed only one pet, then
'Fred buys a dog' and 'Fred buys a cat' name mutually exclu-

sive events. But that list may not jointly exhaust all the possibilities: he may buy a goldfish instead.

mystical experience argument for God's existence   The existence and nature of the mystical experiences some people have are sometimes taken to provide evidence for God's existence. One criticism of this argument is that even though this experience sometimes provides compelling motivation for belief in God, this is not reliable as evidence. The relevance of mystical experience was explored at length by JAMES.

mysticism   A variety of religious practice that relies on direct experience which is often taken to be a union with God or with the divine ground of all being. The content of these experiences is often taken to be INEFFABLE, but we are told that they produce enlightenment or bliss. Mystics often advocate exercises or rituals designed to induce the abnormal psychological states in which these experiences occur.

myth of the cave   *See* CAVE.

myth of the given   SELLARS' phrase for what he took to be the mistaken view that all knowledge is based upon the indubitable FOUNDATION of what is GIVEN by experience.

N

Nagel,   Ernest (1901-1985) American philosopher, influenced by PRAGMATISM and LOGICAL POSITIVISM, did important work on philosophy of science and LOGIC.

Nagel,   Thomas (1937-2001) American philosopher; his central concern was the contrast between the personal/subjective and the external/objective points of view.

naïve realism   What's supposed to be the ordinary view about perception: that it (usually) reveals external objects to us directly, the way they really are. The implication is that this "naïve" view is overturned by philosophical sophistication (*see*, for instance, the ARGUMENT FROM ILLUSION). Also called 'common-sense realism' or 'direct realism'. Contrasts with critical realism (*see* CRITICAL IDEALISM / REALISM) and IDEALISM[2]; *see also* REALISM). [Those two dots over the 'i' are optional]

name, proper / logically proper   *See* PROPER NAMES.

narrow content   *See* WIDE / NARROW CONTENT.

natural   Be very careful when using this word—it has a variety of meanings. It can mean 'pertaining to nature' (in the narrow sense of trees and bugs, or in the wider sense as contrasted with what we create), 'original', 'PRIMITIVE', 'spontaneous', 'undisguised', 'physical', 'INNATE', 'usual', 'accepted', or 'the way things ought to be'. When the word occurs on food labels, it means nothing at all.

natural / conventional rights   *See* RIGHTS.

natural deduction   Natural DEDUCTION is a system for DERIVA-

TION supposed to match relatively closely the ways we actually think. It has rules of INFERENCE but no AXIOMS.

naturalism   This term names the view that everything is a NATURAL entity, and thus to be studied by the usual methods of natural science. Naturalistic or "naturalizing" theories in philosophy try to apply ordinary scientific categories and methods to philosophical problems. For example, a "naturalized EPISTEMOLOGY" (Quine's term) might try to explain when our beliefs are justified by referring to the sorts of belief-production which have been evolutionarily selected because of their survival value; or perhaps it abandons the ideas of justification, rationality, and likelihood to arrive at truth altogether, and interests itself instead only in the belief-forming mechanisms we actually have. A naturalized philosophy of mind includes the belief that mental phenomena are (or are caused by) the neurophysiological processes in the brain. Some philosophers think that ethical characteristics can be explained naturally; *see* ETHICAL NATURALISM / SUPERNATURALISM / NONNATURALISM.

naturalism, ethical   *See* ETHICAL NATURALISM / SUPERNATURALISM / NONNATURALISM.

naturalistic fallacy   *See* ETHICAL NATURALISM / SUPERNATURALISM / NONNATURALISM.

naturalized epistemology etc.   *See* NATURALISM.

natural kind   We can see the world as divided into all sorts of categories, but many philosophers think that only some of these divisions correspond to the way nature really is divided, "cut nature at the joints". Classically, a natural kind is a kind that things belong to necessarily: thus, *human being* is a natural kind because Fred is necessarily human; but *living within fifty miles of the Empire State Building* is not: Fred might move further away; or, if he doesn't he might have. Some contemporary thinkers (e.g.,

KRIPKE and PUTNAM) hold that natural kinds are the ones that support certain MODAL implications needed in science; but NOMINALISTS including QUINE think there are no natural kinds—all kinds are artificial—though they agree that some sorts of categorizations will be more important in science than others. Scientific REALISTS who believe in natural kinds need to explain what makes a kind one of these. (*See also* UNIVERSALS.)

natural languages   *See* ARTIFICIAL / NATURAL LANGUAGES.

natural law   There are several philosophically relevant senses of this phrase. Its ambiguity is due partly to the variety of meanings of 'LAW'. A natural law can be: **1.** A law of NATURE—i.e., a formulation of a regularity found in the natural world, the sort of thing science discovers. **2.** A principle of proper human action or conduct, taken to be God-given, or to be a consequence of "human nature"—our structure or function. In this sense, there are "natural law" theories in ethics and in political philosophy. THOMAS AQUINAS is closely associated with these. **3.** The view that the validity of the laws of a legal system depends on their coherence with God-given or otherwise objective morality (*see* SUBJECTIVE / OBJECTIVE); it says, in other words, that social law depends on natural law in sense **2**, just above; compare for example LEGAL POSITIVISM.

natural philosophy   *See* SCIENCE.

natural religion   The search for religious truth relying on reasoning and perception, not on inspiration or REVELATION. 'Natural theology' is natural religion applied to truths about God, thus including the ARGUMENTS FOR GOD'S EXISTENCE.

natural rights   *See* INTRINSIC / INHERENT / INSTRUMENTAL / EXTRINSIC.

natural selection   *See* EVOLUTION.

natural theology   *See* NATURAL RELIGION.

nature, state of   *See* STATE OF NATURE.

necessary / contingent truth   In ordinary talk we say things like 'It's necessary that I go to the bathroom', but in philosophy a necessary truth is a statement that is true and could not possibly be false; a contingent truth could be false (but isn't, just as a matter of fact). You might not go to the bathroom, so your going is contingent. Such statements as '7 + 5 = 12' and 'All bachelors are unmarried' and 'Every event has a cause' are often thought to be necessary. 'Pigs don't fly', 'More than a million grains of sand exist', and 'The Earth is bigger than Mars' are contingent truths. (Similarly, there are necessary and contingent falsehoods.) Many philosophers think that the necessity or contingency of some fact is a METAPHYSICAL matter—is a matter of the way the external world is—but some philosophers think that this difference is merely a matter of the way we think or talk about the world—that a truth taken to be necessary is merely a CONCEPTUAL or LOGICAL or analytic truth (*see* ANALYTIC / SYNTHETIC; *see also* LOGICISM). A necessary truth is also called a 'necessity', a contingent truth a 'contingency', and a necessary falsehood an 'impossibility'.

necessary / sufficient condition   **x** is a sufficient condition for **y** when: if **x** is true, then **y** must also be true. This is the same as saying: **x** can't be without **y**. For example, the fact that something is a pig is sufficient for that thing to be an animal. **x** is a necessary condition for **y** when: if **y** is true, then **x** must also be true. In other words, **y** can't be without **x**. Thus the fact that something is a pig is not necessary for that thing to be an animal, for something can be an animal but not a pig. But the fact that something is an animal is necessary for something to be a pig. **x** is necessary and sufficient for **y** when both are true: if **x** is true, **y** is true, and if **y** is true, **x** is true. In other words, you can't have one without the other. Thus, the complex condition that something is flammable, heated above a certain temperature, and in the presence of oxygen is (roughly—perhaps you can think of exceptions) necessary and sufficient for the thing to catch on fire. Saying that **x** is sufficient for **y** is the same thing as saying the conditional statement 'If **x** then **y**', and saying that **x** is necessary for **y** is the same as saying 'If **y** then **x**' (*see* CONDITIONAL).

Necker cube   The Necker ('reversing') cube is an ILLUSION often referred to in the course of discussion of issues in the philosophy of perception. It appears to reverse as you stare at it. (It's named for the nineteenth-century scientist Louis Albert Necker, who saw them in crystal structures he was observing.)

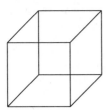

(*See also* MÜLLER-LYER ILLUSION, *and* DUCK-RABBIT.)

negation   The negation of a sentence is obtained by putting 'It's not the case that' in front of it (or by removing that phrase). Negation is often symbolized by the TILDE (~). (*see* SYMBOLS OF SENTENTIAL LOGIC).

neo-   This prefix means 'new' or 'a later version of'. It is put in front of the name of some philosophical movements to signify a later movement based on the earlier one, but including significant changes, for example, 'neo-PLATONISM', 'neo-KANTIAN'.

net, neural   *See* CONNECTIONISM.

neural net   *See* CONNECTIONISM.

Neurath, Otto (1882-1945) Austrian sociologist and philosopher, one of the members of the VIENNA CIRCLE which developed LOGICAL POSITIVISM. "Neurath's boat" is an analogy he proposed for the process of knowledge-building: it's like, he said, repairing a boat at sea: you can't tear it all down and rebuild it from the bottom up; you have to replace only small bits at any one time, leaving the rest intact. This position is thus anti-FOUNDATIONALISTIC. ['NOY-rat']

neutral monism Monism (*see* DUALISM / MONISM / PLURALISM) which takes the one basic substance to be neither physical nor mental. Defended by JAMES and RUSSELL.

Newcomb's paradox Suppose you are faced with the following choice. Box A contains either a cheque for $1 million or nothing (you don't know which). Box B contains a check for $1 thousand. You can take the contents of box A alone, or the contents of both boxes. A very smart computer has been fed information about you; if it predicted you'll take both, it has already put nothing in box A, but if it predicted you'll take only A, it has already put $1 million in there. The computer has almost always been right in predicting other people in the past. What should you do? The paradox arises from two equally convincing contrary strategies: (1) What's in box A won't change depending on your choice. If you take just A, you'll get whatever's in there; if you take both, you'll get that plus the thousand in B. Take both boxes. (This is the DOMINANCE strategy.) (2) The computer has almost certainly predicted you correctly, so if you pick both boxes, it very probably has put nothing in there, and you'll get only $1 thousand. If you pick only A, again the computer most likely predicted this, so you'll very probably get $1 million. Pick only A. (This strategy calculates EXPECTED UTILITY.) Is (1) or (2) the better strategy? Endless debate about the right answer has led to interesting general considerations in DECISION THEORY. The paradox appears to have been invented by William Newcomb, a twentieth-century physicist.

new riddle of induction   *See* GRUE.

Newton,   Isaac *See* SCIENTISTS.

Niebuhr,   Reinhold (1892-1971) American Protestant theologian and social critic. ['NEE-bur']

Nietzsche,   Friedrich (Wilhelm) (1844-1900) German philosopher famous for his attacks on Christianity, LIBERALISM, DEMOCRACY, and SOCIALISM as "SLAVE MORALITY", and for his proclamation of the "death of God". He advocated a morality appropriate to a superior individual, the "SUPER-MAN", who is above the common herd and embodies the "WILL TO POWER"—to self-assertion and self-mastery. ['NEE-chuh', though often carelessly pronounced 'NEE-chee']

nihil ex nihilo fit   Latin: "Nothing comes from nothing." This metaphysical principle, thought to be traceable to PAR-MENIDES, is related (if not equivalent) to the PRINCIPLE OF UNIVERSAL CAUSATION. Religious thinkers would claim supernatural action as an exception to this rule. ['NEE-heel ex NEE-heel-oh feet']

nihil in intellectu nisi prius in sensu   Latin: "Nothing is in the intellect unless previously in the senses." Motto for EMPIRI-CISTS. ['NEE-heel in een-tay-LECK-too NEE-see PREE-yus EEN SAIN-SOO']

nihilism   The name of various sorts of negative belief: that nothing can be known, or that nothing generally accepted in science, religion, or ethics is correct, or that the current social order is worthless, or that nothing in our lives has any real value. ['NY-' or 'NEE-' + 'al-izm']

nirvana   The state of enlightenment thought by Buddhists to occur when the self is extinguished.

noble savage   Characterization of the denizens of "PRIMITIVE" societies, seen as leading happy, peaceful lives in harmony with each other and with their surroundings. This idea, which may not have much connection with reality, sees our problems as arising from our nasty "civilized" societies. ROUSSEAU held a version of it. It is the converse of HOBBES's view.

nomic   Means 'having to do with LAW[3]'. A nomic regularity is distinguished from a mere (accidental) regularity or coincidence, in that the first represents a law of nature. One way this difference is explained is by saying that a nomic regularity supports COUNTERFACTUALS: it's not only the case that all A's are B's, but it's also the case that if something were an A, it would be a B. [synonym: 'nomological']

nominal / real definition / essence   **1.** A nominal definition is one that is merely arbitrarily stipulated, as opposed to one that reveals the already-existing conventional meaning of the term; thus identical to the distinction 'STIPULATED / LEXICAL DEFINITION'. **2.** A real definition is supposed to reveal the "real nature" or essence of the kind of thing being defined. A nominal definition merely gives us accidents that happen to be ways of recognizing that sort of thing. (*See* ESSENCE / ACCIDENT.) Thus the real definition of 'water' is that the term refers to H_2O; but a nominal definition tells us that the term refers to colourless tasteless liquid found in lakes and suitable in its pure form for drinking. (*See* list of other sorts of DEFINITION.)

nominalism   *See* UNIVERSALS.

nomological   *See* NOMIC.

nomological dangler   A supposedly objectionable condition of an item in a theory when it appears in various laws, but when it, and the laws it appears in, are unexplained. This term was coined as an argument for the IDENTITY THEORY OF MIND, which was supposed to give a physicalist REDUCTION—explanation—for (otherwise dangling) mental items and their regular causal connections with stimuli and behaviour.

nomos   *See* PHYSIS / NOMOS / TECHNE.

nonbeing   *See* NOTHING / NOTHINGNESS.

noncognitivism   *See* COGNITIVISM / NONCOGNITIVISM.

non-contradiction, law of   *See* LAWS OF THOUGHT.

nonnaturalism   *See* ETHICAL NATURALISM / NONNATURALISM / SUPERNATURALISM.

nonreflexive   *See* REFLEXIVE / IRREFLEXIVE / NONREFLEXIVE.

nonsense   *See* VERIFIABILITY CRITERION[1].

non sequitur   (Latin: "it does not follow") An ARGUMENT in which the conclusion is not supported by the premises, or a statement that is supposed to follow logically from some others but does not. ['non SEK-wuh-ter']

nonsymmetric   *See* SYMMETRIC / ASYMMETRIC / NONSYMMETRIC.

nontransitive   *See* TRANSITIVE / INTRANSITIVE / NONTRANSITIVE.

norm / normative   A norm is a standard for morally correct action. 'Normative' means prescribing a norm. When somebody says, "We think abortion is wrong". that statement may be descriptive—informing you what a group's views are, or normative—morally condemning abortion. *See* ETHICS.

notation, Polish   *See* POLISH NOTATION.

nothing / nothingness   Sometimes philosophers wondered whether there could be perfectly empty space, a "void";

some argued that the universe must be a "plenum"—filled at every point with something or other. It's less easy to make sense of the worry others had about whether 'nothing' names a thing. Some puzzlement has been occasioned by HEIDEGGER'S famous statement, *"Das Nichts nichtet"*—"The nothing noths". EXISTENTIALISTS distinguish "nothingness" from mere emptiness: the former is a perceived lack of being—a gap that we might find where we need or expect or would think of something.

noumena   *See* PHENOMENA / NOUMENA.

noûs / dianoia / doxa / theoria / techne / phronesis   All these Greek terms refer to different sorts of knowledge. *Noûs* is knowledge of the highest kind (involving, for PLATO, wordless direct intuition of the FORMS[1]); *dianoia* is the kind of knowledge humans more typically get—not direct intuition, but indirect, involving reasoning and argument; *doxa* is mere opinion, the lowest kind. Aristotle divided *dianoia* (by which he seems to mean knowledge in general) into *theoria* (contemplation, theoretical knowledge), *techne* (knowhow, art, craft, technique), and *phronesis* (practical and moral wisdom). ['noose', 'dee-uh-NOY-uh', 'DOX-ah', 'thee-oh-REE-ah', 'TEK-nay', 'fro-NEE-sis']

Nozick,   Robert (1938-2002) American philosopher with a broad scope of interests and publications; but most (in)famous for his enthusiastic defense of a rather extreme LIBERTARIANISM[2].

null set / class   *See* SET.

numbers, law of large   *See* LAW OF LARGE NUMBERS.

numerical identity   *See* IDENTITY[3].

Nussbaum,   Martha [Craven] (b. 1947) American philosopher with specialties in classical and moral philosophy and the philosophy of the emotions.

O

objective / subjective   *See* SUBJECTIVE / OBJECTIVE.

objectivism   **1.** The opposite of RELATIVISM. **2.** The opposite of subjectivism; *see* SUBJECTIVE / OBJECTIVE. **3.** The position of Ayn Rand (*see* WRITERS).

object language   *See* META-LANGUAGE / OBJECT LANGUAGE.

obligation   Generally, something one morally must do, a synonym for 'duty'. What one *must* do is perhaps not all there is to morality. Some good things are supererogatory—above and beyond the call of duty—for example, working as a volunteer in a soup kitchen for the homeless: wonderful if you did, but nobody would blame you if you didn't.

obverse / obversion / obvertend   *See* CONVERSE / OBVERSE.

Occam   *See* OCKHAM

occasionalism   The most extreme occasionalists (for example, MALEBRANCHE) hold that all causal power resides not in matter but in God, who is constantly intervening in the world to bring about change. Occasionalists about mind and body deny that the two interact: they are arranged by God on each occasion to move in parallel. *See also*: PARALLELISM, PRE-ESTABLISHED HARMONY.

Ockham   (or Occam), William of (c. 1285-1347) He and THOMAS AQUINAS are front-runners for the title of greatest MEDIEVAL philosopher. Thomas, however, was accepted as official doctrinal source for the Church, while Ockham was excommunicated; so the former has been far more influential. Ockham's work ranged all over philosophy, but most attention has been given to his LOGIC, his METAPHYSICS, and his theory of meaning. He's best known for his nominalism (*see* UNIVERSALS) and for Ockham's razor, the general principle of EXPLANATION he made much use of: everything else being equal, the correct or preferable explanation is the one that is simpler—i.e., that needs fewer basic principles or fewer explanatory entities. (Also known as the principle of PARSIMONY.)

omissions and acts   *See* ACTS / OMISSIONS.

omnibenevolent   Totally, perfectly good. Often thought to be a characteristic of God. Considered together with God's OMNI- SCIENCE and OMNIPOTENCE, this leads to the PROBLEM OF EVIL.

omnipotent   All-powerful, able to do anything. Often thought to be a characteristic of God, though some philosophers won- der whether this notion makes sense: could God make a con- tradiction true, or change the past, or manufacture a stone too heavy for Him to lift? (These are sometimes called the 'para- doxes of omnipotence'.) ['om-NIP-o-tent']

omnipresent   Everywhere at once, or influential in everything. Pantheists (*see* MONOTHEISM / POLYTHEISM / PANTHEISM) sometimes believe that God is omnipresent.

omniscient   All-knowing. Often thought to be a characteristic of God. To be omniscient is to know everything not only past and present, but also future. Theologians have wrestled with this problem: if God knows what I'm going to do tomorrow, then do I really have a choice? ['om-NISH-ent']

ontological argument for God's existence   A variety of argu- ments that rely on the CONCEPT of God to prove His exis- tence. In the best-known version it is supposed that part of the concept of God is that He is perfect: since something would not be perfect if it did not exist, it follows that God exists. A famous version of the ontological argument is due to ANSELM.

ontological commitment   *See* ONTOLOGY.

ontological parsimony   *See* PARSIMONY.

ontological relativism   A RELATIVISTIC position about ONTOL-OGY. Ontological relativists hold that there is no external fact about what things exist, or what the basic things are: we decide what we are going to count as an existing thing, or as basic, depending on context and what way of thinking suits us.

ontology   The philosophical study of EXISTENCE or being. Typical questions are: What basic sorts of things exist? What are the basic things out of which others are composed? How are things related to each other? The ontology (or the "ontological commitment") of a THEORY is the list of the sorts of things whose existence is PRESUPPOSED or required by that theory. QUINE argued that the answer to the METAPHYSICAL question "What is there?" is "Whatever is required by our best scientific theories." (Adjective form: 'ontological'.)

opaque / transparent   A (referentially) transparent CONTEXT is that part of a sentence surrounding a TERM^2 (a noun or noun phrase), which is such that any other term referring to the same thing may be replaced in it *SALVA VERITATE*, i.e., without changing the truth or falsity of the sentence. For example, the underlined part of this true sentence
    Terry kicked <u>Tabitha</u>.
is in a transparent context—Tabitha is Fran's cat, so
    Terry kicked Fran's cat.
must also be true. Compare, however, the underlined part of this true sentence:
    Terry said, "To hell with <u>Tabitha</u>!"
Replacement yields this false sentence:
    Terry said, "To hell with Fran's cat!"

Quotational contexts are opaque; and it is often thought that belief contexts are too. Thus, if Terry doesn't know that Tabitha is Fran's cat, then

Terry believes Tabitha is here

might be true, while

Terry believes Fran's cat is here

is false. (*See also* INTENTIONAL[3].)

open question argument   An argument against ETHICAL NATURALISM due to G. E. MOORE. Ethical naturalists suppose that an ethical term is synonymous with some natural term, for example, that 'the right action' is synonymous with 'the action that produces the greatest happiness'. But Moore argued against this synonymy (and any synonymy with a natural PREDICATE[1]) by claiming that even though it's clear that some action had this (or any) natural property, it could still be an open question (not a question thereby settled) whether that action was the right action.

open sentence   *See* SYMBOLS OF QUANTIFIER LOGIC.

operational definition   Defines by giving an account of the procedures or measurements used to apply the word. For example, one might describe weighing procedures and outcomes to define 'weight'. (*See* list of other sorts of DEFINITION.)

operationalism / instrumentalism   Operationalism is the view that scientific CONCEPTS should have OPERATIONAL DEFINITIONS, and that any terms not definable in this way should be eliminated from science as meaningless. For example, to be an operationalist about sub-atomic particles is to think that there's nothing we mean by saying they exist except that certain kinds of visible effects exist under certain experimental conditions. Instrumentalists are operationalists who are explicitly anti-REALISTS about THEORETICAL ENTITIES. They say that electrons, for example, don't really exist; electron-talk is about nothing but what's observable. 'Instrumental-

ism' is also the name of the view associated with PRAGMA-
TISM, especially with John DEWEY, that emphasizes that our
thinking arises through practical experience, and should be
judged as a tool for coping with our environment rather than
in terms of truth or falsity.

opposition   *See* SQUARE OF OPPOSITION.

oppression   Subjugation, coercion, persecution, tyrannical
rule, cruelty, injustice, especially as applied to a group. This
is a concept frequently encountered in contemporary social
philosophy.

O proposition   *See* A / E / I / O PROPOSITIONS.

optimism   *See* PESSIMISM / OPTIMISM.

ordered pair / n-tuple   An ordered pair is a RELATION between
two things where the order of the things mentioned is significant. For example, we might symbolize '**x** is bigger than **y**'
by B<**x**,**y**>; here the positions of **x** and **y** make a difference:
B<**y**,**x**> means '**y** is bigger than **x**'. An ordered n-tuple is a
similar relation involving n objects.

ordinary language philosophy   A branch of twentieth-century
philosophy (most closely associated with WITTGENSTEIN and
J. L. AUSTIN) that held that philosophical problems arose
because of confusions about, or complexities in, ordinary
language, and might be solved (or dissolved) by attention to
the subtleties of actual language. Thus, for example, problems about FREE WILL might be solved (or shown to be
empty) by close examination of exactly how we use words
like 'free' and 'responsible'.

original position   To explain what sorts of social arrangements
would be just ones, RAWLS asks you to imagine yourself in an
"original position" prior to any social rules, under the VEIL
OF IGNORANCE as to which position you occupy in this orig-

inal society or in the resulting organized one; the social rules you would choose given this ignorance are the just ones. This is a version of contractarianism—*see* SOCIAL CONTRACT.

original sin   The innate depravity thought by Christians to inhere in everyone as a consequence of Adam's disobedience.

Ortega y Gasset,   José (1883-1955) Spanish essayist and philosopher, associated with PERSPECTIVISM and EXISTENTIALISM.

orthodox / heterodox   An orthodox belief is one that is officially accepted, or conventional, or traditional; a belief that is not orthodox, or is contrary to orthodoxy, is called 'heterodox'.

O statement   *See* A / E / I / O PROPOSITIONS.

ostensive definition   *See* VERBAL / OSTENSIVE DEFINITION.

Other   The Other (often with an upper-case 'O'), is for some philosophers other people: the basic problem here is how one knows about this Other, in its subjective experience. In the writing of the HEIDEGGERIANS and EXISTENTIALISTS, the Other takes on wider and grander significance.

other minds, problem of   *See* PROBLEM OF OTHER MINDS.

overdetermination   An event is overdetermined when two or more events have happened, each of which is individually a sufficient condition (*see* NECESSARY / SUFFICIENT CONDITION) for it. Thus someone's death is overdetermined when he is given a fatal dose of poison and then shot through the heart. (Compare this with UNDERDETERMINATION.)

overman   *See* SUPERMAN.

Oxford philosophy   *See* ANALYTIC PHILOSOPHY.

P

panpsychism The position that everything in the universe, not just people, contains "mind"—is somehow psychological. A few of the philosophers whose views are at least related to this position are THALES, PLOTINUS, LEIBNIZ, SCHOPEN-HAUER and WHITEHEAD.

pantheism *See* MONOTHEISM / POLYTHEISM / PANTHEISM.

paraconsistent logic In ordinary logic, every sentence FOL-LOWS from a CONTRADICTION. But this appears not to map ordinary good reasoning: we often have some contradictions in the beliefs we reason from, but we don't conclude just anything. Paraconsistent logic attempts to provide a FORMAL MODEL for reasoning from inconsistent premises. (*See* ARGUMENT *and* CONSISTENT; *see also* RELEVANCE LOGIC.)

paradigm **1.** A paradigm case is a clear and typical example of a kind of thing. The paradigm case ARGUMENT tries to solve SCEPTICAL doubts about the existence of something by point-ing at a paradigm of that sort of thing. Often the reasoning here is: if a word or phrase has rules for use, and fully accept-able actual uses, it must refer to something real. **2.** A MODEL, a set of assumptions or basic way of seeing things which is relatively immune to disconfirmation (*see* CONFIRMATION / DISCONFIRMATION) from experience. KUHN saw the history of science as a succession of paradigms. ['PAR-uh-dime', where the 'a' sound is as in 'pat', the adjectival form is 'par-adigmatic', pronounced 'PAR-uh-dig-MAT-ic']

paradox A clearly false or SELF-CONTRADICTORY conclusion deduced apparently correctly from apparently true ASSUMP-TIONS[1]. Philosophers often find principles of wide-ranging importance while trying to discover what has gone wrong in a paradox. You'll find accounts of some well-known paradoxes in the following entries:

parallelism Because of the difficulties in INTERACTIONISM some philosophers were led to the belief that mind and body events don't cause each other, but just run along independently; they are coordinated, however, in some possibly inexplicable way, or perhaps GOD sets them up in advance (OCCASIONALISM) to run in parallel, like two clocks set in advance

to chime the hour simultaneously. [Psychophysical] paral-
lelists thus believe in the PRE-ESTABLISHED HARMONY of
mind and body. LEIBNIZ was a parallelist.

paralogism   In general, an error in reasoning; in KANT, more
particularly, four errors that result from reasoning beyond the
boundaries of possible experience. ['par-AL-uh-gizm']

paranormal phenomena   A collection of kinds of events and
human abilities about whose existence mainstream science is
sceptical. You'll find definitions in this dictionary of:

CLAIRVOYANCE
EXTRA-SENSORY PERCEPTION (ESP)
TELEKINESIS (also called teleportation)
TELEPATHY
PRECOGNITION
REINCARNATION

The study of these alleged phenomena is called parapsychol-
ogy or paranormal psychology or psychical research. Also
investigated are reincarnation, ghosts, spiritual healing,
auras, contact with the dead ('spiritualism'), and the mysterious powers of pyramids and crystals. Most of the literature
on paranormal phenomena can be found at supermarket
checkout counters. A synonym for 'paranormal' is 'psi' [pro-
nounced 'sigh' or 'psigh', sometimes abbreviated by the
Greek letter psi, 'ψ']

Pareto,   Vilfredo *See* SCIENTISTS.

Pareto principle / efficiency / optimality   The Pareto principle
is that if everyone in a certain society is indifferent between
x and **y**, then for that society, **x** is equal in value to **y**; but if
everyone is indifferent except for one person who prefers **x** to
y, then **x** is better than **y** for that society. This sounds like a
reasonable starting point for determining social value on the
basis of individual preference, but it doesn't help with hard
cases. Pareto efficiency, also called Pareto optimality, is the
state of affairs in which nobody can be made better off with-

out someone's being made worse off. Both ideas are due to Vilfredo Pareto (*see* SCIENTISTS).

Parfit, Derek [Antony] (b. 1942) English philosopher, best known for his surprising arguments that continuity of personal traits is more important to us than narrow PERSONAL IDENTITY.

Parmenides of Elea (born c. 510 B.C.) PRE-SOCRATIC Greek philosopher. His central doctrine was that reality did not change.

parsimony Means 'economy', in the sense of 'using restricted means'; the principle of parsimony (also known as 'OCK-HAM'S Razor'), counts this as a virtue in theories. One sort is ontological parsimony: the reliance on a comparatively small number of basic kinds of things, or a minimum of THEORET-ICAL ENTITIES. ['PAR-si-mo-nee']

participation **1.** *See* FORM[1]. **2.** In a DEMOCRATIC society, the active involvement by citizens in the processes of government.

particulars *See* INDIVIDUAL.

particular statement / proposition A statement that says something about some but not all the members of a SET; contrasted with a GENERALIZATION or UNIVERSAL PROPOSITION.

part / whole *See* MEREOLOGY.

Pascal, Blaise (1623-1662) French mathematician, scientist, philosopher. His best known philosophical work raises and attempts to answer skeptical doubts about religion. "Pascal's wager" is his famous argument for belief in God:

> Belief in God might result in infinite benefit—eternal salvation—if He exists, while we risk only a little—wasting some time, and foregoing some pleasures forbidden to

believers—if he doesn't. Conversely, disbelief might result in infinite harm—eternal damnation—if He exists, or could provide a tiny benefit if we were right. So even if there isn't any evidence one way or the other, it's a very good bet to believe.

One problem with this argument is the questionable view that we can choose to believe something because of the potential benefits of belief. If I offered you $100 to believe that London was in France, could you do it?

passive euthanasia   *See* EUTHANASIA.

paternalism   Paternalistic action provides for what is taken to be someone's good, without giving that person responsibility for determining his/her own aims or actions. It arises from a sort of benevolence plus lack of trust in people's ability to decide what's to their own benefit or to act for their own real long-range good. Some critics of paternalism argue that the only way to determine someone's good is to see what that person chooses. Some argue that respect for individual AUTONOMY means that we shouldn't interfere even when someone is choosing badly. This issue arises most importantly in political theory and medical ethics, since governments and physicians often act paternalistically.

pathetic fallacy   The mistake of seeing human emotions, intentions, etc., in things that do not have them. ('Pathetic' here doesn't have the colloquial meaning of 'stupid' or 'dreadful'—it's used more strictly, meaning 'having to do with feelings'.)

patriarchy   Societal and familial institutions are patriarchal when they systematically embody male dominance over women: when they arrange things so that men hold power and women do not. FEMINISTS emphasize the widespread incidence of patriarchal institutions in historical and contemporary families and societies.

patristic philosophy   The philosophy—largely theology—associated with early Christian philosophers, especially the Church Fathers. Includes AUGUSTINE and BOETHIUS.

Peirce,   Charles S(anders) (Santiago) (1839-1914) American philosopher and LOGICIAN; father of PRAGMATISM and a significant contributor to philosophy of science and logic. Very little of his work was published during his life, and he did not hold a regular teaching position; his views were, until recently, unknown except in the version popularized by JAMES. ['purse']

Peirce's law $[(P \supset Q) \supset P] \supset P$. It's a LOGICAL TRUTH, though it doesn't seem like one at first glance. Other surprising logical truths are $[(P \supset Q) \lor (Q \supset P)]$ and $[(P \supset Q) \lor (Q \supset R)]$.

per accidens   *See* PER SE.

percept   *See* CONCEPT.

perception   In its broadest use, this means any sort of mental awareness, but it's more often used to refer to the awareness we get when using the senses. This awareness is thought by the EMPIRICISTS to be the source of all substantial knowledge. Various theories of perception attempt to account for its nature and (possible) reliability. *See :*
    ARGUMENT FROM ILLUSION
    REPRESENTATIONALISM
    NAÏVE REALISM
    critical realism (in entry for CRITICAL IDEALISM / REALISM)
    perceptual REALISM
    ADVERBIAL THEORY OF PERCEPTION.

perfectionism   The view that the highest good is to pursue a perfect ideal of character and action.

performative / constative   Constative utterances are ordinary statements, saying something that is independently true or false. A performative utterance makes what is said true, because uttering it actually performs the act it attributes—for example, when a properly constituted authority says, "I now pronounce you husband and wife." Another example: "I apologize." J. L. AUSTIN discussed performatives while considering problems about meaning. *See also* SPEECH ACTS.

performative theory of truth   Denies that 'truth' is a genuine property; claims that it is the mark of a PERFORMATIVE: when one says something of the form, 'P is true', one is merely performing the act of agreeing with P. (*See* list of competing theories of TRUTH.)

per genus et differentiam   *See* GENUS / SPECIES.

Peripatetic school   ARISTOTLE'S students and followers. The name may be derived from Aristotle's custom of walking about (*peripatein*) while lecturing, or from the *peripatos* ("covered walk") of the Lyceum, the parklike area outside Athens, where he lectured.

perlocutionary act / intention   *See* SPEECH ACTS.

per se   (Latin, "through [i.e., on account of] itself") Means 'by itself', 'INTRINSICALLY'. "This is not a valuable house *per se*—it's so expensive merely because of its good location." Sometimes philosophers say that something has a characteristic *per se* when that characteristic is essential to it, this is contrasted with a characteristic *per accidens* (Latin, "accidentally") (*see* ESSENTIAL / ACCIDENTAL). ['pur say']

person   Philosophers sometimes use this word in such a way that persons do not necessarily coincide with living human organisms. The idea here is that a person is anything that has special RIGHTS (for example, the right to life, or to self-determination) or special dignity or worth. What makes something a person? Perhaps: having a mental SUBSTANCE or CONSCIOUSNESS[3], being self-aware, able to think of one's past or future. If awareness or mental ability is relevant, then a human in a permanent coma would not be a person, and could be killed or left to die without continuation of life-support. Pro-choicers on the abortion issue say that fetuses are living humans, but not yet persons. And it has been argued that some persons are not living human organisms—for example, that the person can survive bodily death. If God and angels exist, they are persons. Perhaps certain higher animals exhibit the characteristics that give them the special personal rights and dignity we have—thus they might also be persons. *See also* PERSONAL IDENTITY.

personal identity   **1.** The IDENTITY[1] of a person—whatever it is that makes you *you*. Is it your body, your mind, your personality, your memories, or something else? **2.** The IDENTITY[4] of a person—whatever it is that makes this person now the same person as that one, earlier. Is it a continuing body, or mind, or personality, or that this later stage remembers the experiences that happened to the earlier one?

personalism   The view that PERSONS constitute a basic category for ONTOLOGY and EXPLANATION.

personal supposition   *See* SUPPOSITION.

perspectivism   The idea that truth is "perspectival"—relative to the perspective of the knower. This view has a long history, but it has recently become especially popular among the POST-MODERNS, who tend to hold that truth varies with one's culture, history, language, social class, or gender.

persuasive definition   A definition (usually a STIPULATIVE re-definition) designed to influence the hearer's attitudes: "I define 'abortion' as the heartless murder of a defenseless innocent little baby." (*See* list of other sorts of DEFINITION.)

pessimism / optimism   Optimism is a hopeful attitude, or the view that things are fundamentally good, or will improve, or can be fixed; an extreme version of optimism holds that this is the BEST OF ALL POSSIBLE WORLDS. Pessimism is the reverse of any of these views. Some philosophers argue that these optimistic and pessimistic views are not just ways we might happen to FEEL, but that religious or METAPHYSICAL considerations offer rational grounds for or against them. LEIBNIZ was a philosophical optimist, SCHOPENHAUER a pessimist.

Peter Aureol   (variants: Petrus; Auriol, Aureolus, Aureoli, Oriole) (c. 1275–1322) French Franciscan philosopher and theologian, known for his SCEPTICAL and EMPIRICAL tendencies.

petitio principii   *See* CIRCULAR REASONING / DEFINITION.

phallocentric   Means "penis-centered"—refers to attitudes or institutions which consider only males, or are associated especially with them, or are dominated by them.

phenomenalism   Phenomenalists believe (on the basis, for example, of the ARGUMENT FROM ILLUSION) that all we're ever aware of is appearances or SENSE-DATA, the mental events we have when using our senses. Accepting the EMPIRICIST rule that we're entitled to believe in only what's given by our senses, they deny the existence of external objects independent of perception. Ordinary "objects" like tables and chairs are thus thought to be collections of these appearances—actual and perhaps possible ones. Thus, this is a form of IDEALISM[2]. HUME, MILL, MACH, and RUSSELL were phenomenalists.

phenomena / noumena   Philosophers sometimes use 'phenomenon' in the ordinary sense, referring merely to something that happens, but often it's used in a more technical way, referring to a way things seem to us—to something as we perceive it. Noumena are, by contrast, THINGS-IN-THEMSELVES—things as they really are. These are unavailable to the senses, but perhaps rationally comprehensible; though

KANT argued that they are unknowable. [singular 'phenomenon', 'noumenon', plural: 'phenomena', 'noumena']

phenomenology 'Phenomenologically' means 'as it basically appears to us'. Phenomenology is a very diverse school of philosophy, deriving from the thought of BRENTANO. HUSSERL, and HEIDEGGER and continued by MERLEAU-PONTY and SARTRE. Phenomenologists believe that INTUITIONS or direct awarenesses form the basis of truth, and the FOUNDATION on which philosophy should proceed: by INTROSPECTION, BRACKETING, and exploration of the "inner", subjective world of experiences: that is, of consciousness without PRESUPPOSITIONS, including that the external world exists.

philia See AGAPE / PHILIA / EROS.

philosopher-king This term is associated with PLATO'S idea that the characteristics needed for the best kind of ruler—real wisdom and knowledge of the good—are to be found only in philosophers. Don't you think he's right?

Philosopher, The MEDIEVAL PHILOSOPHERS found ARISTOTLE'S thought so important that they called him 'The Philosopher'.

philosophes (French: "philosophers") Refers to the eighteenth-century French philosophers (ROUSSEAU, DIDEROT, Voltaire (*see* WRITERS), and others). ['fill-oh-soff']

philosophy Oddly, philosophers have a great deal of difficulty defining this word, partly because they disagree so much about what they should be doing. The word comes from Greek roots, and originally meant 'love of wisdom', but this definition is very unhelpful. Better but still inadequate definitions say that it is the study of first or most general principles, or of the PRESUPPOSITIONS behind ways of thought, or of ultimate reality. The best way to understand what philosophy is is to take a look through this book, or through a general philosophy text, to see what kinds of things are done. Most philosophers agree that ordinary folks' uses of this word don't have much to do with their discipline: for example, in 'a philosophical attitude'—a feeling of acceptance or resignation based on a generalized or detached standpoint— or in 'my philosophy', which usually refers to a cliché about how to live. Good advice for using this word in the company of philosophers: don't confuse philosophy with what might be written on a bumper sticker.

For entries on various divisions of philosophy, *see*:

ANALYTIC PHILOSOPHY
ANCIENT PHILOSOPHY
CONTINENTAL PHILOSOPHY
MEDIEVAL PHILOSOPHY
MODERN PHILOSOPHY
NATURAL PHILOSOPHY
ORDINARY LANGUAGE PHILOSOPHY
PATRISTIC PHILOSOPHY
SPECULATIVE PHILOSOPHY.

phonetics   The study of the sounds of a spoken language.

phronesis   *See* NOÛS / DIANOIA / DOXA / THEORIA / TECHNE / PHRONESIS.

physicalism   *See* MATERIALISM.

physis / nomos / techne   '*Physis*' is a Greek term for nature, the way things really are, the active principle behind being, or something's ESSENCE. It is the root of the word 'physics'. *Nomos* is, by contrast, convention or law, and *techne* is what is created by humans. ['FIZ-is' or 'FOOZ-is', 'NO-mos', 'TECK-nay']

Piaget,   Jean *See* SCIENTISTS.

picture theory of meaning   The idea that a sentence (or a thought) has meaning in something like the way a picture represents reality: with a correspondence between the elements and structure of the picture and what it represents. WITTGENSTEIN considered this idea in the *Tractatus*, and later rejected it.

PK   Abbreviation for 'psychokinesis'. *See* TELEKINESIS.

Planck,   Max *See* SCIENTISTS.

Plantinga,   Alvin (b. 1932) American philosopher known for his surprising and subtle application of logic and META-PHYSICS in defense of traditional religious belief.

Plato   (c. 428-348 B.C.) (original name Aristocles) Ancient Greek philosopher, student of SOCRATES, possibly the greatest philosopher of all time. His writings, which often take the form of dialogues with Socrates as one of the characters, contain the first substantial statements of many of the questions and answers in philosophy. It is difficult to know, however, how much of this is due to Plato, and how much to Socrates. Plato's best-known doctrine is the theory of the "FORMS[1]" or "ideas": these are the general or perfect versions of characteristics we ordinarily encounter. To understand ordinary experience, Plato argued, we must first have understanding of these forms, and this must be INNATE, not given by experience. *The Republic* presents his picture of the ideal state: not democratic, but ruled by dictators who have knowledge of the form of the good, and who arrange things in accord with this (*see* PHILOSOPHER-KINGS).

Platonic   The adjectival form of 'PLATO'.

Platonic forms   *See* FORM[1].

Platonic love   This notion actually derives from Plato's theories about love (expressed for example, in his *Symposium*) though for Plato it doesn't exclude sex.

Platonism   Various sorts of views growing from aspects of PLATO's thought. Platonists tend to emphasize Plato's notion of a TRANSCENDENT reality, believing that the visible world is not the real world, and Plato's RATIONALISM—that the important truths about reality and about how we ought to live are TRUTHS OF REASON. [sometimes the 'p' is lower-case]

pleasure-pain calculus   *See* FELICIFIC CALCULUS.

Plekhanov,   Georgii Valentinovich (1856-1918) Russian MARXIST philosopher and revolutionary. His thought, developed from that of MARX and LENIN, was very influential on Soviet philosophy until the 1950s. ['pleh-KHAN-off']

plenitude, principle of   *See* GREAT CHAIN OF BEING.

plenum   *See* NOTHING / NOTHINGNESS.

Plotinus   (c. 204-270) Egyptian-born Roman philosopher, influenced by PLATO, founder of neo-PLATONISM, which emphasized the TRANSCENDENT "One"—the unknowable basis for all existence. ['plo-TIE-nus']

pluralism   **1.** The view that there are several basic kinds of thing (*see* DUALISM / MONISM / PLURALISM). **2.** In general, an attitude of tolerance toward differences; in particular, the view associated with WITTGENSTEIN and POST-MODERNS that different activities are INCOMMENSURABLE, not criticizable, not even understandable, from the outside.

Poincaré,   Henri *See* SCIENTISTS.

Polish notation   A non-standard SYMBOLIC LOGIC notation, so-called because of its introduction by the Polish logician Jan Łukasiewicz (1878-1956). Here are some translations into Polish notation from standard forms:

~P   Np
P & Q   Kpq

P v Q	Apq
P ⊃ Q	Cpq
P ≡ Q	Epq
(x)Fx	ΠxFx
(∃x)Fx	ΣxFx

Conventions for ordering make parentheses unnecessary.

polytheism   *See* MONOTHEISM / POLYTHEISM / PANTHEISM.

pons asinorum   (Latin: "bridge of asses") Originally the name of a difficult proof in Euclid's geometry (that the angles opposite the equal sides of an isosceles triangle are equal). In general, a difficult problem, at least for beginners. Called this because it's supposed to be difficult to get an ass across a bridge. ['pons ass-uh-NOR-um']

Popper,   (Sir) Karl (Raimund) (1902-1994) Austrian-British philosopher of science, known for his emphasis on falsifiability rather than on VERIFIABILITY in science, and for his defence of LIBERALISM in social theory.

posit   *See* AXIOM / POSTULATE / POSIT.

positivism   The philosophy associated with Auguste COMTE, which holds that scientific knowledge is the only valid kind of knowledge, and that anything else is idle speculation. Sometimes this term is loosely used to refer to LOGICAL POSITIVISM, which is a twentieth-century outgrowth of more general nineteenth-century positivism. *See also* LEGAL POSITIVISM.

possible worlds   This world—the collection of all facts—is the actual world. A possible world is a non-actual world, a world in which one or more things are not as they actually are, but are as they might have been. The notion of a possible world has been used to explain and explore MODAL LOGIC and COUNTERFACTUALS, notably by David LEWIS, who has recently argued that possible worlds are real (*see* REALISM).

possibilia Possible things.

postcard paradox Imagine a postcard with this sentence on one side:
> The sentence on the other side of this card is true.

and this sentence on the other side:
> The sentence on the other side of this card is false.

It is impossible to give a consistent TRUTH VALUE assignment to these two sentences. Compare the LIAR'S PARADOX.

post hoc ergo propter hoc *See* FALSE CAUSE.

postmodernism Various late twentieth-century movements, in general characterized by a rejection of FOUNDATIONALISM, an interest in textual interpretation and DECONSTRUCTION, antagonism to ANALYTIC PHILOSOPHY, rejection of the goals of the ENLIGHTENMENT, tendency to PERSPECTIVISM, denial of the applicability of the concepts of reality, objectivity, truth.

poststructuralism A POSTMODERN view, thought of as a successor to STRUCTURALISM. Holds in general that the meaning of words is their relation to other words (in a "text"), not their relation to reality; that human activity is not LAWLIKE, but understood through its relations to power and the unconscious.

postulate *See* AXIOM / POSTULATE / POSIT.

pour soi *See* IN-ITSELF / FOR-ITSELF.

practical reason *See* PURE REASON.

pragmatic implication *See* INFERENCE / IMPLICATION / ENTAILMENT[1].

pragmaticism *See* PRAGMATISM.

pragmatics *See* SEMANTICS / SYNTAX / PRAGMATICS.

pragmatic theory of truth   The theory that truth is what is useful to believe (everything considered, and in the long run). This doesn't mean that anything you'd like to believe is therefore true: usefulness is understood in terms of allowing us to make successful predictions, and in general to function well in life. *See* PRAGMATISM, and, for competing theories of truth, *see* TRUTH.

pragmatism   An American school of philosophy including, in the beginning of the twentieth century, Charles PEIRCE, (who called his version 'pragmaticism'), William JAMES, and John DEWEY. More recently, more loosely associated with the work of QUINE, PUTNAM, and RORTY. The early pragmatists emphasized the relevance of the practical application of things, their connections to our lives, our activities and values. They demanded instrumental definitions of philosophically relevant terms, and urged that we judge beliefs on the basis of their benefit to the believer. *See also* OPERATIONAL-ISM / INSTRUMENTALISM, also PRAGMATIC THEORY OF TRUTH.

praxis   In Greek, "action"; in ARISTOTLE, the ethical and political (as opposed to the theoretical), hence, more generally, custom or practical activity.

preanalytic   *See* INTUITION.

precising definition   *See* STIPULATIVE / PRECISING / LEXICAL DEFINITION.

precognition   Supposed knowledge of events in advance, without the usual kind of physical scientific evidence. A PARA-NORMAL PHENOMENON, about the existence of which mainstream science is sceptical.

predestination   The position of some religions that some or all aspects of our future—our character, what we will do, what will happen to us, our ultimate salvation or damnation—are determined in advance by God, not by our preferences, decisions, efforts, or actions. A religious form of FATALISM; like fatalism, it must be distinguished from DETERMINISM. Also known as 'preordination'.

predeterminism   An ambiguous term, meaning 'DETERMINISM' or 'FATALISM' or 'PREDESTINATION'. Because of this ambiguity, it's probably best avoided.

predicate / predication   **1.** 'Predicate' is sometimes used by philosophers to mean what it does in grammar: the part of the sentence that says something about the subject, including verb, objects, and modifiers of these. Thus the predicate is the italicized part of 'The cat *is on the mat*'. **2.** In TRADITIONAL LOGIC, the predicate (or, more precisely, the predicate term is the part of certain sentences that follows the COPULA ('is', 'are', 'is not', etc.). So it's the italicized part of 'All pigs are *sloppy eaters*'. **3.** Most often these days philosophers use this term to mean any part of a sentence excluding a noun or noun phrase: thus, these italicized parts are predicates: 'The cat *is on the mat*' and '*The cat is on* the mat'. In this use, a predicate is a broader way of saying something about something, or of delimiting a group of things: 'The cat is on ___' delimits a class of things such that the cat is on them. Predicates may be one-place ('unary' or 'monadic'), two-place ('binary' or 'dyadic'), etc. The above are one-place predicates (i.e., they contain one blank to be filled with a term); '___ is on ___' is a two-place predicate; '___ owes ___ to ___' is three-place. One-place predicates are words that name properties (*see* QUALITY / ATTRIBUTE / PROPERTY), predicates with more than one place name RELATIONS. Predication is saying that a predicate applies to something. In the sentence above, '___ is on the mat' is predicated of the cat, and 'The cat is on ___' is predicated of the mat.

predicate logic / calculus   *See* QUANTIFIER LOGIC.

prediction paradox   *See* SURPRISE QUIZ PARADOX.

pre-established harmony Those like LEIBNIZ who didn't believe in ACTION AT A DISTANCE needed to explain the apparent interaction of separated things, and argued that God had arranged, in advance, their apparent coincidence of behaviour. *See also* OCCASIONALISM, PARALLELISM.

pre-existence The existence of the soul before unification with a body. *See* RECOLLECTION.

preface paradox In the preface to their books, authors sometimes own up to whatever errors occur in their books. The statement 'This book contains at least one error' is clearly correct when there's an error elsewhere in the book, but what about when there isn't? Then that statement itself is an error. So there is one error—that statement itself—so it's true. One gets oneself tied up in knots here, as is typical in paradoxes of SELF-REFERENCE.

premise *See* ARGUMENT.

premise, major / minor *See* MAJOR / MIDDLE / MINOR TERM / PREMISE.

preordination *See* PREDESTINATION.

prescriptivism *See* EMOTIVISM.

"present king of France" example *See* DEFINITE DESCRIPTION *and* PRESUPPOSITION.

pre-Socratics The ancient Greek philosophers before SOCRATES, that is, of the sixth and fifth centuries B.C. Their thought marks the beginning of the Western philosophical tradition. The earliest on record is THALES (c. 580 B.C.); others with entries in this dictionary are
    ANAXIMANDER
    ANAXAGORAS
    DEMOCRITUS

EMPEDOCLES
HERACLITUS
PARMENEDES
PROTAGORAS
PYTHAGORAS
ZENO OF ELEA.

presupposition   A necessary condition for the truth of a statement, assumed beforehand by the speaker, but not itself stated. The speaker of 'The present king of France is bald'
believes that there is a present king of France. Because there
isn't, the statement is not true, but is it false, or rather inappropriate and lacking a truth value? RUSSELL and STRAWSON
had a well-known debate about this question. This should be
distinguished from conversational implicature (*see* INFER-
ENCE / IMPLICATION / ENTAILMENT[2]). If you're looking for a
pencil and I say "I've got one" the conversational implicature
is that I'm going to offer it to you. But if I do have a pencil
and don't offer it to you, what I've said is nevertheless true.

prima facie   (Latin: "at first appearance") Based on the first
impression: what would be true, or seem to be true, in general, or before additional information is added about the particular case. Thus, philosophers speak of 'prima facie duties',
those things that by and large people are obliged to do, but
that might not turn out to be real duties in particular cases,
given additional considerations; and 'prima facie evidence'
that can be overridden by contrary considerations. [usually
'PRY-ma FAY-sha' or '-shee']

primary / secondary qualities   LOCKE (and others) argued that
some characteristics we perceive are really as perceived in
external objects (the primary qualities), whereas others (the
secondary qualities) don't exist as perceived in the real
world, but are just powers of external objects to produce
ideas in us which don't resemble what's out there. For example, the dimensions of something are really objective characteristics of it (*see* SUBJECTIVE / OBJECTIVE), but its colour is

not really out there; we attribute colours to things just because of sensations caused in us by some other real (primary) characteristics.

prime   Philosophers sometimes use a notation to distinguish between an original and an amended version of something by writing a single-quote or apostrophe (') after the name of the second. Read this 'prime'. Thus, if Definition D is amended, one might get Definition D' (read 'D prime'). Further amendment might result in D'' ('D double-prime'), etc. A similar convention would call the amendment D* (read 'D star').

prime mover   *See* UNMOVED MOVER.

primitive   This word means behaviour, cultures, or people that are comparatively undeveloped or simple; nowadays, it is sometimes thought politically unacceptable and derogatory to call a tribe or culture 'primitive'. Philosophers often use this word (acceptably) to refer to what is simple and basic in the ANALYSIS of something.

principia   (Latin: "principles") Sometimes used as the first word of the title of books. Two such books are titled *Principia Mathematica*, one (1687) by Newton (*see* SCIENTISTS), the other (1910-1913) by RUSSELL and WHITEHEAD. Each is sometimes called 'the *Principia*' for short. Another philosophically important *Principia* is MOORE'S *Principia Ethica* (1903). ['prin-KIP-ia']

principle, in   *See* IN PRINCIPLE.

principle of ...   *See* (in many cases) under what follows 'of', or under LAW OF ... .

principle of charity   **1.** One of the principles used in "translating" others' statements—that is, in understanding what they mean by what they say (if they're speaking another language, or even what seems to be your own). This principle says that we should understand their words in a way that maximizes the number of true statements they are taken to say. It's not merely a matter of being nice—it's supposed to be a necessary step in getting the right translation. This can't be the only principle for translation (if it were we could simply translate everything as 'Snow is white' and it would all be true). DAVIDSON and QUINE discuss this principle. **2.** Logic includes a similar principle of charity: when trying to understand the structure of someone's argument, we should fill in the details in a charitable way—i.e., in a way that would make the argument a good one.

principle of dominance   *See* DOMINANCE.

principle of double effect   *See* DOUBLE EFFECT.

principle of identity   *See* LAWS OF THOUGHT.

principle of identity of indiscernibles   *See* LAW OF THE INDE-SCERNABILITY OF IDENTICALS.

principle of indeterminacy   *See* UNCERTAINTY PRINCIPLE.

principle of induction   *See* PROBLEM OF INDUCTION.

principle of liberty   The first principle of justice in RAWLS'S theory. It says that each person has an equal right to the most extensive total system of equal basic liberties compatible with a similar system of liberty for all. *See also* DIFFERENCE PRINCIPLE.

principle of plenitude   *See* GREAT CHAIN OF BEING.

principle of sufficient reason   Says that something exists if and only if it has a complete or full reason or EXPLANATION.

principle of uniformity of nature   *See* PROBLEM OF INDUCTION.

principle of universal causation   The principle that every event has a cause. *See also* DETERMINISM.

principle of utility   *See* UTILITARIANISM.

prior   **1.** Earlier than. **2.** More fundamental or basic than.

prior probability   *See* PROBABILITY.

prisoner's dilemma   A situation in which two or more people (or groups) face a decision analogous in structure to the one in the following story. Suppose you and an accomplice have committed a crime. The police have evidence sufficient only to give each of you a short jail sentence, and they want to get a confession fully implicating both of you. They separate you, and tell you that if your accomplice doesn't confess you'll get one year in jail if you confess, but two years if you don't confess. If your accomplice does confess, then you'll get three years if you confess, and four years if you don't confess (*see* the table in DECISION MATRIX for a summary of the situation). They also say that the same deal is being offered to your accomplice. You reason that whether he confesses or not, you'll get a shorter sentence if you confess (*see* DOMINANCE). Confessing here—the dominant option—is called "defection", as contrasted with "cooperation". He reasons similarly, so he confesses too; thus, both of you get three years. But something has gone wrong: if neither of you confessed, both of you would be better off (two-year sentence). So this is a somewhat paradoxical situation, since selfishness on each of your parts has resulted in an outcome worse for each than an alternative; perhaps RATIONAL SELF-INTEREST prescribes cooperation. Many philosophers think that prisoner's dilemmas of this sort are an important MODEL for thinking about real-choice problems in political and ethical theory. [Sometimes the apostrophe is placed after the final 's'] *See also* TRAGEDY OF THE COMMONS, *and* TIT FOR TAT.

privacy   **1.** The private realm, in political theory, is that area of our lives (if any!) supposed to be immune from public regulation. Does government have any business in our bedrooms? **2.** (EPISTEMIC) privacy is the supposed fact that your own mental states can be known directly only by you. (*See also* PRIVILEGED ACCESS.)

private language argument   Ludwig WITTGENSTEIN'S argument that, if there were PRIVATE[2] events, we would be unable to name, categorize or talk about them. For it to be possible to name or categorize something, there must exist rules of correct naming and categorization. Without the possibility of public check, there would be no distinction between our feeling that we named something correctly and our really doing so, so nothing could count as our doing so correctly or incorrectly. Thus, there could be no such thing as a "private language"—a language naming private events without possibility of public check. (*See also* BEETLE IN THE BOX.)

privileged access   The special way that you alone (it is supposed) can find out about the contents of your mind. Other people need to infer what's in your mind from your external behaviour, but you can discover your mental states directly. CARTESIANS and others suppose that this access is IMMEDIATE, INCORRIGIBLE, and CERTAIN. *See also* INTROSPECTION *and* PRIVACY[2].

pro attitude   A mental state (a desire, feeling, wish, value, etc.) that is favourable about something. EMOTIVISM holds that ethical utterances are expressions of pro- (and con-) attitudes.

probabilism   The position that emphasizes the fallibility of any of our beliefs: the best we can hope for is high probability of truth.

probability   Something is probable when it is neither impossible nor definite, but likely to some degree. Probability is standardly measured on a scale between 0 (impossible) and 1 (definite). To say that something is probable may be to say that it has a probability of more than .5. There has been philosophical controversy about what it really means to say that an event has a certain probability. Some philosophers argue that saying that the probability of heads is .5 when flipping a fair coin means that the frequency of heads in a large number of flips will tend toward .5 (*see* LAW OF LARGE NUMBERS); this is the frequency theory of probability. But what if a coin is flipped only once? A competing theory, the subjectivist theory, holds that .5 is the justified degree of strength of the belief that it will come up heads. Probability theory distinguishes between conditional and unconditional (also known as *A PRIORI* or prior) probability. Suppose it rains where you live on average one out of five days, the unconditional probability that it rains (which might be symbolized as '**P(r)**') is thus .2. But suppose that it rains in April one day in four; then the probability that it rains given that it is April—"conditional upon" it's being April—symbolized as '**P(r/a)**' or '**P(ra)**', is .25. The system of calculating probabilities is called the 'probability CALCULUS'.

problematic   *See* APODEICTIC / ASSERTORIC / PROBLEMATIC.

problem of evil   A problem for religious believers: God is supposed to be all-powerful (He can do anything He wants), benevolent (He wants whatever is good for us), and all-knowing (He knows everything that goes on). Evil is what is bad for us, so God must eliminate all evil. But there clearly is evil. So a God with all of these features does not exist. *See also* THEODICY.

problem of future contingents   *See* FUTURE CONTINGENTS.

problem of identity   Actually several problems: how we establish the IDENTITY[1] or the IDENTITY[4] of things or people. *See also* PERSONAL IDENTITY *and* "BALL OF WAX" EXAMPLE *and* SUBSTANCE.

problem of induction   Everyone believes that the basic regularities we have observed in the past will continue into the
future; this principle is called the 'principle of induction' or
the 'principle of the uniformity of nature'. It is difficult to
see, however, what good grounds we have for believing
this; perhaps it's merely an unjustifiable habit of mind, as
HUME argued. The problem of justifying this belief is called
the 'problem of induction'. (There is also a somewhat different "new" problem [or "riddle"] of induction, due to GOOD-
MAN—*see* GRUE *and* PROJECTIBILITY.)

problem of other minds   If you suppose that your mind and its
contents can be "perceived" directly only by you (*see* PRIVA-
CY^2), this raises the problem of what ground (if any) you
have for thinking that anyone else has a mind, and is not, for
example, just a body with external appearance and behaviour
much like yours. Some philosophers (for example, RYLE)
think that the absurdity of this problem shows that there's
something wrong with the view of the mental that leads
to it.

procedure, decision / effective   *See* ALGORITHM.

process philosophy   *See* WHITEHEAD.

product of sets   *See* INTERSECTION / UNION OF SETS.

product theorem / rule (of probability)   *See* MULTIPLICATION
THEOREM / RULE.

projectibility   We sometimes think that the fact that all A's have
been B's so far justifies us in believing that future A's will be
B's. Thus, being a B is a projectible property. But we don't
count all properties as projectible: being GRUE isn't projectible. Philosophers (most famously, GOODMAN) have discussed the possibility of finding the difference between projectible and unprojectible properties. Goodman called this
the "new riddle of INDUCTION".

projectivism   The view that we project characteristics of a certain sort on to external objects when in fact these are purely in our minds. One might make this claim about colours, for example, or ethical properties.

proletariat   *See* BOURGEOISIE / PROLETARIAT.

proof   *See* ARGUMENT.

proof, indirect   *See* INDIRECT PROOF.

proper names   Is the term 'Mt. Everest' defined as the highest mountain? Then if it turned out that Mt. Schmidlap was a little higher, then Mt. Schmidlap would actually be Mount Everest. But it wouldn't. MILL argued that no proper names have definitions; none is equivalent in meaning to any set of descriptions. Rather, their REFERENCE comes from their direct connection with their object. KRIPKE'S version of this "direct reference" theory argues that the connection between name and named is CAUSAL, and that proper names are RIGID DESIGNATORS. RUSSELL agreed that "logically proper names" (like 'this') refer directly, that is, not via definitionally associated descriptions; but he thought that ordinary proper names aren't "logically proper" but are equivalent to descriptions (the 'descriptivist theory' of proper names).

properties, dispositional   *See* DISPOSITION.

properties, emergent   *See* SUPERVENIENCE.

properties, essential and accidental   *See* ESSENCE / ACCIDENT.

properties, primary / secondary   *See* PRIMARY / SECONDARY QUALITIES.

properties, relational and intrinsic   *See* RELATIONAL / INTRINSIC PROPERTIES.

property   *See* QUALITY / ATTRIBUTE / PROPERTY.

proposition   This term has been used in a confusing variety of ways. Sometimes it means merely a sentence or a statement. Perhaps the most common modern use is the one in which a proposition is what is expressed by a (declarative) sentence: an English sentence and its French translation express the same proposition, and so do 'Seymour is Marvin's father' and 'Marvin's male parent is Seymour'. (A proposition then might be ANALYZED as a SET of POSSIBLE WORLDS.)

propositional attitudes   These are our mental states which are, so to speak, directed at PROPOSITIONS. For example, toward the proposition *It will snow on Christmas,* one can have the propositional attitude of wishing ("I wish that it will snow on Christmas"), believing, fearing, and so on. Compare these with mental states which are not directed at propositions: feeling happy, enjoying an ice cream, remembering Mama.

propositional logic / calculus   *See* SENTENTIAL LOGIC.

propositions, A / E / I / O   *See* A / E / I / O PROPOSITIONS.

propositions, atomic   *See* ATOMIC PROPOSITIONS.

Protagoras   of Abdera (c. 490-421 B.C.) Most famous of the ancient Greek SOPHISTS, known for his doctrine that "man is the measure of all things".

protasis   *See* APODOSIS / PROTASIS.

protocol sentences   Those sentences that express (what are supposed to be) the basic facts we learn IMMEDIATELY[2] by sense-experience and which form the FOUNDATION of our EMPIRICAL knowledge.

proviso, Lockean   *See* LOCKEAN PROVISO.

proximate / remote cause   Imagine a series of events in which each causes the next. The first event is a remote cause of the last (separated by intervening events in the series of causes), but the next-to-last is a proximate (near) cause. *See also* CAUSAL CHAIN.

Proudhon,   Pierre Joseph (1809-1865) French political theorist, associated with UTOPIAN SOCIALISM.

psi   *See* PARANORMAL PHENOMENA.

psychical research   *See* PARANORMAL PHENOMENA.

psychological behaviourism   *See* BEHAVIOURISM.

psychological egoism   *See* EGOISM.

psychological hedonism   *See* HEDONISM.

psychologism   The view that the rules of logic are psychological LAWS OF THOUGHT.

psychology, folk   *See* FOLK PSYCHOLOGY.

psychophysical parallelism   *See* PARALLELISM.

public / private   *See* PRIVACY.

punishment   It is difficult to define this word. Must punishment be unpleasant? If so, then a judge who sentenced someone to not-unpleasant corrective therapy wouldn't be punishing. Must punishment be given in response to a previous bad act? But this would mean that a jail sentence given to an innocent person, either by mistake or to set an example for future wrongdoers, wouldn't count as punishment. A continuing philosophical problem is the attempt to justify the existence of punishment, either in the cases of legal, state-imposed punishment, or in personal instances, as when a parent punishes a child. For major theories, *see* DETERRENCE *and* RETRIBUTIVISM *and* REHABILITATION.

pure reason   **1.** Pure reason is often taken to be reason working on its own, as contrasted with practical reason which connects facts with desires and yields conclusions about what we ought to do. **2.** Pure reason is sometimes spoken of in contrast to EMPIRICAL reason; thus it's *A PRIORI* reasoning, supposedly independent of what we get from the senses. *See* TRUTH OF REASON.

putative   Means 'supposed', with the suggestion that what is supposed is debatable or false.

Putnam,   Hilary (b. 1926) American philosopher with important contributions to philosophy of LOGIC, mathematics, and mind: an early proponent of FUNCTIONALISM.

Pyrrhonism   Originally the extremely SCEPTICAL doctrines of the Greek philosopher Pyrrho (c. 360-270 B.C.) and his followers, hence, any extreme scepticism. ['PEER-on-ism']

Pythagoras   (c. 572-510 B.C.) A PRE-SOCRATIC Greek philosopher and mathematician, supposed to be the discoverer of the theorem about the length of the sides of a right-angled triangle, founder of a mystical religious cult that believed that relations between numbers were at the core of reality.

Q

Q.E.D.   Stands for '*quod erat demonstrandum*' (Latin: "that which was to be demonstrated"). Sometimes written after the conclusion of an ARGUMENT to mark it as the conclusion.

qua   (Latin, "as") Means 'considered as a...'. Thus, one might say that Fred is essentially rational *qua* human being.

quale   *See* QUALIA.

qualia   **1.** = characteristics (old-fashioned use). **2.** = SENSE-DATA. **3.** The characteristics of sensations (of sense-data), distinguished from characteristics of things sensed; for example, the flavour of an apple, as tasted, or the feel of a headache. The existence of qualia is sometimes supposed to be a problem for FUNCTIONALISM. ['Qualia' is plural, pronounced 'QUAH-lee-a'. Its singular is 'quale', pronounced 'QUAH-lay' or 'QUAH-lee']

qualitative identity   *See* IDENTITY[2].

quality / attribute / property   These words are synonyms. They each mean a characteristic of something, anything named by a PREDICATE[3]. Some philosophers argue that a thing cannot be composed entirely of qualities; there must be something else, the thing itself, which these are qualities of, in which these qualities are said to "inhere". *See* SUBSTANCE *and* "BALL OF WAX" EXAMPLE.

quality, essential / accidental   *See* ESSENCE / ACCIDENT.

quality / quantity (of a proposition)   In TRADITIONAL LOGIC, every PROPOSITION is affirmative or negative; these are the 'qualities' of propositions. The A and I propositions have affirmative quality, and the E and O negative. (These letter-names are thought to come from the Latin *AffIrmo*, 'I affirm', and '*nEgO*', 'I deny'.) The quantity of a proposition is either UNIVERSAL (A and E) or PARTICULAR (I and O). *See* A / E / I / O PROPOSITIONS.

quality, primary / secondary   *See*   PRIMARY / SECONDARY QUALITIES.

quantifier   *See* SYMBOLS OF QUANTIFIER LOGIC.

quantifier calculus   *See* QUANTIFIER LOGIC.

quantifier logic   The part of LOGIC that deals with sentences using logical terms such as 'all', 'some', 'no', 'there exists at least one'. Also called 'quantified logic', 'predicate logic', 'predicate calculus', and 'quantifier calculus'. In first-order quantifier logic, quantifiers range only over indivi-duals; in second-order logic, they also range over functions and properties of individuals; in third-order over proper-ties of properties, etc. *See also* SYMBOLS OF QUANTIFIER LOGIC.

quantitative identity   *See* IDENTITY[3].

quantum logic   A LOGIC that attempts to deal with the puzzling sorts of things said in quantum physics. For example, sup-pose that a particle is 50% likely to be in location A, and 50% likely to be in position B; quantum physicists insist that it's neither true that it is in one location nor true that it's in the other. *See* SCHRÖDINGER'S CAT.

quasi-quotes   *See* CORNER QUOTES.

question, begging the   *See* CIRCULAR REASONING / ARGUMENT.

quiddity   In (not terribly) ordinary talk this means 'quibble' or 'trivial subtlety'. In philosophical talk the ESSENCE of a thing is its quiddity.

Quine, Willard Van Orman (1908-2000) American philosopher, author of several important works in LOGIC, METAPHYSICS, and philosophy of language. An EMPIRICIST, but his attack on the "two dogmas of empiricism" (VERIFICATIONISM and the ANALYTIC / SYNTHETIC distinction) has been enormously influential, along with his HOLISM about meaning (*see* INDETERMINACY OF TRANSLATION) and his NATURALISM.

quotational context   *See* OPAQUE / TRANSPARENT.

R

race course paradox   *See* ZENO OF ELEA.

radical translation / interpretation   The process of understanding a language initially totally unknown to you. The notion is associated with QUINE, who argued for the INDETERMINACY OF TRANSLATION on the basis of his discussion of radical translation.

Ramsey,   Frank (Plumpton) (1903-1930) English mathematician and philosopher. Influential works in the philosophy of mathematics and of science. A "Ramsey sentence" is a sentence of the form "There exists something with [this, that, and the other] characteristics." This is intended for substitution in scientific theories for statements about THEORETICAL ENTITIES which otherwise would PRESUPPOSE their existence, or suggest that we know what they are.

Rand,   Ayn *See* WRITERS.

random   *See* CHANCE.

ratiocination   A fancy term meaning 'reasoning'.

rationale   One's reasons for doing something, or the support for some claim.

rational / irrational   Mean, loosely, 'reasonable' / 'unreasonable'. These terms can refer to people, to their beliefs and attitudes, and to their methods of getting beliefs and attitudes. It is possible to distinguish between rationality of means ('instrumental rationality') and rationality of ends: a means is rational when it achieves rational ends. It is more difficult to give a suitable test for the rationality of ends.

rationalism   Broadly, any philosophical position which makes reasoning or rationality extra-important. More particularly the view, contrasted with EMPIRICISM, that reason alone, unaided by sense experience, is capable of reliable and substantive knowledge; rationalists also tend to believe in INNATE ideas. Sometimes by "the rationalists" one means the MODERN CONTINENTAL rationalists DESCARTES, LEIBNIZ, and SPINOZA.

rationality   *See* RATIONAL / IRRATIONAL.

rational self-interest   Acting from self-INTEREST is seeking one's own benefit. Some philosophers have sometimes argued that sometimes one can achieve this only by fulfilling some interests of others too; so they argue that RATIONAL self-interest often involves more than narrow selfishness. *See* PRISONER'S DILEMMA.

raven paradox   When you see a green leaf you see something which is non-black and which is a non-raven. So this CONFIRMS (to a small extent) the general statement that all non-black things are non-ravens. Now, it seems reasonable to think that anything that confirms a general statement **S** also confirms any statement logically equivalent to **S** (*see* BICONDITIONAL). "All non-black things are non-ravens" is logically equivalent to "All ravens are black." So this green leaf confirms (to a small extent) the statement, "All ravens are black." But that seems clearly false: the leaf offers no confirmation at all for that statement. What has gone wrong? This problem for confirmation theory is due to Carl HEMPEL, and is also known as Hempel's paradox.

Rawls,   John (b. 1921) American philosopher, his work *A Theory of Justice* is among the most influential twentieth-century works on ethical and political theory. *See* DIFFERENCE

PRINCIPLE *and* ORIGINAL POSITION *and* VEIL OF IGNORANCE *and* PRINCIPLE OF LIBERTY.

real definition / essence   *See*   NOMINAL / REAL DEFINITION / ESSENCE.

realism / antirealism   In philosophical use, 'realism' does not have its ordinary sense of "free from illusion". It's the view that some sort of entity has external existence, independent of the mind; anti-realists think that that sort of entity is only a product of our thought, perhaps only as a result of an artificial convention ('conventionalism'). Realists quarrel with anti-realists in many philosophical areas. *See* the following entries:

LEGAL REALISM
METAPHYSICAL REALISM
MODAL REALISM
MORAL REALISM
perceptual realism *see* NAÏVE REALISM *and* CRITICAL
   IDEALISM / REALISM
SCIENTIFIC REALISM.

reasoning by analogy   *See*   ANALOGY.

reason, pure   *See*   PURE REASON.

reasons / causes   You sometimes have reasons for doing something, but is this to be understood causally? That is, does that mean that there is a special sort of cause for your action? One reason to think that reasons are not causes is that talk about reasons often mentions the future, but a cause of **x** must occur before **x** does. This is a controversy in ACTION THEORY. *See also* EXPLANATION.

recollection   According to Plato, it is impossible to learn certain things by experience (*see* LEARNER PARADOX); so this sort of knowledge must already be in the mind—remembered, as it were, from the soul's PRE-EXISTENCE before birth among the forms. Also called 'anamnesis'.

recursive   Something (for example, a DEFINITION or a FUNC-
TION) is recursive when it is to be applied over and over again
to its own previous product. For example, one can define
'integer' by saying that 0 is an integer, and if **x** is an integer,
then **x** + 1 is an integer. Thus, applying the second part of this
definition to the first, 1 is an integer, applying the second part
to this result, 2 is an integer, and so on. *See* RECURSIVE.

reductio ad absurdum   **1.** Rules of INFERENCE: (P ⊃ ~P) therefore ~P; and (~P ⊃ P) therefore P. **2.** = INDIRECT PROOF.

reduction   To reduce some notion is to define (or ANALYZE) it
in terms of others, and thus to eliminate it from the list of
basic entities in the field under discussion. Reductionism
about some notion is the idea that that notion can be
reduced—can be given a "reductive analysis". Reductionists
in social science, for example, hold that any statement about
a social phenomenon may be reduced to talk about what individual people do, and social theory may be reduced (at least
IN PRINCIPLE, if not in practice) to psychology (*see*, by contrast, HOLISM). Other reductionisms include psychology to
physiology, biology to chemistry; chemistry to physics;
arithmetic to logic. "Micro-reduction" is reduction to talk
about small (perhaps invisibly small) entities, as sometimes
happens in physics. But reduction can as well go in the other
direction: INSTRUMENTALISTS sometimes argue that talk
about these tiny invisible items in physics should be reduced
to talk about visible large-scale phenomena and measurements.

reductive analysis   *See* REDUCTIONISM.

redundancy theory of truth   This theory claims that 'It's true that
it's raining' means no more than 'It's raining'. That's all there
is to say about 'true'; truth is not a special deep and mysterious
property. (There are genuine questions, however, about how we
find things out.) One redundancy theory is known as the 'disquotational' theory of truth, because it explains the sentence

'The cat is on the mat' is true.

as being equivalent to a sentence which removes the quotation marks:

The cat is on the mat.

Reduncancy theories are sometimes also known as 'deflationary' theories, because they deflate what was taken to be a deep question with a simple answer. A variety of redundency theory, associated with TARSKI, is the semantic theory of truth. For competing theories, *see* TRUTH.

reference   The connection between a noun or noun phrase and something in the world—e.g., between the word 'pig' and any particular pig.

reference, indeterminacy / inscrutability of   *See* INDETERMINACY OF TRANSLATION / REFERENCE.

referentially opaque / transparent   *See* OPAQUE / TRANSPARENT.

reflection   **1.** The process of calm reconsideration, which may lead to a better view of things. **2.** *See* INTROSPECTION. [A chiefly British alternative spelling is 'reflexion.']

reflective equilibrium   A goal sometimes thought to guide one in the construction of theories. A theory is in reflective equilibrium when the basic general principles of the theory square with the particular facts the theory is supposed to explain. We start with beliefs about particulars, and construct some general principles to explain these. Alterations might then be made in other beliefs about particulars when they conflict with the principles, or in the principles when they conflict with beliefs about particulars. Mutual adjustments continue until equilibrium is achieved. GOODMAN proposed this as an account of the construction of a theory of INDUCTION; RAWLS elaborated it for theory-building in ethics.

reflexion   *See* REFLECTION.

reflexive / irreflexive / nonreflexive   A RELATION is reflexive if everything must have that relation to itself. For example, 'is the same age as' is reflexive, because everything must be the same age as itself. But 'has a different address than' is irreflexive, because nothing has a different address than itself. And 'likes' is nonreflexive, because things might or might not like themselves.

refutation   The demonstration by means of ARGUMENT that some position is mistaken. Philosophy students often misuse this word to refer to any attempt to rebut a position: "The Church refuted Galileo's claim that the earth travelled around the sun by appealing to Scripture." Something is refuted, properly speaking, only when it is successfully shown to be false.

regress, infinite   *See* INFINITE REGRESS.

regulative rule   *See* CONSTITUTIVE / REGULATIVE RULE.

rehabilitation   One possible justification for PUNISHMENT: that it will reform the character of the wrongdoer. (This motive is reflected in names for prisons: 'reformatories', and 'penitentiaries', where prisoners are supposed to become "penitent"—to feel remorse for their crimes.) Is this really what we're after? We know that our jails do a terrible job of this, but we want to jail criminals anyway. What if pleasant surroundings reformed criminals better than nasty jails? If reform were our motive, then this should be how we "punish" them—but then the word seems misapplied. For alternative attempts to justify punishment, *see* DETERRENCE *and* RETRIBUTIVISM.

Reichenbach, Hans (1891-1953) German-born American philosopher of science, with important contributions to philosophy of physics and PROBABILITY theory. ['RYE-CHen-baCH']

Reid, Thomas (1710-1796) Scottish philosopher. Founder of

Scottish "COMMON SENSE²" school in reaction against the
SCEPTICISM of British EMPIRICISTS.

reification   The mistaken way of thinking about some abstract
notion as if it were a real thing. (*See* ABSTRACT / CONCRETE
ENTITIES / IDEAS.) Thus, it could be argued that although it
makes sense to talk about something as being absolutely (i.e.,
completely) such-and-such, the way some philosophers think
of the ABSOLUTE, as if it were a real thing, is merely a reification. ['REE-uh-fih-KAY-shun'] 'Hypostatization' is a more
or less synonymous term, though it sometimes suggests the
ascription of material existence in particular. ['hy-POS-tuh-ti-
ZAY-shun'] *See also* CONCRETE.

reincarnation   The reappearance of the soul or mind or person,
following bodily death, in a different body. Also called
'metempsychosis' and 'transmigration [of souls]'.

relational / intrinsic properties   A property is intrinsic if things
have that property in themselves, rather than in relation to
other things. Thus being 100 meters tall is an intrinsic
property, but being the tallest building in town is a relational property, because this is relative to the heights of
other buildings in town. *See* CAMBRIDGE CHANGE / PROPER-
TY; *see also* INTRINSIC / INHERENT / INSTRUMENTAL /
EXTRINSIC.

relation of ideas   *See* MATTER OF FACT / RELATION OF IDEAS.

relations   Connections, comparisons, or associations between
two or more things. Thus 'smaller than' names one sort of
relation, in this case a two-place ('binary' or 'dyadic') relation. There are also three-place relations (e.g., the one named
by the PREDICATE '____ is located between ____ and ____ '),
four-place, and so on. The items related by a relation are
called its 'relata'. [plural; singular form is 'relatum'] For
some logical types of relations *see*:
    REFLEXIVE / IRREFLEXIVE / NONREFLEXIVE

SYMMETRIC / ASYMMETRIC / NONSYMMETRIC
TRANSITIVE / INTRANSITIVE / NONTRANSITIVE.

relations, internal / external *See* INTERNAL / EXTERNAL
RELATIONS.

relative identity Whether **x** (at one time) and **y** (at another) are
IDENTICAL[4] depends, some philosophers argue, on what sort
of things **x** and **y** are identified as. If a bronze statue was
melted and cooled, then the statue has been destroyed; so **x**
(the statue) is not identical with the resulting lump of bronze.
But, considered as a piece of bronze, **x** is still around: it's **y**.
So identity is relative to what sort of thing we count objects
as.

relativism / absolutism Relativists argue that when certain
views vary among individual people and among cultures
('cultural relativism') there is no universal truth: there is
instead, only "true for me (or us); false for you (or them)".
This contrasts with absolutism (sometimes called 'objectivism'): the position that there is an objectively right view.
The most common relativist views concern morality ('ethical
relativism'), but some philosophers have been relativists
about a number of other matters, including the nature of reality itself (*see* ONTOLOGICAL RELATIVISM; *see also* SUBJEC-
TIVE / OBJECTIVE *and* MORAL REALISM).

relevance logic In ordinary logic, any PREMISES, even irrelevant ones, IMPLY a TAUTOLOGY; and CONTRADICTORY
premises imply any conclusion, even an irrelevant one. Relevance logics attempt to exclude these cases by restricting
logical implications to cases in which the premises are relevant to the conclusion. The problem they face is to give a
good account of what relevance is.

reliabilism For **S** to know that **p**, **S** must believe **p**, and **p** must
be true. But this is not enough, because a guess that happens
to be true is not knowledge. What else to add? Reliabilists
add that **S** must have come to believe **p** by a generally reli-

able process—one that usually yields true belief. (But note that on this simple version of reliabilism, the problem of GETTIER EXAMPLES still arises.) *See also* TRACKING THE TRUTH.

religious experience argument for God's existence   *See* MYSTICAL EXPERIENCE ARGUMENT FOR GOD'S EXISTENCE.

remote cause   *See* PROXIMATE / REMOTE CAUSE.

Renaissance   The period (fourteenth through sixteenth century) characterized by the diminution of the authority of the Church in favour of a new HUMANISM, and the rapid growth of science.

representationalism   Theories that hold that mental contents— thoughts, perceptions, etc.—represent reality. If these representations are the only thing directly available to the mind, how do we know that the external world is actually being represented—and what it is really like? DESCARTES and LOCKE were among the representationalists.

Rescher,   Nicholas (b. 1928) Astoundingly productive American philosopher who has published over fifty books and innumerable articles. He calls his philosophical system "PRAGMATIC IDEALISM".

res cogitans / res extensa   (Latin: "thinking thing" / "extended thing") Having established the CERTAINTY of his own existence (*See COGITO ERGO SUM*) DESCARTES asked, "But what am I?" and answered that he has established the existence of himself only as a thing-that-thinks—a *res cogitans*. The contrast is with "extended things"—the other category of existence— physical stuff. ['RACE CO-gee-tans' / 'RACE EX-TENS-uh']

residues, method of   *See* MILL'S METHODS.

responsibility   We are said to be responsible when it is "up to us" what we do. Moral responsibility is responsibility for morally relevant (good or bad) actions; we can be praised or blamed only for those actions for which we are morally responsible. *See also* FREE WILL *and* COLLECTIVE RESPONSIBILITY *and* DIMINISHED RESPONSIBILITY.

resurrection   Rising again from the grave. Christians think that Christ was resurrected, and that resurrection of the dead will occur at the Last Judgment.

retributivism   The DETERRENCE and REHABILITATION theories claim PUNISHMENTS are justified when they have good effects: for example, the prevention of future bad acts through the deterrent threat of punishment to others, or the reform of the wrongdoer. Retributivists claim that such uses of punishment are immoral, and that punishment is justified for wrongdoers merely because wrongdoing demands it—because it's JUSTICE—or a restoration of the moral order—to inflict punishment on wrongdoers. Retributivists also claim that the severity of punishment should fit the severity of the crime, sometimes they go so far as to advocate that the criminal's suffering should equal that caused by the crime ("An eye for an eye, a tooth for a tooth"). Versions of retributivism are advocated by KANT and HEGEL. This position is sometimes criticized as merely advocating revenge.

retrocausation   "Backward" causation, in which the effect occurs before the cause. The possibility of retrocausation is debatable.

retrodiction   Means 'prediction backwards'—"prediction" of the past. A historian might retrodict, for example, on the basis of certain historical documents, that a battle took place centuries ago at a certain location. This retrodiction can be CONFIRMED by present evidence, for example, by artifacts of war dug up at that site.

return, eternal   *See* ETERNAL RETURN.

revelation   Knowledge revealed to us directly by God (or through Jesus or the Bible) distinguished from what we find out by using our senses, or by reasoning—the techniques used by NATURAL RELIGION.

rhetoric   **1.** Persuasive or expressive, showy or elaborate language, or the study of this. Sometimes ("mere") rhetoric is distinguished from genuine ARGUMENT, when it is supposed that the former is not a good means for persuasion. SOCRATES accused the SOPHISTS of substituting rhetoric for argument. But there are legitimate uses of persuasive language, so the theory of rhetoric is an important area of LOGIC. **2.** A rhetorical question is one that is asked when no answer is expected, or when the answer is obvious. Some students have the bad habit of over-using the rhetorical question in their papers, where they are supposed to answer questions, not merely ask them.

Ricoeur,   Paul (b. 1913) French philosopher and theologian, known for his HERMENEUTIC approach to topics such as the will and evil.

right   *See* GOOD / RIGHT.

rights   You are said to have a right to do or have something when it is thought that nobody should be allowed to keep you from it. Thus, we can speak of a right to property, or to vote, or to life. Having a right to do something doesn't mean you ought to do it, but merely that you're allowed to do it if you want. UTILITARIANS might be able to justify according certain rights, but usually rights-theorists insist that a right is independent of UTILITY: that someone morally can exercise a genuine right even if it is contrary to the general welfare. (For reasons like this, the arch-utilitarian BENTHAM called talk of rights "nonsense upon stilts".) An "inalienable right" is a right that one cannot give up or get rid of. Thus, the right to my car is alienable; I can give it up by selling it. But on some theories the right not to be enslaved is something one cannot give up (for example, by selling one's self into slavery) even if one wanted to. A civil right is a right that is (or ought to be) guaranteed and enforced by government. (Nobody thinks that government ought to enforce all our rights; I have the right to whistle in the shower, but I don't want or need government enforcement for this.) Conventional rights are rights produced or guaranteed by society (by government or agreement, or just by custom). Natural rights, on the other hand, are rights we are supposed to have just because we are human (perhaps because they are God-given).

rigid / flaccid designator   A rigid designator (Saul KRIPKE'S term) is a term that refers to the same thing in every other POSSIBLE WORLD in which it exists. Kripke argued that PROPER NAMES are normally rigid designators. Thus, to say that Fred might have been bald is to say that there is another possible world in which Fred is bald. DEFINITE DESCRIPTIONS, on the other hand, are usually not rigid designators, so are sometimes called 'flaccid designators'. ['FLAK-sid']. In this world, 'the highest mountain' is Everest, but 'the highest mountain' does not refer to the same thing in other possible worlds. Thus, when we say 'Mount Ranier might have been the highest mountain', we don't mean that there's another possible world in which Mount Ranier is Mount Everest (*see* COUNTERFACTUAL).

ring of Gyges   *See* HOBBES'S FOOLE.

Romanticism   The name of a wide variety of cultural and philosophical movements associated with the period from the late eighteenth through the mid-nineteenth century. Philosophically, this is associated with the distrust of rationality and ANALYSIS, and is thought of as a reaction against earlier ENLIGHTENMENT thought. SCHOPENHAUER is a good example of a Romantic philosopher.

Rorty,   Richard (b. 1931) American PRAGMATIST philosopher, the author of a good deal of influential work; famous (or infamous) for his defense of the dreaded CONTINENTALS to the ANALYTIC school, and for his rather POSTMODERN methodology.

Ross, W[illiam] D[avid] (1877-1971) English classical scholar and ethical theorist.

Rousseau, Jean-Jacques (1712-1778) French ENLIGHTENMENT philosopher, one of the ENCYCLOPEDISTS, responsible for important works in moral theory and for the view that society corrupts the natural goodness of humans (*see* NOBLE SAVAGE), but is legitimated by a SOCIAL CONTRACT that represents the GENERAL WILL. His views were influential on the French Revolution.

Royce, Josiah (1855-1916) American philosopher, the leading American IDEALIST of his time.

rule / principle Sometimes the distinction is made in philosophy of LAW between a rule and a principle of (civil) law: a rule is strict, without exceptions or borderline cases, but a principle is more VAGUE and may be overridden. It is a principle (not a rule) of certain systems of law, for example, that one can't profit from one's illegal acts; but one is nevertheless allowed to keep the money one has earned while out of jail because of having escaped. Against this distinction, it has been argued that nothing in law should—or even could—be exceptionless, anticipating all possible exceptions.

rule of inference A rule for reasoning from one statement to another, for example, *MODUS PONENS*.

rule utilitarianism *See* UTILITARIANISM.

Russell, Bertrand (Arthur William) (1872-1970) British philosopher, perhaps the best-known philosopher of the twentieth century. Founder (with WHITEHEAD) of contemporary SYMBOLIC LOGIC; leader (with MOORE) of the twentieth-century revolt against IDEALISM[2], though some of his views—for example his PHENOMENALISM about our knowledge of externals—tended to be less in accord with COMMON SENSE[2] than Moore's. A controversial public figure because of his pacifism, his criticism of Christianity, and his advocacy of freer sexual morality; because of his views he was fired from teaching positions and jailed. "Russell's paradox" asks us to consider the SET of sets that are not members of themselves. Is this set a member of itself? If it is, it isn't. If it isn't, it is. Consideration of Russell's PARADOX has resulted in some complications in set theory. For Russell's own reaction, see THEORY OF TYPES.

Ryle, Gilbert (1900-1976) English (Oxford) philosopher, leading early figure in ANALYTIC and ORDINARY LANGUAGE philosophy. Important works in philosophy of LOGIC and of mind; in *The Concept of Mind* he argued that CARTESIAN DUALISM was based on a CATEGORY MISTAKE.

S

Saint ... *See* under name that follows 'Saint' *or* 'St.'. E.g., for Saint Augustine, *see* AUGUSTINE.

Saint Petersburg paradox Flip a fair coin till tails turns up. The payoff is 2^n, where n is the number of flips. The EXPECTED UTILITY of this game is $(1/2 \times \$2) + (1/4 \times \$4) + (1/8 \times \$8)$ ... This is an infinite amount, so you should be willing to pay any amount, no matter how large, to play. What has gone wrong with this reasoning?

Saint-Simon, (Claude-Henri de Rouvroy,) Comte de (1760-1825) French social (and SOCIALIST) philosopher, influenced MARX.

Salmon, Wesley (b. 1925) American philosopher of science and logic, with influential work on explanation and scientific methodology.

salva veritate (Latin: "saving the truth") Means 'keeping the truth or falsity (of a sentence) the same'. A TERM may always be replaced in a transparent context *salva veritate*, but not in an opaque context (*see* OPAQUE / TRANSPARENT). ['SAL-vuh ver-uh-TAH-tay']

sanction A good or bad result of an action that motivates (or is designed to motivate) us to do it (or not to), sometimes as provided by civil LAW.

Sandel, Michael (b. 1953) American political theorist, interested in the relations between the individual and the community; critic of liberal individualism. (*See* HOLISM / INDIVIDUALISM.)

Santayana, George (1863-1952) (Original name Jorge Augustin Nicolas Ruiz de Santayana) Philosopher and literary writer, born in Spain but grew up and worked in the U.S. His views were a blend of MATERIALISM and PLATONISM, with emphasis on the AESTHETIC viewpoint.

Sartre, Jean-Paul (1905-1980) Widely known French proponent of EXISTENTIALISM; author of important philosophical and literary works expressing the view that humans have no fixed ESSENCE, but live in, and constantly attempt to escape from, a terrifying FREEDOM[1]. [The closest English-speakers usually can get to the French pronunciation of his name is 'sar-truh']

satisfice To satisfice is to accept what is good enough, rather than to hold out for what would be the best. Sometimes satisficing is the better strategy for decision making. It's an alternative to the maximization proposed in the theories of some UTILITARIANS and economists.

Saussure, Ferdinand de (1857-1913) Swiss linguist and philosopher, founder of structural linguistics and influential on later more general STRUCTURALISM. ['so-soor']

scepticism The view that knowledge in some area is not possible. Philosophical scepticism doesn't come just from a FEELING or personality quirk: it needs to be supported by ARGUMENT. Someone who holds this view is called a sceptic; the Sceptics were a group of (sceptical!) Greek philosophers, including PYRRHO and his followers. HUME is the champion of modern scepticism. Sceptics often don't actually doubt the truth of the belief about which they are sceptical: their central claim is that we don't have JUSTIFICATION[1] for that belief, and thus can't be said to know it. [may also be spelled 'skepticism' and 'skeptic'; spellings with 'scep-' are preferred by the British] *See also* DOUBT.

Schelling, Friedrich Wilhelm Joseph von (1775-1854) German idealist philosopher; combined ROMANTIC and KANTIAN approaches.

schema   A rule or category that we use to organize, understand, and formulate what we think about. [plural 'schemata']

Schleiermacher   Friedrich (Daniel Ernst) (1768-1834) German philosopher. His influential writing on religion proposed that it be seen as primarily emotional rather than rational. A founder of HERMENEUTICS. ['SCHLY-er-maCH-er']

Schlick,   [Friedrich Albert] Moritz (1882-1936) German founder of the VIENNA CIRCLE, leading figure in the development of LOGICAL POSITIVISM. Killed by one of his students!

scholasticism   Characterizes MEDIEVAL philosophy as done by the scholastics—"schoolmen"—in medieval European universities: both strongly Christian and heavily reliant on the ancients, especially ARISTOTLE. ANSELM, THOMAS AQUINAS, DUNS SCOTUS, and OCKHAM were scholastics. The adjective 'scholastic' has come to have pejorative overtones, suggesting pedantry, dogmatism, and endless debate over the number of angels capable of dancing on the head of a pin. But the scholastics also produced a great deal of genuinely important philosophy.

Schopenhauer,   Arthur (1788-1860) German philosopher, known for his emphasis on "Will" in the world—an irrational and blind force behind all change—and for his advocacy of an attitude of detached PESSIMISTIC resignation. ['SHOW-pen-how-er']

Schrödinger's cat   The Austrian physicist Erwin Schrödinger (1887-1961) gave his name to this example, which vividly illustrates a paradoxical consequence of quantum physics: Imagine a cat in a closed box will be killed by a mechanism activated by a certain quantum-indeterminate event. Until someone looks into the box, the cat is neither wholly alive nor wholly dead, but rather alive and dead each to a certain degree. *See also* QUANTUM LOGIC.

science   Science and philosophy have always been closely connected. Until recent centuries, the two disciplines were not separated: there was no "science", as such, just "natural philosophy". Since then fundamental science and philosophy, though distinguishable disciplines, nevertheless have had a great deal of mutual influence. And the line between the two is blurred by recent tendencies to NATURALIZE philosophy, and to emphasize the moral, METAPHYSICAL, and *A-PRIORI* aspects of scientific theory-building, especially when that theory is basic and revolutionary.

science, unity of   *See* UNITY OF SCIENCE.

scientific image   *See* MANIFEST / SCIENTIFIC IMAGE.

scientific realism   Scientific realists sometimes hold that THEORETICAL ENTITIES are mind-independent, or that LAWS in science reflect external realities (so are not just constructed by us), or that the categories of successful science are real and mind-independent NATURAL KINDS. (*See also* REALISM.)

scientists   Several thinkers whom we think of now primarily as scientists deserve mention in this dictionary. In many cases, they dabbled in philosophical speculation rather extrinsic to their scientific work, but this work is rarely noteworthy. What has made each of them philosophically important is either the philosophical work they did connected closely to their science, or the philosophical implications, drawn by others, of their scientific theories and methods.

> Arrow, Kenneth Joseph (b. 1921) American economist and social theorist.
> Bohr, Niels (1885-1962) Danish physicist with very important (and philosophically provocative) work in atomic theory and nuclear physics.

Boyle, Robert (1627-1691) English chemist/physicist. Theory of gasses: Boyle's Law.

Copernicus, Nicolaus (1473-1543) Polish astronomer, considered responsible for the adoption of the view that the earth goes around the sun, not vice versa.

Darwin, Charles (Robert) (1809-1882) English naturalist. Theory of evolution.

Duhem, Pierre (Maurice Marie) (1861-1916) French theoretical physicist. Work on the nature of scientific LAWS and THEORIES.

Durkheim, Émile (1858-1917) French sociologist. The foundations of sociology.

Eddington, (Sir) Arthur (Stanley) (1882-1944) British astronomer / physicist. The EPISTEMOLOGY of physics.

Einstein, Albert (1879-1955) German-born American theoretical physicist. Theory of Relativity.

Fanon, Franz (1925-61) Psychiatrist born in Martinique, known in philosophical circles for his writing on violence and colonialism.

Faraday, Michael (1791-1867) British chemist/physicist. Conservation of energy law; electricity and magnetism.

Freud, Sigmund (1856-1939) Austrian psychologist. Psychoanalysis; the unconscious. ['froyd']

Galileo (Galilei) (1564-1642) Italian astronomer/physicist. Taken as a hero of scientific SCEPTICISM and the battle for scientific autonomy. Celestial and mechanical theory.

Gilligan, Carol (b. 1936) American psychologist. Her claims that women characteristically think in terms of caring rather than justice have influenced many FEMINIST ethicists.

Hayek, Friedrich August von (1899-1992). Known primarily as an economist; his SCEPTICISM about the possibility of individual knowledge led to a defense of conservative social policy.

Heisenberg, Werner (1901-1976) German atomic physicist. The UNCERTAINTY PRINCIPLE.

Helmholtz, (Baron) Hermann (Ludwig Ferdinand) von (1821-1894) German physician/physicist/mathematician. Work on perception, EMPIRICISM, philosophy of physics.

Huxley, Thomas Henry (1825-1895) British biologist. Philosophy of Science, anti-religious MATERIALISM; champion of Darwinism.

Jung, Carl (Gustav) (1875-1961) Swiss psychologist. Postulated a "collective unconscious" with innate "archetypes" structuring our mental lives; speculated influentially on mythology, religion. ['yung']

Kepler, Johannes (1571-1630) German astronomer/ physicist / mathematician. Elliptical planetary motion; gravitation.

Keynes, John Maynard (first Baron Keynes) (1883-1946) British economist. His economics has influenced social theory; important work, in addition, on INDUCTION, PROBABILITY. ['kaynz']

Lamarck, Chevalier de (title of Jean Baptiste Pierre Antoine de Monet) (1744-1829) French naturalist. An early scientific theory of evolution.

Laplace, Pierre-Simon, (Marquis de) (1749-1827) French mathematician / astronomer. DETERMINISM, PROBABILITY theory.

Leonardo da Vinci (1452-1519) Florentine engineer/ artist. The "mathematization" of science.

Malthus, Thomas (Robert) (1766-1834) English economist. Moral philosophy, theology.

Maxwell, James Clerk (1831-1879) Scottish physicist. Colour vision, molecular theory, and electromagnetic theory.

Newton, Sir Isaac (1642-1727) English mathematician/ scientist. The Newtonian revolution in physics.

Pareto, Vilfredo (1848-1923) French-born Italian economist/sociologist. ['pa-RAY-to']

Piaget, Jean (1896-1980) Swiss psychologist; his hypotheses about cognitive development have been an important influence on some EPISTEMOLOGISTS. ['pee-ah-zhay']

Planck, Max (Karl Ernst Ludwig) (1858-1947) German physicist. The "quantized" nature of radiation. ['plonk']

Poincaré, Jules Henri (1854-1912) French mathematician / physicist. ['pwAN-ca-ray']

Sen, Amartya K. (b. 1933) Indian philosopher/economist working in the US

Skinner, B(urrhus) F(rederic) (1904-1990) American psychologist. Behaviourism.

Smith, Adam (1723-1790) Scottish political economist.

Watson, J(ohn) B(roadus) (1878-1958) American psychologist. The foundations of behaviouristic psychology.

Weber, [Karl Emil] Max[imilian] (1864-1920) German sociologist / historian. ['vAY-bair']

scientific image   *See* MANIFEST / SCIENTIFIC IMAGE.

scientific realism   *See* REALISM.

Scottish common sense philosophy   *See* COMMON SENSE².

Scotus   *See* DUNS SCOTUS.

sea battle example   *See* FUTURE CONTINGENTS.

Searle, John [Rogers] (b. 1932) Contemporary American philosopher best known for his work on the SPEECH ACT theory in philosophy of language, and for the CHINESE ROOM EXAMPLE in philosophy of mind.

secondary qualities   *See* PRIMARY / SECONDARY QUALITIES.

second-order logic   *See* QUANTIFIER LOGIC.

self-caused   *See* CAUSE-OF-ITSELF.

self-consciousness   In ordinary use, a self-conscious person is one who feels embarrassed or behaves unnaturally, as if under critical observation by others. In philosophical use, this often means the sort of knowledge one has of one's self that one gets by adopting the perspective that others might have of one; or else the sort of self-awareness one gets by INTROSPECTION. The EXISTENTIALISTS thought that self-awareness made for FREEDOM[1].

self-contradiction   A statement is self-contradictory when it asserts and denies the same thing ('It's raining and it's not raining'), or when it's logically false (*see* LOGICAL TRUTH / FALSITY). An inconsistent set is self-contradictory (*see* CONSISTENCY). Sometimes (more loosely, and rather incorrectly) a statement that is analytically false (*see* ANALYTIC / SYNTHETIC) is called a self-contradiction: for example, 'Fred is a married bachelor'.

self-deception   The process of convincing yourself (or trying to) of the truth of what you know is false (or vice versa), because you want to believe it. For the EXISTENTIALISTS, BAD FAITH is a typical form of attempted self-deception. A problem: can you really succeed in convincing yourself that something is true while you also really believe it's false?

self-defeating belief   *See* SELF-FULFILLING / DEFEATING.

self-evident   Obviously true, so in need of no JUSTIFICATION[1].

self-fulfilling / defeating   A self-fulfilling belief is one that makes itself true, or tends to. For example, the belief that other people think you're strange will often make you act strangely, and will as a result make people think you're strange. On a positive note, the belief that you will do well in an exam will sometimes be self-fulfilling, if as a result of this belief you go into the exam relaxed and confident, and thus do well. The belief that you have a belief is self-fulfilling (having that belief makes it true). A related concept is the 'self-fulfilling prophecy'. A self-defeating belief is one that tends to make itself false. A procedure is self-defeating when it makes achievement of its own goals less likely. For example it has been argued that UTILITARIANISM is self-defeating, because a society of people pursuing happiness will have a reduced total quantity of happiness in it.

self-interest   *See* SELFISHNESS *and* RATIONAL SELF-INTEREST.

selfishness   Someone who is selfish is interested only in his/her own benefit, that is, self-interest (*see* EGOISM). This is nasty when it involves seeking one's own benefit only, and at others' expense; but some philosophers argue that the rational pursuit of one's own benefit would necessitate sometimes looking after others' benefit as well (*see* RATIONAL SELF-INTEREST).

self-reference   Something is self-referential when it REFERS to itself. The word 'word' refers to itself (among other things). The sentence 'This sentence is false' is self-referential. Synonyms for 'self-referential' are 'autological' and 'homological'; 'heterological' means non-self-referential. Self-reference can lead to logical puzzles and PARADOXES; *see*, for example,

BARBER PARADOX
LIAR'S PARADOX
GRELLING'S PARADOX
PREFACE PARADOX.

Sellars,   Wilfrid (1912-1989) American philosopher, influential as a critic of FOUNDATIONALIST EPISTEMOLOGY and as an advocate of FUNCTIONALISM about mind.

semantics / syntax / pragmatics   These terms name aspects of language and the study of these aspects. Semantics is that part of language which has to do with meaning and REFERENCE. Syntax has to do with GRAMMAR or LOGICAL FORM. Syntax, then, can tell you whether a sentence is formed correctly (for example, 'Is the on but but' is not formed correctly), but cannot tell you what a correctly formed sentence means, or what conditions would make it true. Pragmatics concerns the relations between bits of language and their uses by language-users.

semantic theory of truth   *See* REDUNDANCY THEORY OF TRUTH. For competing theories, *see* TRUTH.

semantic holism   *See* HOLISM / INDIVIDUALISM.

semiotics   The general study of symbols in language. For a description of its branches, see SEMANTICS / SYNTAX / PRAGMATICS. ['seh' or 'see' + 'mee' or 'my' + 'AH-ticks']

sensa / sensum   *See* SENSE-DATA.

sense-data   The DATA of the senses—what they give us: the internal event or picture or representation we get when perceiving external objects—or sometimes, as when we dream or hallucinate, even in their absence. A straight stick half under water looks bent; we then have a bent sense-datum, the same sort of internal picture we would have if we saw a bent stick out of water. The ARGUMENT FROM ILLUSION is supposed to show that all we really directly (IMMEDIATELY[2]) perceive are sense-data, and that we only infer external objects from these. The term was invented by MOORE. Note that 'sense-data' is plural: the singular form is 'sense-datum'. Also known as 'sensa' (singular 'sensum').

sense qualia   *See* QUALIA[2].

sense / reference   *See* DENOTATION / CONNOTATION.

sensible knave   *See* HOBBES'S FOOLE.

sensibles   *See* SENSIBILIA.

sensibilia   Things not being perceived, but capable of being perceived. Realists count unperceived external objects as these; but those who believe that SENSE-DATA are the only direct objects of perception sometimes think that sensibilia are unsensed sense data—a highly problematic notion. 'Sensibilia' is plural; the singular is 'sensibile'. Sensibilia are also called 'sensibles'.

sentence, open   *See* SYMBOLS OF QUANTIFIER LOGIC.

sentences, protocol   *See* PROTOCOL SENTENCES.

sentential logic   'Sentential' is the adjectival form of 'sentence'. Sentential LOGIC (also called 'the sentential CALCULUS', 'the TRUTH-FUNCTIONAL calculus', 'the propositional calculus', etc.) is that part of logic which deals with the way sentences are combined to form other sentences. For example, 'Snow is white' and 'Pigs fly' may be combined by logical connectives to form such sentences as 'Snow is white or pigs don't fly' and 'If snow is white, then pigs fly and snow isn't white'.

set   A collection of things (called its 'members'). Set theory is the abstract study of the way we reason about sets. A unit set is a set with exactly one thing in it (e.g., the set of first presidents of the US). The null set is the set with nothing in it—the empty set. Sometimes 'class' is used synonymously with 'set', but they can be distinguished in one or the other of these ways: (1) A set is any old collection (for example, there is a two-member set consisting of the Eiffel Tower and your left big toe), whereas a class is a collection of things defined by a common characteristic. (2) Set theorists sometimes say that sets can be members of other sets, but classes cannot. (*See also* INTERSECTION / UNION OF SETS.)

sets, fuzzy   *See* FUZZY SETS / LOGIC.

sex   *See* GENDER / SEX.

sexism   By analogy with the word 'racism', this is the set of attitudes and practices involving discrimination and oppression on the basis of sex, most often against women. A central concern of FEMINISM has been to expose and combat sexism.

Sextus Empiricus   (c. 200) Greek philosopher, the best-known ancient SCEPTIC. His best-known view is that real knowledge is impossible.

shepherd, Lydian   *See* HOBBES'S FOOLE.

Sheffer stroke   A non-standard SYMBOL OF SENTENTIAL LOGIC: (P | Q) means 'not both P and Q'. With this alone one can symbolize all TRUTH-FUNCTIONAL relations. ~P is (P | P); (P v Q) is (P | P) | (Q | Q), and so on.

ship of Theseus   A story (found in HOBBES'S writing and elsewhere) used to raise a puzzle about IDENTITY[4]: Suppose that Theseus owns a wooden ship, which is renovated while in use by replacing one plank at a time, till everything has been replaced; the removed planks are stored, and when the renovation is complete, the stored planks are used to build a second ship just like the first. Which of the two is the original ship?

Shoemaker, Sydney (b. 1931) American philosopher, with influential writings on METAPHYSICS and mind.

Sidgwick, Henry (1838-1900) English philosopher and economist. He is best known for his books on ETHICS in which he argued that none of the major ethical theories alone is adequate.

simple / complex ideas   A COMPLEX IDEA is one that can be analyzed into simpler ideas. 'Brother', for example, names a complex idea that is "composed" of the ideas of male and sibling; but 'green' perhaps names a simple idea.

simple supposition   *See* SUPPOSITION.

simpliciter   (Latin: "simply") Without qualification, not just in certain respects. ['sim-PLISS-uh-tur']

simplification   A rule of INFERENCE that permits inference from (P & Q) to P or to Q.

Simpson's paradox   Its surprising result is that something can be true of each subset of a group but false of the whole. For example, it's possible that Fred has a lower batting average than Sam against left-handed pitchers, and a lower batting average than Sam against right-handed-pitchers, but a higher overall batting average. How can that be? Here's a possible scenario in which it's true:

	FRED	SAM
Against lefties	28/100 = .280	6/20 = .300
Against righties	9/50 = .180	20/100 = .200
Overall	37/150 = .246	26/120 = .216

Singer,   Peter [Albert David] (b. 1946) Australian CONSEQUEN-TIALIST ethicist whose views on "animal liberation" have made him quite visible outside the confines of academic philosophy.

Sinn   *See* DENOTATION / CONNOTATION.

situation ethics   Holds that there is no general ethical standard that can be uniformly applied; there is no characteristic such that any act with that characteristic is wrong. Each situation should be considered on its own, in all its specificity. This position caused a bit of a scandal a few decades ago in more conservative religious circles when it was popularized by some unconventional theologian/moralists. Nowadays, something like it is advocated by some FEMINISTS.

skepticism   *See* SCEPTICISM.

Skruijü, Kristu (Latin name Cristus Scruius) (4th century) Albanian theologian, known for his anticipation of the HEGELIAN DIALECTIC[5]. ['SKROO-you']

slave / master morality   NIETZSCHE thought that there were two sorts of "moralities"—ways of thinking about the self, right and wrong, and society. Slave morality involves cooperation and self-negation, fear of change and obedience. Master morality reflects the WILL TO POWER, and is appropriate for the "SUPERMAN".

slice, time   *See* IDENTITY[4].

slippery slope   A form of moral reasoning in which it is argued that some act or practice is undesirable not because it's bad in itself, but because its acceptance will or might lead to a series of other acts that differ from each other in small ways, and eventuate in something clearly bad. It might be argued, for example, that a city's allowing street vendors on one corner isn't in itself bad, but this might gradually lead to more and more permissiveness, resulting eventually in the clogging of city sidewalks by all sorts of undesirables. This sort of reasoning is a form of SORITES argument.

Smart, J[ohn] J[amieson] C[arswell] (b. 1920) English/Australian philosopher best known for his enthusiastic MATERIALISM about mind, but also important for his ethical non-COGNITIVISM, and energetic UTILITARIANISM.

Smith, Adam *See* SCIENTISTS.

social choice theory   The study of various methods for aggregating the preferences of many different individuals to yield a collective GENERAL WILL.

social contract   A way of justifying the LEGITIMACY of a ruler or government, or the restrictions imposed by government or by moral rules, on the basis of an agreement (whether explicit or tacit) of the people involved. It is supposed that people agree (or would agree) to these restrictions because of the resulting long-range benefits to everyone. This agreement is called a 'social contract'. Thinking about this (often merely hypothetical) social contract is intended to provide not an actual history of the origin of these rules, but rather a JUSTI-FICATION[1] of their existence and of their binding force. This is the sort of justification of rules given by contractarians, among whom are HOBBES, LOCKE, ROUSSEAU, and RAWLS. *See also* STATE OF NATURE *and* VEIL OF IGNORANCE.

social Darwinism   *See* EVOLUTION.

socialism / communism   In general, both socialists and communists advocate that there be a classless society, that there be public ownership of the means of production. Both terms are closely associated with the thought of MARX and with the former Eastern bloc countries, though both systems have existed (in various partial forms) elsewhere and at other times. In some uses, 'communism' (especially with a capital 'C') is a more restricted term, referring only to Marxist-LENINIST societies; communism is thought to be more AUTHORITARIAN than socialism, and to use more extreme and repressive measures (one hears the phrase 'democratic socialism' but not 'democratic communism'). Sometimes the two are distinguished by the communist addition to socialism that people work according to their abilities and receive goods according to their needs. In a popular inaccurate use, 'communism' refers to any radical view regarded as revolutionary or subversive.

Socrates   (c. 470-399 B.C.) Athenian philosopher whose debates were chronicled by PLATO. Extremely influential for what's now called "Socratic method": his continual questioning of his opponents, leading them to analyze their own assumptions and to reveal their inadequacy. PARADOX was an important philosophical tool for SOCRATES, sometimes as a way of showing the absurd consequences of a view he wanted to argue against, but sometimes just as an unresolved puzzle. So 'Socratic paradox' might refer to a number of different ones; but often what's referred to is Socrates' position that nobody ever does wrong knowingly. (This is an odd view, but perhaps not exactly a paradox.) He rejected the SCEPTICAL and RELATIVISTIC views of the professional debaters of the day, urging a return to ABSOLUTE ideals. He was condemned to death for impiety and for corrupting youth.

soft determinism   *See* FREE WILL.

solipsism   The position that the self is the only thing that can be known, or, more extremely, that one's own mind is the only thing that exists in the universe. Nobody sane ever believed this latter view, but it is philosophically interesting to try to REFUTE it. Someone who believed solipsism would be called a 'solipsist'. ['SAHL-ip-sism', 'SAHL-ip-sist'] (*See also* METHODOLOGICAL SOLIPSISM.)

solipsism, methodological   *See* METHODOLOGICAL SOLIPSISM.

solo numero   (Latin: "by number alone") Two things differ *solo numero* when they are precisely alike in every detail, but are two distinct things (i.e., are "numerically"—quantitatively—distinct) (*see* IDENTITY[3]). The existence of difference *solo numero* is impossible according to the law of the identity of indiscernibles. *See* LAW OF THE INDISCERNIBILITY OF IDENTICALS.)

sophism   An ARGUMENT that is subtle and convincing, but mistaken (though sometimes 'sophism' refers in particular to the FALLACIES of AMBIGUITY). Sophistry is arguing using sophisms. Named after the Sophists, ancient Greek travelling philosophers who taught for a fee, because they were thought to use such arguments. Protagoras and Thrasymachus are two of the better-known Sophists. ['SOF-ism']

Sophists   *See* SOPHISM.

sorites   An ARGUMENT consisting of a chain of smaller arguments. This sort of argument is involved in the sorites PARA-
DOX, an example of which follows:
  (1) Someone 3 feet tall is short.
  (2) If someone is short, then anyone .0001 feet taller is
      also short.
  (3) Therefore someone 3.0001 feet tall is short.
Applying premise (2) to step (3) yields a further conclusion,
to which premise (2) is applied again; application of (2) to
succeeding conclusions in this way, over and over, eventually yields the obviously false final conclusion, 'Someone 7
feet tall is short'. What has gone wrong? The obvious step to
criticize is premise (2), but if you think this is false, you need
to produce some height such that a person of that height is
short, but a person .0001 feet taller is not short; and there is,
it seems, no such height. It's difficult to figure out what
exactly has gone wrong here, and there are interesting consequences for LOGIC of various proposals. The sorites paradox has something to do with the involvement of a VAGUE
CONCEPT (of being short, in this case). The sorites paradox is
also known as the 'paradox of the heap': 'sorites' means
'heap' in Greek, and the classical version of the paradox
involves removing grains of sand, one at a time, from a heap.
Another version, 'the bald man' considers a man with a full
head of hair: removing one hair would not make him bald.
['suh-RIGHT-eez']

sortal   *See* COUNT / MASS TERM / SORTAL.

sound   *See* ARGUMENT.

soundness   *See* ARGUMENT.

space, absolute   *See* ABSOLUTE SPACE AND TIME.

species   *See* GENUS / SPECIES.

specism   By analogy with the word 'racism' (and later, 'SEX-

ISM'), this term was coined to refer to the way we tend to restrict certain considerations of moral treatment to our own species. Some philosophers—most notably Peter SINGER—have argued in favour of according certain RIGHTS to animals, and against certain widespread ways they are currently treated. Some philosophers prefer the term 'speciesism'; a substitute for either ugly word is 'anthropocentrism'—the restriction of consideration to humans. ['SPEESH' or 'SPEES' + '-ism']

spectrum, inverted   *See* INVERTED SPECTRUM.

speculative philosophy   A style of philosophy that some ANALYTIC PHILOSOPHERS claim to find among some CONTINENTALS: it is said to ignore empirical evidence, rigorous argument, clarity, and analysis of concepts, in its characteristic attempts to construct grand schemes to unify all of reality. HEGEL'S thought is taken as a good example of this.

speech acts   Acts done with language (written or spoken). J. L. AUSTIN distinguished these:
1. A locutionary act is merely the utterance of noises (or written marks) associated with a language.
2. Examples of illocutionary acts are *informing* somebody of something, *asking* somebody about something, *ordering* somebody to do something, and so on. These are done by means of locutionary acts. They are accomplished merely by the hearer's understanding the speaker's intention to inform, ask, order, etc.—the speaker's illocutionary intention.
3. Of course, often we have further intentions regarding the hearer: when I say 'Please close the door' I intend not only to perform the illocutionary act of requesting that you close the door, but also to perform the further act of getting you to close the door because of this request. This further act is a perlocutionary act, and the intention behind it is a perlocutionary intention.

This act is getting you to respond in some way because of my illocutionary act and your recognition of it.

Austin, SEARLE, and others argue that a good way to explain the meanings of parts of a language is to specify how the rules of the language create the potential for each bit to perform illocutionary acts—give it, in other words, its illlocutionary force.

Spencer, Herbert (1820-1903) English philosopher who emphasized EVOLUTION as the unifying force behind all of nature, and as the principle of unification of all the sciences.

spheres, music / harmony of the, *see* MUSIC OF THE SPHERES.

Spinoza, Benedict (or Baruch) (1632-1677) Dutch Jewish philosopher. He argued that nature is a unity, equivalent to a highly abstract and all-pervasive God, and that its facts are necessary, and can be derived by a method of rigorous "proof" (as in geometry). Believing that humans were part of nature, he was a thoroughgoing DETERMINIST; given this, he concluded that emotions such as regret and anger were mistaken. He argued that love of knowledge was the highest good.

spirit, absolute *See* ABSOLUTE.

split brain A surgical severing of the corpus collosum—the connection between the two hemispheres of the brain—results in awareness, or control of various functions, by one or the other hemisphere independently. These facts have provoked philosophical speculation about the general differences in function of the "right-brain" and "left-brain", and against the supposed unity of the person with an unsevered hemisphere connection.

square of opposition A diagram showing the logical relationships (called 'oppositions') of the sentences in traditional logic. (*See* all the terms in the diagram.)

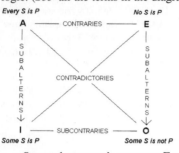

St ... *See* under person's surname. E.g., for St. Augustine, *see* AUGUSTINE.

St. Petersburg paradox *See* SAINT PETERSBURG PARADOX.

stage, temporal *See* IDENTITY[4].

Stalnaker, Robert C[ulp] (b. 1940) American philosopher of mind and logic best known for his views on COUNTERFACTUALS.

standpoint theory A collection of related views, all of which begin with the uncontroversial idea that how you see things depends on (among other things) your "standpoint"—your position in society. Some standpoint theorists go on to make more controversial claims, for example, that there is no real absolute standpoint-free truth; or that the view from the standpoint of a repressed group is likely to be truer than others, because it is free from the dominant ideology.

state of nature The condition of human societies before we invented governmental or conventional rules regulating conduct, or the state we would be in without such rules. HOBBES argued that in such a state there would be constant warfare of each against all, and life would be "solitary, poor, nasty, brutish, and short"; so moral and political restrictions on our natural freedom are justified (*see* SOCIAL CONTRACT).

statements, basic   *See* BASIC STATEMENTS.

statements, lawlike   *See* LAWLIKE STATEMENTS.

statements, protocol   *See* PROTOCOL STATEMENTS.

Stevenson, C[harles] L[eslie] (1908-1979) American philosopher who introduced and popularized in the the the US the EMOTIVIST ethical theory developed by the LOGICAL POSITIVISTS in Vienna and England.

stipulative / precising / lexical definition   A stipulative definition creates the meaning of a freshly-coined term, or a new meaning for an old term. A precising definition stipulates a new meaning when the old one was insufficiently precise. A lexical definition, by contrast, defines words as they really are (already) used. (*See also* NOMINAL / REAL DEFINITION *and* list of other sorts of DEFINITION.)

stochastic   Means "having to do with PROBABILITY". A stochastic (as opposed to DETERMINISTIC) law predicts outcomes as only probable. ['stuh-KAS-tik']

Stoicism   The views of the Stoics, an ancient Greek and Roman school. They held that VIRTUE is the highest good, and stressed control of the passions and indifference to pleasure and pain (thus the ordinary use of 'stoic'). Well-known stoics are ZENO of Citium, CHRYSIPPUS, EPICTETUS, and MARCUS AURELIUS. (Spelled with a capital S when referring to that school.)

straw man   Straw man argument or reasoning (or "setting up a straw man") is a bad form of reasoning in which one argues against some position by producing and REFUTING a false and stupid version of that position: a "scarecrow" that can easily be knocked over.

Strawson, (Sir) P(eter) F(rederick) (b. 1919) English philosopher, leading practitioner of ANALYTIC PHILOSOPHY, especially in its ORDINARY LANGUAGE version.

strict implication *See* CONDITIONAL.

structural ambiguity *See* AMBIGUITY.

structuralism Wide-ranging and controversial largely French twentieth-century philosophical school of thought. Its central idea is that cultural phenomena should be understood as manifesting unchanging and universal abstract structures or forms; their meaning can be understood only when these forms are revealed. Associated with this movement are LÉVI-STRAUSS, Piaget (*see* SCIENTISTS), ALTHUSSER, LACAN, BARTHES, and FOUCAULT.

structure, deep / surface *See* DEEP / SURFACE STRUCTURE.

subalternation In TRADITIONAL LOGIC, the A statement ("All **S** is **P**") implies the I statement ("Some **S** is **P**"), and the E statement ("No **S** is **P**") implies the O statement ("Some **S** is not **P**"). These relationships are called 'subalternation', relating the 'superaltern' (A or E) to the 'subaltern' (I or O) it implies. (*See* A / E / I / O PROPOSITIONS *and* SQUARE OF OPPOSITION.)

subcontraries Two statements are subcontraries if they cannot both be false. In TRADITIONAL LOGIC, the I statement ("Some **S** is **P**"), and the O statement ("Some **S** is not **P**") are subcontraries. (*See* A / E / I / O PROPOSITIONS *and* SQUARE OF OPPOSITION *and* CONTRADICTION / CONTRARY.)

subjective probability *See* PROBABILITY.

subjective / objective Whether something is objective—a feature of the real external mind-independent world, or subjective—in our minds only—is a perennial and pervasive topic in all areas of philosophy. Examples: ETHICAL subjectivism, for example, holds that our ethical "judgments" reflect our own feelings only, not facts about externals. AESTHETIC subjectivism puts beauty (and other aesthetic properties) in the eye of the beholder. ('OBJECTIVISM' has other senses; *see* that word. *See also* RELATIVISM.)

sublime   Something is sublime when it produces feelings of overwhelming awe. The idea of the sublime played an important part in eighteenth and nineteenth century AESTHETICS.

subset   *See* SET.

subsistent entity   MEINONG and BRENTANO argued that some INTENTIONAL objects (such as Santa Claus) and ABSTRACT objects (for example, those of mathematics) exist, though not in the usual way; subsistence is this peculiar mode of "existence".

sub specie aeternitatis   (Latin: "under the aspect of eternity") Spinoza's description of real knowledge—gotten by PURE REASON[2], contemplating the eternal and NECESSARY, as opposed to the temporary and contingent. [Often anglicised as 'SUB SPEESH-ee uh-TURN-uh-tas' but you might try the classical pronunciation 'SOOB SPAKE-ee-ay eye-TAIR-nee-tas']

substance   Any basic, independently existing entity or subject; the stuff of which things are made. Thought sometimes to be unavailable to our senses, but conceptually necessary as that which "underlies" or "supports" characteristics we can sense (*see* QUALITY / ATTRIBUTE / PROPERTY), and as that which is responsible for things existing through time despite changes in characteristics (*see* "BALL OF WAX" EXAMPLE, in which DESCARTES argued for the existence of substance). DUALISTS believe that there are two substances: physical and mental. Physical substance is also called 'material', 'corporeal', or 'extended' (*see* EXTENSION[2]) substance. It's what physical things are made of—that to which material qualities (size and shape, weight or mass, etc.) apply. Mental (or immaterial or incorporeal) substance is what mental or spiritual things are made of, and to which a different group of qualities apply: thinking of something, desiring something, feeling pain, etc.

substitution instance   *See* INSTANTIATION.

substratum   Synonymous with 'SUBSTANCE', in the sense in which this is supposed to be necessary as what underlies properties. Also called 'substrate'.

success word   Application of such a word entails the achievement of some result. For example, to say that someone has "refuted" a position implies that the person has succeeded in showing it false.

sufficient   *See* NECESSARY / SUFFICIENT CONDITION.

sufficient cause   A causal condition that is sufficient for its effect (*see* NECESSARY / SUFFICIENT CONDITION). Some causal conditions are not (by themselves) sufficient: striking a match is not a sufficient cause for the match lighting: it also has to be dry, for instance.

sufficient reason   *See* PRINCIPLE OF SUFFICIENT REASON.

summum bonum   (Latin: "highest good") The central principle of all that one should strive for.

sum of sets   *See* INTERSECTION / UNION OF SETS.

supererogatory   *See* OBLIGATION.

superman   Not Lois Lane's boyfriend, but, according to NIETZSCHE, a person who represents the highest type. This sort lives a self-disciplined, creative, and joyful life, manifests the

WILL TO POWER, and deserves to rule over the "common herd". Translates Nietzsche's German term, "*Übermensch*," more literally translated as "overman". *See also* SLAVE / MASTER MORALITY.

supernaturalism, ethical   *See*   ETHICAL NATURALISM / SUPERNATURALISM.

supervenience   Things of kind A supervene on things of kind B (the 'supervenience base') when the presence or absence of things of kind A is completely determined by the presence or absence of things of kind B; there can be no difference of sort A without a difference in sort B (though there may be differences in B without differences in A). A clear example is the supervenience of the biological on the chemical: things have biological properties in virtue of their chemical properties, and there can be no biological difference without a chemical difference. It is sometimes thought that ethical properties supervene on physical ones; this means that there can be no ethical difference without a corresponding physical difference in things, so the physical determines the ethical; but the same ethical property can be realized in a variety of physical ways. It is also sometimes thought that the mental supervenes on the physical. Supervenience is distinguished from reduction: when to be something of sort A actually is nothing but something of sort B (*see* REDUCTIONISM). Those who think the mental supervenes on the physical argue that mental categories are not identical with or reducible to any physical categories. Thus, there is no mental difference without a physical difference, but mental categories are not equivalent to physical ones (*see* ANOMALOUS MONISM). The term 'supervenient property' has now mostly replaced its synonym 'emergent property', a term associated with nineteenth-century ROMANTICS, who found emergent properties everywhere in connection with their anti-scientific views; but the number of apparent non-reducibles has shrunk with scientific progress.

supposition (In Latin: *suppositio*) MEDIEVAL designation for what a term in the subject position of a sentence stands for. In "personal supposition", that term stands for some individual thing or things (not necessarily a person), as in "The cat is on the mat". In "simple" supposition, it stands for a kind of thing, as in "Chocolate is one kind of ice cream"; in "material" supposition, to a bit of language ("'cat' has three letters").

surface grammar / structure *See* DEEP / SURFACE STRUCTURE.

surprise quiz paradox Suppose your teacher announces that there will be a surprise quiz (i.e., one whose date you can't predict—you'll know when it happens only at the moment it happens) on one of the next five meeting-days of the class. Now, you know it can't be day 5, because if it hasn't happened by the end of day 4, you'd be able to predict then, in advance, that it will happen during day 5, so it wouldn't be a surprise. But it also can't be day 4, because if it hasn't happened by the end of day 3, you already know it won't happen on day 5, so you'd be able to predict it would happen on day 4, so it wouldn't be a surprise. Similarly, you can predict that it won't happen on day 3, or on day 2. So you can predict that it must happen during day 1; but therefore it won't be a surprise! So the PARADOXICAL conclusion is that it's logically impossible that there be a surprise quiz. QUINE and others have considered some complicated matters in MODAL LOGIC that lead to this paradox. Also known as the 'unexpected examination paradox' and 'prediction paradox'. A variant known as the 'hangman's paradox' or 'executioner's paradox' imagines that someone is sentenced to death, but told that the day on which this execution is to be carried out will be a surprise.

survival This often refers to survival of death.

syllogism A DEDUCTIVE CATEGORIAL ARGUMENT that has two premises (*see* MAJOR / MIDDLE / MINOR TERM / PREMISE). For example: No reptiles are sloppy animals; all pigs are sloppy animals; therefore no pigs are reptiles. Categorizing and explaining valid and invalid syllogisms was a primary concern of TRADITIONAL LOGIC (also called 'syllogistic logic').

syllogism, hypothetical   *See* HYPOTHETICAL SYLLOGISM.

symbolic logic   The main sort of LOGIC studied in the twentieth century, replacing TRADITIONAL LOGIC, and much more powerful and general than what it replaced. It uses symbols (*see* SYMBOLS OF QUANTIFIER LOGIC *and* SYMBOLS OF SENTENTIAL LOGIC) to represent LOGICAL FORM, and certain of its special areas are closely related to mathematics.

symbols   Philosophers often use symbols to abbreviate logical connections (*see* SYMBOLS OF QUANTIFIER LOGIC *and* SYMBOLS OF SENTENTIAL LOGIC), and letters to stand for terms or sentences. Using these abbreviations is useful when showing the form of a complicated argument, or as shorthand when you're going to use them several times, but avoid doing this otherwise. If you merely want to say that a man crosses a street, it will impress no one to say, "A man M crosses a street S".

symbols of quantifier logic   Predicates (or predicate-letters) stand for properties (*see* QUALITY / ATTRIBUTE / PROPERTY): for example, suppose 'B' stands for the property of being bald. Constants stand for particular INDIVIDUALS. If 'f' stands for Fred, 'Bf' stands for the sentence, 'Fred is bald'. Variables stand for any individual thing. They are said to be 'bound' by quantifiers. The two quantifiers are the universal quantifier ('all') and the existential quantifier ('some', i.e., 'at least one'), sometimes symbolized by '$\forall$' and '$\exists$', respectively. Thus in '$(\forall x)(Bx)$', 'x' is a variable bound by the universal quantifier, and the sentence means 'Everything is bald'. '$(\exists x)(Bx)$' means 'Something is bald'. (Alternate symbolization: '(Λx)' or simply '(x)' for universal, '(Vx)' for existential quantifiers.) '(Bx)' all by itself is not a meaningful sentence—it's called an 'open' sentence, because it lacks a quantifier, so the variable is unbound (also called 'free'). The equals sign (=) symbolizes IDENTITY[3]: 'a = b' means 'a is identical with b'. The iota-operator 'ι' (sometimes upside-down) symbolizes the DEFINITE DESCRIPTION, so '(ιx)(Bx) = f' means 'The one and only thing that is bald is Fred'. '((∃!x)' (sometimes read 'E shriek x') means 'There exists exactly one thing'; so '((∃!x)(Bx)' is the false statement that there exists exactly one bald thing.

symbols of sentential logic   The symbols used to stand for logical TRUTH FUNCTIONAL connections between sentences in SENTENTIAL LOGIC. The sentences themselves are usually abbreviated by capital letters. The connectives are:

The ampersand (&) and the dot (·), less commonly the carat (∧) are used to stand for 'and'. Connecting two sentences P and Q with one of these makes a CON-JUNCTION[1], and means 'P and Q'.

The horseshoe (⊃) and the arrow (→), both commonly used for 'if...then'. Connecting two sentences P and Q with one of these makes a material CONDITIONAL whose antecedent is 'P' and consequent is 'Q'; it means 'if P then Q'.

The wedge or vee (v) stands for the inclusive 'or'. 'P v Q' is a DISJUNCTION whose disjuncts are P and Q, and means 'P or Q'.

The tilde or curl (~) stands for 'not' or 'is not the case that'. ~P is a negation, and means 'it is not the case that P'. Other negation symbols are '–' and '¬'.

The triple-bar (≡) or the double-arrow (↔) stand for 'if and only if'. 'P ≡ Q' is called a BICONDITIONAL or material equivalence, and means 'P if and only if Q'.

The assertion-sign or single-bar turnstile (⊢) was introduced by FREGE as the sign of a sentence that was being claimed to be true, and was not merely being mentioned (*see* MENTION/USE). Often it is used to mean that the sentence that follows can be DERIVED from the sentences preceding it; or, if no sentences precede it, that it is a THEOREM.

The double-bar turnstile (⊨) means that the sentence that follows is IMPLIED by the sentences that precede it. Thus {P, Q} ⊨ R means that it is impossible for P and Q to be true and **R** be false. If no sentences precede the double-bar turnstile, it says that what follows is a LOGICAL TRUTH.

symmetric / asymmetric / nonsymmetric (Alternatively, 'symmetrical / asymmetrical / nonsymmetrical'.) Characteristics of certain RELATIONS. A relation is symmetric if it IMPLIES the relation in reverse order. For example, 'is the same age as' is symmetric, because the statement 'Fred is the same age as Zelda' implies 'Zelda is the same age as Fred'. But 'wants to know' is nonsymmetric, because 'Fred wants to know Zelda' doesn't imply either 'Zelda wants to know Fred' or 'Zelda doesn't want to know Fred'. And 'is taller than' is asymmetric, because 'Zelda is taller than Fred' implies the falsity of 'Fred is taller than Zelda'. Saying that a relation is 'commutative' is the same as saying it's 'symmetric'.

sympathy / empathy / benevolence These three terms are sometimes used synonymously, but there are subtle differences. Sympathy is taking on the same feeling another person has, or of feeling as they would feel. Empathy is a state in which we understand the feelings of someone else, but don't necessarily share those feelings. Benevolence is having a feeling of kindness toward others. All three of these have at times been thought to provide a psychological FOUNDATION for ETHICS, an antidote to mere self-interest.

syncategorematic / categorematic A categorematic word (or concept) is a word (or concept) that is meaningful when standing alone ('cat'); a syncategorematic word (or concept) needs a categorematic ('on', 'while'). It is sometimes argued that to say that something is "good" doesn't make sense: it has to be a good **x**—a good action, a good apple, etc. This would make *good* a syncategorematic concept.

synchronic / diachronic 'Synchronic' means 'at the same time'; 'diachronic' means 'at different times'. So we can speak of synchronic IDENTITY[3]—when **x** (at some time) is **y** (at that same time). For example, George W. Bush in 2001 is (synchronically) identical with the President of the United States in 2001. Or we can speak of diachronic IDENTITY[4]: when **x** (at one time) is identical with **y** (at another). For example, the person you see here and now is (diachronically) identical with the little boy in 1950 in that photograph.

syntax   *See* SEMANTICS / SYNTAX / PRAGMATICS.

synthesis   *See* DIALECTIC[5].

synthetic   *See* ANALYTIC / SYNTHETIC.

systems, formal   *See* FORMAL SYSTEMS.

T

tabula rasa   (Latin: "blank slate") The term is associated with LOCKE; he and others opposed to INNATENESS think that at birth our minds have no concepts or beliefs in them—they are "blank slates" that will get things "written" on them only after, and by, sense experience. [Usually 'TAB-you-la RAZ-uh'; classically 'TAB-oo-la']

tacit   Means 'silent'. Contractarians admit that people never agreed by word or signature to the SOCIAL CONTRACT, but suppose that by recognizing the advantage of society and participating in it, we give it 'tacit consent'. We understand 'tacit' rules of language, of social etiquette, and so on.

Tarski,   Alfred (1902-1983) Polish-born American LOGICIAN, best known for his semantic theory of truth (*see* REDUNDANCY THEORY OF TRUTH).

tat for tit   *See* TIT FOR TAT.

tautology   *See* LOGICAL TRUTH / FALSITY.

Taylor   [Mill], Harriet [Hardy] (1807-1858) English philosopher, an early advocate of the rights of women, and an influence to some extent on the writings of her husband John Stuart Mill.

techne   *See* NOÛS / DIANOIA / DOXA / THEORIA / TECHNE / PHRONESIS; *see also* PHYSIS / NOMOS / TECHNE.

technical term   *See* ART.

Teilhard de Chardin,   Pierre (1881-1955) French Jesuit paleon-

tologist and philosopher whose thought, a mixture of EVO-
LUTIONARY science and religion, received some popular
attention. ['tay-ar duh shar-dAN']

telekinesis The supposed ability to move things at a distance
by power of the mind alone, without physical contact.
A PARANORMAL PHENOMENON about whose existence
mainstream science is sceptical. Sometimes called 'teleportation' or 'psychokinesis' (abbreviated 'PK'). ['tel-uh-kuh-
NEE-sis']

teleological   *See* TELEOLOGY.

teleological argument for God's existence   Arguments based
on the apparent goal-directedness of things in nature. Here is
a common version: Living things are adapted to their environment—they are built in complex and clever ways to function well in their surroundings. This could not have happened
merely by the random and mechanical processes of nature.
They must have been constructed this way, with their functions in mind, by a creator much more clever and powerful
than humans; thus they are evidence for God's existence. The
usual reply to this argument is that Darwinian EVOLUTION-
ARY theory provides a scientific account of how these things
arose merely by the mechanical processes of nature, so one
need not take the large step of POSITING something unseen
and supernatural to account for them.

teleology The study of aims, purposes, or functions. Much
ancient philosophical and scientific thought saw teleology as
a central principle of things, and a very important basis for
explanation. Teleology is much less important in contemporary thought, but philosophers are still interested in what
teleology remains (for example, scientific talk about what the
pancreas is for, or about the function of individual organisms
in the ecosystem): is this REDUCIBLE to MECHANISTIC talk?
How are 'aims' or 'functions' in nature to be identified or
understood? Teleological ethics sees the aim of actions—

good results—as the basic concept, from which the notions of right action and good person can be derived (*see also* CON-SEQUENTIALISM).

telepathy Supposed communication by "mind reading" or "sending one's thoughts" directly to another person's mind. A PARANORMAL PHENOMENON about whose existence mainstream science is sceptical.

teleportation *See* TELEKINESIS.

telishment *See* PUNISHMENT.

temporal Having to do with time. 'Temporal priority' means the characteristic of being earlier in time. 'Temporally proximate' means 'next in time'. Temporal logic is the branch of MODAL LOGIC dealing with sentences involving 'before', 'after', 'never', etc.

temporal stage *See* IDENTITY[4].

term **1.** Loosely, any group of words. **2.** More narrowly, a noun or noun phrase. *See also* MAJOR / MIDDLE / MINOR TERM / PREMISE.

term of art *See* ART.

term, technical *See* ART.

Thales of Miletus (c. 640-546 B.C.) The earliest known Greek philosopher, whose view—reputedly that all matter was constituted of one element, water—was a very early attempt to provide a natural, as opposed to supernatural account of natural phenomena.

theism *See* ATHEISM / THEISM / AGNOSTICISM.

theodicy The study whose aim is to reconcile the goodness of

God with the apparent existence of evil in His creation. *See* PROBLEM OF EVIL *and* BEST OF ALL POSSIBLE WORLDS. ['thee-ODD-uh-see']

theology   The study of religion, or of religious truths, especially those having to do with God.

theorem   In logic, a theorem is a sentence that can be proven in a logical system by DERIVATION from the empty set of premises. In some areas of mathematics, however, something is called a theorem of a system when it can be derived from the AXIOMS of that system.

theorem, Arrow's   *See* VOTER'S PARADOX[2].

theorem, De Morgan's   *See* DE MORGAN.

theorem, Gödel's   *See* GÖDEL.

theoretical entities / constructs   Theoretical (or hypothetical) entities (or constructs) are things we do not sense directly, but whose existence is assumed or argued for by a THEORY. Atoms and their components are theoretical entities of modern physics. The word 'constructs' may suggest the controversial view that such things were constructed—thought up—for the purposes of the theory; that is, they aren't real (*see* REALISM).

theoria   *See* NOŪS / DIANOIA / DOXA / THEORIA / TECHNE / PHRONESIS.

theory   In an ordinary way of speaking, saying that something is "just a theory" is a way of saying that it is just a guess or HYPOTHESIS without proof. Scientists and philosophers use this term differently, however: some theories are extremely well founded. Usually 'theory' refers to a system of interrelated statements designed to explain a variety of phenomena. Sometimes a theory is distinguished from a LAW or set of laws insofar as a theory postulates the existence of THEORETICAL ENTITIES.

theory, axiomatic   *See* AXIOM / POSTULATE.

theory of action   *See* ACTION THEORY.

theory of games   *See* GAME.

theory of knowledge   *See* EPISTEMOLOGY.

theory of types   In response to the RUSSELL PARADOX, RUSSELL himself proposed that we see the elements of any SET of objects as arranged in a hierarchy of types: the lowest consisting of INDIVIDUALS, the next of SETS of individuals, next are sets of sets, etc; and to deal with the paradox, we disallow statements containing names of items in different types.

Theseus, ship of   *See* SHIP OF THESEUS.

thing for-itself   *See* IN-ITSELF / FOR-ITSELF.

thing-in-itself   **1.** Something as it really exists, as opposed to as it is perceived (*see* PHENOMENA / NOUMENA). A term associated with KANT; in German, '*Ding an sich*'. **2.** For a different use (SARTRE'S), *see* IN-ITSELF / FOR-ITSELF.

Thomas Aquinas,   Saint (c. 1225-1274) Italian-born SCHOLASTIC theologian; he and OCKHAM are the leading candidates for the title of greatest MEDIEVAL PHILOSOPHER, but the Catholic Church's choice of Thomas as an official doctrinal source certainly makes him the more influential. His thought is based on ARISTOTLE, modified to fit Christianity; for him, Aristotle's thought represents philosophical truth, which cannot conflict with the revealed truths of Christianity. Thus, for example, he provided rational proofs of God's existence (*see* his FIVE WAYS), which were adapted from Aristotle. Like Aristotle, he argued that the good life was based on the VIRTUES of reason, but added that these are subordinate to (though not in conflict with) the theological, Christian virtues.

Thomistic   Having to do with the philosophy of THOMAS
AQUINAS. 'Thomism' is the name of the doctrines of Aquinas,
or of the philosophers, including many in the late nineteenth
and twentieth centuries, deeply influenced by him. ['toe-
MIST-ic', 'TOE-mism']

Thomson,   Judith Jarvis (b. 1929) American philosopher,
author of a widely-read article defending the right to abortion, and of other articles applying RIGHTS-theory to practical
situations.

thought experiment   A state of affairs or story we are asked to
imagine to illustrate or test some philosophical point. For
example, imagine that the brains of two people were inter-
changed; what you would then say about the location of the
two might have implications for the principles of PERSONAL
IDENTITY. (Sometimes encountered in its German translation, *Gedankenexperiment*.)

thought, language of   *See* LANGUAGE OF THOUGHT HYPOTHESIS.

tilde   The symbol '~', used for the negation; it means 'not' or
'it's not the case that'. *See* SYMBOLS OF SENTENTIAL LOGIC.

Tillich,   Paul (Johannes) (1886-1965) German-born American
theologian and educator; his thought, influenced strongly by
EXISTENTIALISM, has had a good deal of attention recently in
some religious circles.

time, absolute   *See* ABSOLUTE SPACE AND TIME.

time-slice   *See* IDENTITY[4].

time travel   Interesting to philosophers because it seems to
involve PARADOXES and impossibilities. Imagine, for example, that you traveled back to the time when your grandfather
was a little boy and killed him then. This would mean you
never would have been born; but then who killed your grand-

father? Would you be unable to kill him? Or does this show that time travel is impossible?

tit for tat   The strategy used in playing iterated PRISONER'S DILEMMA games (that is, several games in a row with the same players) in which one cooperates on the first play, and subsequently does whatever the other player did in the previous interaction. Empirical studies have shown that this is a very good strategy. The same strategy except that one defects on the first interaction is called 'tat for tit'.

token   *See* TYPE / TOKEN.

token physicalism / identity   *See* TYPE / TOKEN.

total utilitarianism   *See* AVERAGE / TOTAL UTILITARIANISM.

tracking the truth   **S**'s belief that **P** is said to track the truth, roughly speaking, if the belief is true and depends on **P**; that is to say, if **P** were not the case, **S** would not believe that **P**. It is sometimes argued that a belief constitutes knowledge if it tracks the truth. This perhaps provides an answer to the problems posed by GETTIER EXAMPLES. (*See also* RELIABILISM.)

Tractatus   (Latin: "tract") The first word of the title of several philosophical works. When one speaks of 'the *Tractatus*' nowadays, this usually refers to Ludwig WITTGENSTEIN'S *Tractatus Logico-Philosophicus*, a short but hugely influential book on thought and language. ['trak-TAY-tus' or 'trak-TAH-tus']

traditional logic   Logic before the twentieth century, also called "classical logic" or "ARISTOTELIAN logic". Largely concerned with cataloging and describing some of the correct and incorrect forms of reasoning, including the FALLACIES and the SYLLOGISM. Contemporary SYMBOLIC LOGIC has largely replaced it.

tragedy of the commons   Consider a public resource, such as open land on which cattle can graze. It is in the interest of each individual user of this common resource that it not be exploited beyond the level at which it can replenish itself. But if you take as much as you can, this will not (by itself) lead to the depletion of the resource beyond the point of no return. And you can't save it from this depletion if it's headed that way, merely by restraining your use. So it's in your interest to take as much as you can. But if everyone reasoned this way and acted accordingly, the resource will be destroyed and nobody would get any. This parable represents a general and central problem of ethics and social philosophy. It's a case of the PRISONER'S DILEMMA.

transcendence   *See* TRANSCENDENT / IMMANENT.

transcendental   The sort of thought that attempts to discover the (perhaps universal and necessary) laws of reason, and to deduce consequences from this about how reality must be understood by any mind. KANT used this sort of reasoning— the "transcendental argument"—to account for *A PRIORI* METAPHYSICAL truths. (*See also* TRANSCENDENT / IMMANENT.)

transcendental analytic   The section of Kant's *Critique of Pure Reason* which deals with the principles of understanding and the necessity of the application of the CATEGORIES.

transcendental ego   *See* EMPIRICAL / TRANSCENDENTAL EGO.

transcendentalism   This term can refer to the philosophy of KANT and his followers, or (more usually) to New England transcendentalism, the American mid-nineteenth-century school centred around Emerson (*see* WRITERS), influenced by Kant and later German IDEALISTS, more noteable as a literary than as a philosophical movement.

transcendent / immanent   'Transcendent' means 'higher than, existing apart from or beyond'. To think of God as transcendent is to think of Him as separate from the ordinary universe, in a different and higher realm. This is contrasted with an immanent God, who exists in His creation. 'Transcendent' truths were for KANT those that are unknowable, not the proper business of philosophy; he contrasted these with 'TRANSCENDENTAL' ones, which he thought his transcendental reasoning could discover. 'Transcendence' is SARTRE'S term for people's plans and hopes for their futures.

transitive / intransitive / nontransitive   Transitivity is a characteristic of some relations, such that if **A** has that relation to **B** and **B** to **C**, then it follows that **A** has that relation to **C**. For example, 'taller than' names a transitive relation, because if Arnold is taller than Bernie, and Bernie is taller than Clara, it follows that Arnold is taller than Clara. 'Is a friend of' names a nontransitive relation, because it's possible that Arnold is a friend of Bernie, and Bernie is a friend of Clara, but Arnold is not a friend of Clara. 'Is the father of' names an intransitive relation, because if Arnold is the father of Bernie, and Bernie is the father of Clara, then it follows that it's false that Arnold is the father of Clara.

translation, indeterminacy of   *See* INDETERMINACY OF TRANSLATION / REFERENCE.

translation, radical   *See* RADICAL TRANSLATION / INTERPRETATION.

transmigration of souls   *See* REINCARNATION.

transparent context   *See* OPAQUE / TRANSPARENT.

transposition   A rule of INFERENCE of the form: P ⊃ Q therefore ~Q ⊃ ~P.

triple-bar   The symbol '≡', meaning 'if and only if'. *See* SYMBOLS OF SENTENTIAL LOGIC.

trivial   Something that is obvious or insignificant, so not worth saying. Logicians speak of 'trivial' proofs in this sense. Courses in three liberal arts (grammar, RHETORIC, and LOGIC) in MEDIEVAL universities were called 'trivia', though the subject matter was not obvious or insignificant (and neither did it consist of obscure facts about sports records and movie stars); the word here derives from its Latin use, meaning "place where three roads meet", and contrasts with 'quadrivia', the other four courses in their liberal arts curriculum (arithmetic, geometry, astronomy, music).

trope   **1.** In classical logic, one of the forms of valid ARGUMENT. **2.** A figure of speech, a non-literal use such as irony or metaphor. **3.** An "abstract particular"—an instance of a UNIVERSAL at a particular place and time. For example, the red of the skin of the apple on my desk: it's not the universal redness, but neither is it a concrete particular.

truth   To define this term is to give a THEORY of what it is that makes a sentence or belief true. Here are some major theories of truth defined in this dictionary:

CORRESPONDENCE THEORY OF TRUTH
COHERENCE THEORY OF TRUTH
disquotational or deflationary or semantic theory—*see*
    REDUNDANCY THEORY OF TRUTH
IDEAL LIMIT THEORY OF TRUTH
PERFORMATIVE THEORY OF TRUTH
PRAGMATIC THEORY OF TRUTH.

truth conditions   The facts in the world that would make a sentence true. Some theories count truth conditions as constituting the meaning of the sentence.

truth-functionality   A truth-function is a FUNCTION whose arguments and values are *True* and *False*. A sentence constructed out of two sentences connected with 'and' is a truth-function when its truth or falsity depends systematically on the truth or falsity of the component sentences and on nothing else (it's true whenever both components are true, false otherwise). When a sentence of this sort is a truth-function, 'and' is said to be used truth-functionally. But 'and' sometimes isn't used truth-functionally, as when it's used to mean 'and then'. 'Fred went to the store and Fred lost $5' might be thought false if Fred lost $5 before he went to the store. It's often a mistake to think of uses of 'if... then' constructions in English as being truth-functional (*see* CONDITIONAL for a discussion of this). 'Truth-functional logic' is a synonym for 'SENTENTIAL LOGIC', in which truth-functional connectives are studied.

truth of reason   KANT used 'reason' to refer to our intellect in general, not to 'reasoning' in the sense of argumentation or problem-solving in particular. A truth of reason is a truth that can be discovered by the operations of PURE REASON[2] alone, that is, which does not rely on sense-experience. Thus this is synonymous with '*a priori* truth'. (*See* A PRIORI / A POSTERIORI.) EMPIRICISTS and RATIONALISTS disagree on the extent to which truths of reason are possible: empiricists usually limit these to CONCEPTUAL TRUTHS, analytic statements (*see* ANALYTIC / SYNTHETIC), and LOGICAL TRUTHS; but rationalists characteristically believe that there are more truths of reason.

truth table   A diagram used in SENTENTIAL LOGIC to display the systematic way the truth or falsity of a TRUTH-FUNCTIONAL sentence depends on the truth or falsity of its component sentences. The following truth table demonstrates the way the truth or falsity of a complex expression 'P v (~Q ⊃ ~P)' depends on the truth or falsity of its components, 'P' and 'Q':

P	Q	P v (~Q ⊃ ~P)
T	T	T
T	F	T
F	T	T
F	F	T

Note, in this case, the complex expression is true no matter what TRUTH VALUES P and Q have; thus it is shown, by this truth table, to be a LOGICAL TRUTH. Truth tables can also be used to prove certain other logical claims.

truth, theory of   *See* TRUTH.

truth, vacuous   *See* VACUOUS.

truth value   Truth or falsity. The truth value of a true sentence is *True*; of a false sentence, *False*.

***tu quoque* argument**   *See* AD HOMINEM.

Turing,   A(lan) M(atheson) (1912-1954) English mathematician known for pioneering work in the theory of computing. The 'Turing machine' is a generalized and simple form of computer he described. Rarely actually built, this machine would read a tape containing symbols; the symbols cause changes in the machine's internal states, and these changes cause it to erase and print symbols on the tape. It can be proven that this simple machine can do anything any complicated computer can do, so showing how a problem can be solved by a Turing machine proves that it can be computed. Analyzing a sort of behaviour as a complicated series of actions by a Turing machine is giving a calculational explanation of it. Can human behaviour be given a Turing machine ANALYSIS? The 'Turing test' (also known as the 'imitation game') was proposed by Turing as an answer to the question "Can a machine think?" Imagine two computer terminals: you can type questions into either, and get answers back on their screens. One of them is connected to a person in another room reading and answering your questions; the other to a machine. If you can't tell which is connected to the person and which to the machine, the machine has passed the test for thinking.

turnstile   *See* SYMBOLS OF SENTENTIAL LOGIC.

twin-earth   An imaginary planet just like our Earth, in a thought-experiment invented by Hilary PUTNAM. If on Earth, John loves Mary, then on Twin-earth, John's look-alike (call him Twin-John) loves Twin-Mary. But this shows that Earth and Twin-earth aren't exactly alike, because John and Twin-John aren't exactly alike: the former loves Mary, but the latter doesn't—he loves Twin-Mary instead. Earth and Twin-earth also differ in INDEXICAL facts. Are John and Twin-John psychologically alike? (*See* METHODOLOGICAL SOLIPSISM.) Their thoughts have the same narrow content but different WIDE CONTENT. Suppose twin-water has all the same obvious properties that water does, but it's XYZ, not H_2O; then 'water', Putnam argued, would have a different meaning in Twinglish.

two-place predicate   *See* PREDICATE[3].

types, theory of   *See* THEORY OF TYPES.

type / token   Two different things that are both of a certain sort are said to be two tokens of one type. Thus, in the sentence 'The cat is on the mat' there are six word tokens, but only five word types. Token physicalism (sometimes known as the token-token identity theory of mind) is the view that each particular mental event is IDENTICAL[3] with (the same thing as) a particular physical event (e.g., a brain event). Type physicalism (sometimes known as the type-type identity theory) adds that each kind of mental event is also a kind of physical event. FUNCTIONALISTS tend to be token physicalists but not type physicalists. IDENTITY THEORISTS tend to be type physicalists. ANOMALOUS MONISM admits token identity, but denies type identity.

U

Übermensch   *See* SUPERMAN.

Unamuno   (y Jugo), Miguel de (1864-1936) Spanish writer and philosopher of life.

unary predicate   *See* PREDICATE[3].

unbound variable   *See* SYMBOLS OF QUANTIFIER LOGIC.

uncertainty principle   A principle of modern physics, saying that it is impossible to know both the position and the momentum of a basic atomic particle at once. Philosophers wonder whether this means that the position and momentum cannot both simultaneously be real facts, or merely that there is a limit on our knowledge. Also called the Heisenberg uncertainty (or indeterminacy) principle, after Werner Heisenberg (*see* SCIENTISTS).

unconditional probability   *See* PROBABILITY.

underdetermination   Something is underdetermined by a set of conditions if these conditions don't determine how (or that) it will exist. Thus, the striking of a match underdetermines its lighting (because it's not sufficient—*see* NECESSARY / SUFFICIENT CONDITIONS). Compare OVERDETERMINATION. Language behaviour underdetermines a translation manual when different equally adequate translation manuals can be constructed for that behaviour (*see* INDETERMINACY OF TRANSLATION). Scientific THEORY is underdetermined by empirical evidence when two rival HYPOTHESES are both consistent with all the evidence.

undistributed middle (fallacy of)   *See* DISTRIBUTED / UNDISTRIBUTED TERM / MIDDLE.

unexpected examination paradox *See* SURPRISE QUIZ PARADOX.

unextended *See* : EXTENSION / INTENSION², *and* SUBSTANCE.

uniformity of nature, principle of *See* PRINCIPLE OF UNIFORMITY OF NATURE.

union of sets *See* INTERSECTION / UNION OF SETS.

unintelligibility *See* INTELLIGIBILITY / UNINTELLIGIBILITY.

uninterpreted calculus *See* CALCULUS.

unit set / class *See* SET.

unity of science   The view that every science would eventually be REDUCIBLE to a single, most basic science—possibly physics.

universal causation, principle of *See* PRINCIPLE OF UNIVERSAL CAUSATION.

universal generalization   A rule of INFERENCE which allows inferring that everything has property **P** (*see* QUALITY / ATTRIBUTE / PROPERTY) from the statement that an individual has property **P**. This is a valid rule of inference only when used under various restrictions.

universal grammar *See* GENERATIVE GRAMMAR.

universal instantiation   A rule of INFERENCE which allows inferring that a particular INDIVIDUAL has property **P** (*see* QUALITY / ATTRIBUTE / PROPERTY) from the statement that everything has property **P**.

universalizability   True of a particular action when it can be universalized—that is, when the rule behind it can consistently or reasonably be conceived of as a universal law (one that could apply to everyone). The test of consistent universalizability is roughly what KANT thought to be the test of ethically right action (*see* CATEGORICAL IMPERATIVE). The test of *practical* universalizability (not Kant's test) is perhaps what we apply when we think morally about some action by evaluating the consequences if everyone were to do that sort of thing.

universal propositions A PROPOSITION that says something about all the members of a SET—either positively ("All pigs are sloppy eaters") or negatively ("No pigs are reptiles").

universal quantifier *See* SYMBOLS OF QUANTIFIER LOGIC.

universals These are "abstract" things—beauty, courage, redness, etc. The problem of universals is whether these exist in the external world. Thus, one may be a REALIST or anti-realist about universals. PLATO's theory of forms (*see* FORM[1]) is an early and well-known realism about universals; the EMPIRICISTS are associated with anti-realism. Nominalism is a variety of anti-realism that claims that only particulars exist, and that such abstractions are merely the result of the way we talk. Conceptualism claims that they exist only within people's minds, as mental CONCEPTS, not externally. *See* ABSTRACT / CONCRETE ENTITIES / IDEAS; *see also* NATURAL KIND.

universe of discourse Sometimes it is convenient while doing LOGIC to restrict in advance the SET of things one is talking about in a series of statements; one then specifies a "universe of discourse" for those statements. Given the restriction of the universe of discourse to cats, the statement 'Everything is fuzzy' means 'All cats are fuzzy'. An unrestricted universe of discourse is the whole universe.

univocal Means not AMBIGUOUS. ['you-NIV-uh-cul']

unmoved mover That which is uncaused (or CAUSE-OF-

ITSELF); it's the first (or the basic) cause, the entity that existed at the beginning and caused everything else—the 'prime mover'. This is often identified with God. Does motion imply the existence of an unmoved mover? (*See* FIRST-CAUSE ARGUMENT.)

unsound   *See* ARGUMENT.

use / mention   *See* MENTION / USE.

utile   *See* UTILITY.

utilitarianism   Utilitarians think that the moral worth of any action can be measured by the extent to which it provides valued results—usually pleasure or happiness—to the greatest number of people. Thus, their general moral principle is the principle of UTILITY, also known as the 'greatest happiness principle': "Act so as to produce the greatest happiness for the greatest number of people." Act utilitarians hold that moral thinking evaluates each act, in context, separately; rule utilitarians argue that morality is concerned with general rules for action, and that a particular action is right if it is permitted or recommended by a moral code whose acceptance in the agent's society would maximize utility, even if that act in particular does not. The famous classical utilitarians are MILL and BENTHAM.

utility   As used by philosophers (and economists), this term doesn't refer merely to usefulness (or to the electric company). It means the quantity of value or desirability something has. Often it is thought that the utility of something can be given a number (the quantity of "utiles" it possesses), and utilities can be compared or added. *See also* UTILITARIANISM *and* EXPECTED UTILITY.

utility calculus   *See* FELICIFIC CALCULUS.

utility, principle of   *See* UTILITARIANISM.

utopia / dystopia   A utopia is a (usually imaginary) ideal society; a dystopia is the reverse, a (usually imaginary) bad society.

V

vacuous Means 'empty'. In LOGIC, the statement 'All A's are B's' is understood to be equivalent to 'For all **x**, if **x** is an A then **x** is a B'. Suppose there aren't any A's at all. Then it's always false that any **x** is an A: but this makes the CONDITIONAL, 'if **x** is an A then **x** is a B' true. It follows, then, that if there aren't any A's, all statements of the form 'All A's are B's' are true. So, for example, because there aren't any unicorns, the statement 'All unicorns are mammals' is true, and so is 'All unicorns are non-mammals'. This strange kind of truth is called vacuous truth.

vagueness In its ordinary usage, a vague statement or term is one not clearly expressed, or imprecise. Vagueness in this sense differs from ambiguity (*see* EQUIVOCATION): an ambiguous statement or term has two or more meanings that may each be perfectly clear: what is unclear is which one is meant. In a more technical logicians' sense, a term is vague whose application involves borderline cases: thus, 'tall' is vague, because there are some people who are clearly tall, some clearly not tall, and some who are in a borderline area, and are not clearly tall or not tall. Consideration about vague terms leads to problems in LOGIC (*see* SORITES).

valid argument *See* ARGUMENT.

validity *See* ARGUMENT.

valuation *See* CALCULUS.

value, intrinsic / inherent / instrumental / extrinsic *See* INTRINSIC / INHERENT / INSTRUMENTAL / EXTRINSIC.

value of a function   *See* FUNCTION.

value theory   A very broad philosophical study including ETHICS, AESTHETICS, and sometimes even EPISTEMIC values (e.g., justification). Also called 'axiology'.

van Fraassen, Bas[tiaan] C[ornelius] (b. 1941) Dutch/Canadian/American logician and philosopher of science; influential proponent of an EMPIRICIST but anti-REALIST view of science.

variable   *See* SYMBOLS OF QUANTIFIER LOGIC.

vat, brain in a   *See* BRAIN IN A VAT.

vee   The symbol 'v', meaning 'or'. *See* SYMBOLS OF SENTENTIAL LOGIC.

veil of ignorance   John RAWLS argued that JUSTICE might be conceived of as (roughly) what everyone would agree to be the rules of society (*see also* SOCIAL CONTRACT). These rules would not necessarily guarantee each person an equal share of everything, and if you knew that you would be relatively disadvantaged under these rules, you wouldn't agree to them. Thus, he argued that the agreement be conceived as happening under a "veil of ignorance": that you not know in advance which place in the society you would hold. Under these conditions you'd want to make sure that the worst-off (who might turn out to be you) wasn't in a really terrible position.

Venn diagram   Diagrams used to illustrate CATEGORIAL LOGIC, and to do logical proofs. They use interlocking circles to represent SETS; areas of these circles are shaded to assert emptiness, and **x**'s are inserted to assert the existence of one or more thing. Thus, one diagrams:

"All pigs are slobs"

"Some pigs are slobs"

"No pigs are slobs"

One can use three interlocking circles to prove the validity of a SYLLOGISM. On the following, 'All P is R' and 'No R is S' are entered; the truth of the conclusion, 'No P is S' may be read off.

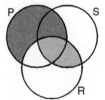

Venn diagrams are named after their inventer, John Venn (British logician, 1834-1923); he adapted them from a somewhat similar technique invented by Leonhard Euler (Swiss logician, 1707-1783). ['oil-er']

verbal dispute   A disagreement that turns out to be merely a matter of words. The dispute about the answer to the old cliché question whether a tree that falls in the forest where nobody hears it makes any sound may be just verbal: the answer depends wholly upon whether you mean by 'sound' an air vibration capable of being heard, or an air vibration actually heard. Verbal disputes aren't real disputes, and are uninteresting unless they reveal significant ambiguities in word use.

verbal / ostensive definition   Verbal definitions define using other words, giving synonymous words or phrases. These are what you find in dictionaries (but note that dictionaries often do more than merely this: they tell you, for example, facts not definitionally associated with these words, and show you pictures). Ostensive definitions, by contrast, define by giving examples. One might define the word 'green' by showing somebody a number of green things, or 'bird' by listing many different sorts of birds. Also called 'DEMONSTRATIVE definition'. (*See* INDEXICAL / DEMONSTRATIVE; *see also* list of other sorts of DEFINITION.)

veridical / falsidical   'Veridical' means 'truthful'; 'falsidical' the opposite. Their most frequent use concerns the "truth" or "falsity" of perceptions: an ILLUSION is a falsidical—non-veridical—perception.

verifiability   A statement is verifiable when there exist (at least IN PRINCIPLE) procedures that would show that it is true or false. 'In principle' is added here because there do not need to be procedures actually available now or ever, as long as we can imagine what they are. So, for example, the statement 'There is a planet on a star seven million light years from here' is unverifiable given our current (and perhaps future) technology, but because we can imagine what would be evidence for its truth or falsity, it is verifiable, in principle.

verifiability criterion / principle   **1.** The verifiability CRITERION for meaningfulness was advocated by LOGICAL POSITIVISTS; their "verifiability principle" said that any statement that was not VERIFIABLE was meaningless. Thus, for example, since it might be thought impossible to find evidence for or against the statement 'God loves us', they would count this statement not as false (or as true), but as meaningless. Similar conclusions were drawn about statements in METAPHYSICS and ETHICS. **2.** Some logical positivists also thought that verification provided an account of what meaning is. The verification theory of meaning says that the meaning of a sentence can be specified by giving its procedures of verification.

verification   *See* CONFIRMATION / DISCONFIRMATION / VERIFICATION / FALSIFICATION.

verstehen   (German: "to understand") German romantic philosophers used this term to apply to the kind of understanding they thought was appropriate for human activities—subjective understanding "from within", not a matter of objective external scientific observation or theorizing. (*See* SUBJECTIVE / OBJECTIVE.) ['fair-SCHTAY-en']

vicious circle   *See* CIRCULAR REASONING / DEFINITION.

vicious infinite regress   *See* INFINITE REGRESS.

Vico,   Giambattista (1668-1744) Italian philosopher mainly known for his views on history, which he saw as a divinely guided development of civilizations along certain regular patterns.

Vienna Circle   A group of philosophers who met in Vienna and elsewhere during the 1920s and 30s. It included SCHLICK, NEURATH, CARNAP and GÖDEL, occasionally AYER and QUINE, and was influenced by WITTGENSTEIN. These philosophers produced the groundwork of LOGICAL POSITIVISM and were deeply influential on future ANALYTIC PHILOSOPHY, especially in Britain and the US, where many members moved during the rise of Hitler.

vindication (of induction)   A PRAGMATIC attempt to deal with the PROBLEM OF INDUCTION not by showing that induction is guaranteed to continue to work, but rather by arguing that if anything will work, induction will; because there is no better strategy, one should continue to use it.

virtue   Moral excellence or uprightness; the state of character of a morally worthwhile person. 'The virtues' are those character traits that make for a good person. Some philosophers think that virtue, not good states of affairs or right action, is the central notion in ethics; this line of thinking ("virtue ethics") derives from ARISTOTLE.

virtuous circle   *See* CIRCULAR REASONING / DEFINITION.

vitalism   Vitalists argue that living things are not just certain sorts of combinations of non-living parts, that they contain a special (and irreducible—*see* REDUCTIONISM) sort of thing (sometimes called, in French, the '*élan vital*' ['ay-lAN vee-tal']) –the "vital impulse" contained by no non-living things, and which drives EVOLUTION. BERGSON is a well-known vitalist.

void   *See* NOTHING / NOTHINGNESS.

volition   The exercise of the will, deciding, desiring, or wanting; a mental event that initiates action.

Voltaire   *See* WRITERS.

voter's paradox   The ambiguous name of two different PARA-DOXES: **1.** In elections with many voters, it's highly unlikely that your vote will make any difference to who wins, so even if you care very much who wins, there's no point in voting. This is true also of every other potential voter. So it seems to follow that there's no point in anyone's voting. **2.** Suppose there are three people who disagree about the relative value of three actions (call them A, B, and C):
Arnold prefers A to B, and B to C.

Beth prefers B to C, and C to A.

Carla prefers C to A, and A to B.

Suppose they agree to decide on what to do by voting on these actions two at a time. First they vote on A and B: Arnold and Carla vote for A. Next they vote on B and C: Arnold and Beth vote for B. Last they vote on C and A: Beth and Carla vote for C. Each "pairwise" decision has a majority favourable vote; yet this clearly does not decide matters. This example shows the surprising result that in certain cases even a majority vote of a group does not give a clear answer about what to do. This is also known as the 'Condorcet paradox', named for the Marquis de CONDORCET who wrote about it. It has been generalized by Kenneth ARROW (b. 1921) into the central problem of SOCIAL CHOICE THEORY. Arrow's Theorem (or "paradox") shows that there is no rule for social choice that satisfies certain apparently minimal conditions for rationality and DEMOCRACY.

W

warranted assertibility   The characteristic an ASSERTION has when it is JUSTIFIED in the proper way. Statements, for example in science, have warranted assertibility when they are CONFIRMED by the appropriate scientific procedures. It seems that a statement with this characteristic might nevertheless be false, but some philosophers of science think that warranted assertibility is really all that we mean by 'truth' in science; this is a kind of scientific antirealism (*see* REALISM / ANTIRE-ALISM).

wax example   *See* "BALL OF WAX" EXAMPLE.

weakness of the will   The character trait in one who knows what is right to do but doesn't do it. This notion is puzzling: doesn't one always do what one really, overall, thinks best? For similar puzzles, *see* BURIDAN'S ASS and SELF-DECEPTION. The Greek word for weakness of the will is *akrasia* (sometimes spelled *acrasia*) "lack of strength", "lack of self control or moderation". ['ah-kra-SEE-ah' or 'uh-KRAY-zha']

Weber,   Max *See* SCIENTISTS.

wedge   The symbol 'v', meaning 'or'. *See* SYMBOLS OF SENTENTIAL LOGIC.

Weil,   Simone (1909-1943) French writer; her writings show an odd combination of left-wing social philosophy, PLATONISM, and Christian MYSTICISM. ['vail']

well-formed formula   In addition to rules for going from one sentence to another, LOGICS give rules for being a sentence (as opposed to a bit of nonsense). These are called 'formation rules', and a sentence formed in conformity with these rules is called a 'well-formed sentence' or 'well-formed FORMULA'. Expressions not in conformity are sometimes called 'ill-formed'. Thus, by application of the formation rules of a common form of SENTENTIAL LOGIC, we can discover that 'P &' is ill-formed, nonsense, not a sentence (because '&' must connect two sentences). 'Well-formed formula' is sometimes abbreviated 'wff' [pronounced 'wiff' or 'woof'].

Weltanschauung   (German: "world view") A very general conception of the way things are. ['velt-on-show-oong', where 'show' rhymes with 'now']

Weltschmerz   (German: "world pain") Generalized romantic pessimistic world-weariness. Try medication. ['VELT-schmairtz']

wff   *See* WELL-FORMED FORMULA.

Whitehead,   Alfred North (1861-1947) English philosopher and logician; developed, with RUSSELL, the first modern systematic SYMBOLIC LOGIC; known also for his "process" philosophy, in which change, not substance, is fundamental, and in which purpose is a feature of the external world.

wide / narrow content   To see what one thinks or expresses as having wide content is to hold that identifying or explaining them must make reference to the external objects and facts in the world that they are about. To see them as having narrow content is to believe that they are identifiable or explainable wholly by reference to what's "inside the head". What is conceived of as having narrow content may have syntax, but won't have semantics. (*See* SEMANTICS / SYNTAX / PRAGMATICS; *see also* METHODOLOGICAL SOLIPSISM.)

will, free   *See* FREE WILL.

will, general   *See* GENERAL WILL.

William of Ockham   (or Occam) *See* OCKHAM.

Williams,   Bernard [Arthur Owen] (b. 1929) English philosopher, best known for his work on PERSONAL IDENTITY and moral philosophy.

will to believe   William JAMES argued that certain beliefs are acceptable despite the lack of good evidence for them, when they are good for us psychologically and help us get on in the world. These are the ones justified by our will to believe them; James even argued that this is what it means for them to be true. *See* PRAGMATIC THEORY OF TRUTH.

will to power   The will to power is the disposition to superiority—power over others, but also over one's self. NIETZSCHE'S term; he thought that this was the character trait that marked the best sort of person.

Winch,   P[eter] G[uy] (b. 1926) English WITTGENSTEINIAN; his most influential work argues that social science is unlike EMPIRICAL physical science.

Wisdom,   [Arthur] John [Terrence] (1904-1993) British philosopher; influenced by WITTGENSTEIN and MOORE; writings on mind and psychoanalysis.

Wittgenstein,   Ludwig (Josef Johann) (1889-1951) Austrian-born, he did much of his work in England, where his thought was greatly influential on recent philosophical trends, especially on LOGICAL POSITIVISM and ORDINARY LANGUAGE PHILOSOPHY, though he never embraced either methodology. He engaged many of the technical problems of contemporary philosophy, but is best known for his view of philosophy as "therapy" designed to cure puzzlement and confusion resulting from misunderstandings of the function of parts of language. ['VIT-gen-stine' or, more correctly, '-shtine']

Wolff, Christian (Freiherr) von (1679-1754) German ENLIGHTENMENT philosopher, influenced by LEIBNIZ. ['volf']

Wollstonecraft, Mary (1759-1797) English schoolteacher, political writer, and novelist; her book *A Vindication of the Rights of Woman* (1792) was an early landmark in FEMINIST thought.

writers Some authors known primarily as writers of literary works or general essays deserve mention here because of the philosophical importance of their thoughts. They are:

Dante (Alighieri) (1265-1321) Italian poet. His *Divine Comedy* is the paradigmatic representation of the MEDIEVAL world-view; in other works, there is a great variety of philosophical discussion.

Dostoyevsky, Fyodor Mihailovich (also spelled in a variety of other ways) (1821-1881) Russian novelist. A forerunner of EXISTENTIALISM.

Emerson, Ralph Waldo (1803-1882) American essayist/ poet. Foremost figure in New England TRANSCENDENTALISM.

Erasmus, Desiderius (c. 1466-1536) Dutch theologian, RENAISSANCE HUMANIST scholar.

Goethe, Johann Wolfgang von (1749-1832) German poet /dramatist. His work often expresses philosophical views on God, humanity, nature. ['GUH-tuh']

Montaigne, Michel (Eyquem) (1533-1592) French essayist. Influential SCEPTIC, forerunner of the ENLIGHTENMENT. ['mon-taine']

Montesquieu, Baron (de la Brède et) de (title of Charles de Secondat) (1689-1755) French writer / political theorist, one of the ENCYCLOPEDISTS. Writing on LOCKEAN political theory, philosophy of history. ['mon-tes-kyuh']

Murdoch, Iris [Jean] (1919-1999) Irish-born writer, known primarily for her novels, she has also published on SARTRE, PLATO, and ethics.

Rand, Ayn (pen name of Alissa Rosenbaum) (1905-1982) Russian-American author of novels and essays expounding OBJECTIVISM[3], an INDIVIDUALISTIC and LIBERTARIAN social philosophy with some popular appeal but limited philosophical influence.

Voltaire (pen name of François Marie Arouet) (1694-1778) French dramatist / poet / historian, one of the ENCYCLOPEDISTS, influential in many areas of philosophy.

Y

yoga   The Hindu system for exercise and meditation designed to produce self-control and spiritual enlightenment. A person who practices this is called a '*yogi*'.

Z

Zeitgeist   (German: "spirit of the time") The supposed general character of an era. ['zyte-geyst']

Zeno   of Citium (c. 336-264 B.C.) Greek philosopher, an influential STOIC.

Zeno   of Elea (5th century B.C.) PRE-SOCRATIC Greek philosopher, student of PARMENIDES, best known for his PARADOXES, which seemed to disprove the existence of motion:

1. Achilles and the Tortoise. Imagine a tortoise in a race with speedster Achilles, with the tortoise starting closer to the goal line. When Achilles has reached the point at which the tortoise started, the tortoise has gone a little further; when Achilles reaches this further point, the tortoise has advanced again; and so on. The ABSURD conclusion is that Achilles will never pass the tortoise.

2. The Arrow. A flying arrow is, at every instant, at a particular place. Something that is at a particular place is at rest. So at every instant, the arrow is at rest. So it doesn't move.

3. The Racecourse (or The Dichotomy). Imagine a horse attempting to cover a one-kilometre course. First it must run halfway—500 metres. Next it must cover half the remaining distance—250 metres. Then 125 metres more, then 62.5. But no matter how many of these segments are added, they will never add up to the whole kilometre.

4. The Moving Blocks (or The Stadium). Imagine three blocks:

A, B, and C have the same width, w. A and C are moving, as indicated by the arrows, in opposite directions at the same speed. A takes time t to pass B, but it takes time t/2 to pass C. So it takes both t and t/2 to travel distance w.

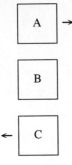

zero-sum game A GAME in which one player's gain is another player's loss.

ziggety!, hot *See* HOT ZIGGETY!

zombies These are, of course, the walking dead of horror movies, starring also in the problem of absent QUALIA which haunts FUNCTIONALISM. In this THOUGHT EXPERIMENT, we are to imagine that zombies show fairly normal stimulus-response connections, but no qualia—no consciousness. The functionalist would have to grant them mentality; this is supposed to show what's wrong with functionalism.